If everyone is carping about industry standards, how come there are so few standards being used? (Test Plans,

Beta Testing for Better Software

Customer?

What would incent you to test?

Beta Testing for Better Software

Michael Fine

Wiley Technology Publishing

Publisher: Robert Ipsen
Editor: Ben Ryan
Managing Editor: Pamela Hanley
New Media Editor: Brian Snapp
Text Design & Composition: Benchmark Productions, Inc.

Designations used by companies to distinguish their products are often claimed as trademarks. In all instances where Wiley Publishing, Inc., is aware of a claim, the product names appear in initial capital or all capital letters. Readers, however, should contact the appropriate companies for more complete information regarding trademarks and registration.

This book is printed on acid-free paper. ∞

Published by John Wiley & Sons, Inc.

Published simultaneously in Canada.

Limit of Liability/Disclaimer of Warranty: While the publisher and author have used their best efforts in preparing this book, they make no representations or warranties with respect to the accuracy of completeness of the contents of this book and specifically disclaim any implied warranties of merchantability or fitness for a particular purpose. No warranty may be created or extended by sales representatives or written sales materials. The advice and strategies contained herein may not be suitable for your situation. You should consult with a professional where appropriate. Neither the publisher nor author shall be liable for any loss of profit or any other commercial damages, including but not limited to special, incidental, consequential, or other damages.

For general information on our other products and services please contact our Customer Care Department within the United States at (800) 762-2974, outside the United States at (317) 572-3993 or fax (317) 572-4002.

Wiley also publishes its books in a variety of electronic formats. Some content that appears in print may not be available in electronic books.

Library of Congress Cataloging-in-Publication Data

Fine, Michael.
 Beta testing for better software / Michael Fine.
    p. cm.
"Wiley Computer Publishing."
 ISBN 0-471-25037-6
 1. Computer software--Testing. 2. Beta I. Title.
 QA76.76.T48 F56 2002

 005.1'4--dc21   2002009966

 Printed in the United States of America.

10 9 8 7 6 5 4 3 2 1

CONTENTS

Michael Fine is director of Corporate Development and a founder of Centercode, an application service provider (ASP) focused on providing tools and services that enable businesses to improve their products through effective beta testing.

Prior to Centercode, Mike was the beta test manager for Megahertz, US Robotics, and ultimately, 3Com Corporation for more than seven years. He was responsible for managing the beta testing of 3Com networking and communication products for three global divisions. During that time, he and his staff performed nearly 300 beta tests.

In addition to his professional experience, Mike is an inventor with two U.S. patents, a former technical writer for Iomega, and a published freelance writer on various subjects including technology. He graduated from Weber State University where he earned a bachelor of arts degree with honors.

In addition to his recognized leadership in the area of beta testing, Mike is a certified technology freak with a passion for innovation. He is also a recognized expert in a variety of fields, including Web programming, wireless and wired communications, networking, quality processes, and new technologies. He loves tinkering in digital video, handhelds, music, DVD, home theatre, and anything new or fascinating.

Originally from Chicago, Mike now makes his home in Utah. He spends his free time with his family skiing, canoeing, geocaching, playing soccer, and enjoying the outdoors. If it weren't for the inconvenient need for sleep, he would spend more time reading, listening to music, and watching films. He was a gate judge for the Women's Downhill during the 2002 Olympic Winter Games.

Definition

 This icon indicates an important word definition.

Warning/Danger

 This icon warns you to take caution or note about a critical issue.

Tip/Hint

 The tip icon provides some additional insight into the discussed topic.

Process

 Flow charts detailed in this book are marked with the process icon.

Case Study

 The case study icon indicates a real world example is being provided.

Note

 The note icon indicates some additional information about the topic is being addressed.

Go To

 When something is covered more effectively somewhere else in the book, the Go-to icon directs you to it.

PART ONE

Understanding Beta

Summary

This first part of the book is designed for people who want the proverbial "10,000-foot" view. It focuses on providing a synopsis of what a beta test is, what it does, what it costs, and why a company should do it. You will want to read this section if any of the following applies to you:

- You are currently deciding whether to perform a beta test on a product.
- You are a decision-maker looking to see the value of beta testing.
- You are trying to understand the costs of deploying a beta test program.
- You want to determine if your beta test program is effective.
- You need to build a beta test program and want to understand what is required.
- You are looking to save money on your development cost and want to see if performing a beta test can help.
- You need to determine where you should place beta test within your organization.
- You want to fix a broken beta test process.
- You want to encourage beta testing in your organization and want good justification for its implementation.
- You don't know what a beta test is and you want to understand how it works.

This part provides you with a better understanding of the value of the beta test process without burying you in the details of its operation. Part Two, "Building a Beta Test Program," goes into extensive detail about its operation, and Part Three, "Making the Results Work," examines how to use the test results effectively.

CHAPTER 1

Listening to the Customer

You might find it strange that a book on beta testing does not actually go into the definition of the test until the second chapter. However, it is my firm belief that before you can understand how to do something, you need to understand why.

This chapter explores the importance of listening to the customer. Although this seems rudimentary, more often than not, companies do not have a good process in place to ensure it is happening. Beta testing is the most effective method to guarantee that you are listening to your customers and making certain their input is integrated into your products.

Are You Listening?

How do you differentiate your product from your competition? Do you have more features? Is your price lower? Do you have an innovative design? Do you really even know? Are you listening?

Listening to your customer remains the single most important aspect of doing business. Any good salesperson will tell you that sales is not about the pitch, but rather listening to the people who want and use your product.

A beta test is the part of the development process that allows a company to effectively "listen" to the customer. No other aspect of the process directly involves the customer like a beta test does, and no other process can effectively gauge a customer's perspective as a beta test can. It is the single most effective way to ensure you are listening.

Beta testing allows you to understand what the customers want, what they need, and how they view your company. It is a powerful tool that allows you to bring the consumer into the fold of the product development process.

By listening, you gain so much. First, listening tells people that you care about them and their issues. A company that employs a method for listening to its customers demonstrates that it values the customers' opinions and that it wants to meet their needs.

Second, listening builds rapport with customers. Longevity in business is based on established relationships. When a company has good rapport with its customers, it can establish long-term relationships and build its business.

Finally, listening is powerful. It conveys confidence, intelligence, and understanding. Good listeners can resolve issues quickly, be decisive, and move more effectively. Using a process designed to listen allows a company to convey the value it places on their customers and builds confidence with those customers in its products.

Who Are Your Customers?

It seems senseless, but companies often make fatal mistakes about who their customers are and what their needs are. Over and over again, companies drive a product to market only to find that there isn't any interest or the product isn't what the market needs. A beta test can help identify, confirm assumptions, and potentially reveal new customers.

Most understand that a customer is defined as one who consumes goods and services. While this definition identifies "what" the person does, it does not state "who" this is. The reason is simple because the answer is not: the customer is as varied as the products or services being sold.

From a child to a corporate executive, from international corporations to a home-based business, customers come in many different forms. While it takes a serious amount of time to refine a product to the point where it is ready for release, it takes even more time to determine your target market.

Investing time and effort to determine who the customer is, is the first step in this process to ensuring a viable product for the market. Even more important, companies must establish a process to ensure that the expectations of these customers are met. By using beta testing, a company can achieve both of these objectives.

Perception Is Reality

In her book, *My Several Worlds*, Pearl S. Buck wrote:

> I learned early to understand that there is no such condition in human affairs as absolute truth. There is only truth as people see it, and truth, even in fact, may be kaleidoscopic in its variety.

As frustrating as it can be, the fact remains that the customer's perception of your product or company is a reality that you must understand and address. If a customer perceives a quality problem with your product, it does not matter if the problem is real or fictional—it becomes real.

Perception is one of the most powerful allies to a product. It can also be one of its worst enemies. The businesses of marketing and public relations are designed to help build and protect a company's image and keep the public perception in a positive light. Nonetheless, one bad product can destroy that work. The following case study (see page 6) examines how perception impacts reality.

In the case study, we see an example of how a customer's perception of a product can impact its design. In this case, the customers perceived the product to be slower than it actually was because of what the product reported when it connected. Whether the product actually worked was irrelevant in this case—it was purely an issue of perception.

Understanding this impact of perception on a product is critical to its success. When a product is released to the market, perceptions are being formed immediately. Whether these perceptions are those of a high-profile media person or your average customer, they all have a direct influence on the future of your product and your company.

While it might seem strange, perception is a manageable risk. It does vary and can be unpredictable at times. However, it can be controlled and influenced with the proper tools. One of the best tools for understanding and managing perception is a beta test.

By listening to beta test results, a company will have an understanding of customer perceptions prior to a product's release. Providing a small glimpse of the future, a beta test simulates the market and allows a company to work through its release process. With this information, a company can prepare for potential issues and promote a plan that will improve the customer's perception.

Communicating with Your Customer

If you could talk to your customers and discover what they think of your product prior to release, wouldn't you do it? If you could simulate the real world and see how your product works compared to your competitor's products, wouldn't that be of value? Doesn't it make sense to communicate with your customers and answer their needs?

The fact is, getting a product into the customer's hands before release is one of the most effective ways of preparing the product for the market. Companies using beta tests are effectively measuring the customer's perception prior to the general release of the product, and performing a form of risk management.

Most products need to have customer interaction prior to release. What person would buy drugs or food products that had no field-testing? While a new piece of software might not mean literal life and death, it can be the life and death of a company.

Case Study: Fast Performer

Cheetah Modem Corporation is about to release its fastest modem ever. Their lab tests conclude that the new auto negotiation software they are using is going to make this product perform 20 percent faster than any other modem on the market.

The unique design of this software is that it quickly negotiates the connection as fast as possible. While connected to the other modem, it re-negotiates the connection to a higher speed. This design provides more stable connections and happens in the background so the customer can get online quickly.

George Thompson, the product manager, is ready to send the product out to magazines so they can start benchmarking performance. He is very excited about the results and feels that a good write-up will take the product to the next level. However, Barbara Collins, lead engineer on the project, feels it is a bit premature.

George argues that there is no risk. All of the testing that the magazines will perform has already been done. In addition, the Product Quality Assurance people have nearly completed testing and their results show no significant issues.

Barbara is still uncomfortable with this as she realizes that there might be some last-minute issues and the product is not ready. She suggests that they give the product to the beta test team to see what the customers think.

George is a bit apprehensive, as timing is critical, and if he misses the window for the magazine reviews, it might impact Christmas sales. Nonetheless, he agrees to the test if they can get the product out and tested in less than two weeks.

Barbara contacts Phil Davis in beta test. Phil has no trouble getting testers immediately lined up. Within three days, the product is distributed into the field and results are coming back. Unfortunately, the reports from beta testers indicate that the customer thinks the product is a slow performer.

Getting customers to look at product builds assures that the product is ready for the real market and that it will succeed. There is no substitute for reality when developing a product. If you can get real information from real people, you have a better shot at winning.

Few of us ever make completely scientific and rational decisions about products. When we go out to shop, our hearts often interfere with our minds. While items such as performance, features, and reliability certainly come into play, we also focus on the appeal of product, what others have said, and even where we are buying it.

Your customers are the people you rely upon for success. They keep you in business and they pay the bills. It only makes sense to give your customers the clearest communication channels possible. Beta testing is best of these channels.

George is dumbfounded! The lab tests show this to be faster than anything out there, and that this is potentially the fastest modem ever. He asks Phil to verify that the proper code was distributed, and he wants some tests performed to ensure that the modem is working properly.

Testing in the field does show that the modem is performing as expected. However, the quick negotiation of this modem shows it connecting at slower speed than what the customer normally sees. For example, people who were connecting at 46666 are now seeing the modem report connections of 44000. To the customers, they have lost performance. It makes no difference that once the modem connects it is faster. Their perception of the product is based on the results being reported, not the actual speed.

George becomes very frustrated. This is simply an issue of the result codes reporting the connect speed, not the actual speed. He is at a loss at how to handle this and wonders if the magazines might report the same findings. He proposes they report the theoretical speed once connected or even the top speed every time. If it is only a matter of perception, what does it matter? However, he quickly realizes that this is not an answer. Changing the product in either of these manners is deceptive and could end up giving the company a bad reputation.

After some discussion, Barbara comes up with a way to solve the problem. Rather than negotiate up, they will reverse the process and have the modem start at the fastest possible speed and then negotiate down if necessary. This will show the customer that the modem connects aggressively and will answer this perception problem. George agrees and new code is distributed to the beta testers.

As soon as the testers upgrade, positive comments come back. In their eyes, the modem performs much better and they are happy. Although no actual changes were made to the performance aspects of the product, the customer perceives this as an improvement and thus, it is an improvement.

Defining Quality

There are certain intangible items in the product development process that impact the overall cost. Items such as product safety, design, and performance are all measurements of a product. While they are intangible, there are always efforts to measure their impact. Critical to the success of any product, quality is, by far, the most important.

Quality is an esoteric business necessity that all corporations aspire to obtain. The reason for this is simple: quality sells. Customers demand it and thus companies are driven to ensure that they have it in their products. However, while many lay claims to having quality, it is difficult to know what "quality" actually encompasses.

Some use factors such as durability, reliability, and safety to measure quality. Others prefer an all-inclusive support structure for the product's components, addressing quality issues by ensuring high customer satisfaction. Many try to demonstrate processes and certifications to their customer. Whatever method, it really comes down to one thing: the perception of the customer.

Therefore, understanding the customer's perspective is a critical aspect of assessing a product's quality. Beta testing allows a company to inexpensively gather this data while adding value to the product. Later in this book, we will examine aspects of the development process that can utilize beta test to reduce the overall cost of the product and add quality.

Nonetheless, understanding the cost of quality and how it impacts the product is critical. By defining a standard for measurement of the product quality and then adhering to that standard, a company can ensure that its software will be successful and will meet the customer's needs. Beta testing can help define the customer side of this process.

Prepare for the Impact

When a product is about to be launched, there are numerous items that have to be addressed. Overwhelming and time consuming, it might seem like getting that product to market will never happen. However, when a company takes the time to listen to the customer, it softens the impact of the release.

Software developers establish a road map of builds and revisions to address issues and implement features so the product can get to market in a timely manner. However, determining what will go into those revisions is a constant struggle. Each organization within a company has a vested interest in a portion of the software.

Marketing might have a feature that it thinks is critical. Engineering might want to manage the number of builds. Support might have a critical issue they need fixed. Whatever the concerns, it is exceptionally difficult to address every need of every organization.

Listening to the customer allows a company to focus its development effort on items that the customer wants or needs. It helps establish priorities, evaluate issues, and understand the impact of the release. With this proper understanding, it is a much simpler process

If a company can gain a valuable focus on those items that need to be released, development time can be effectively reduced. In addition, the revisions are being driven by the customer's demands. Beta testing is an excellent way to gather this information.

The Final Word

Companies build products for customers. If a company does not understand the needs of its customers, how can it possibly design a product? Effective developers recognize that customers are the final word in product design, and make every effort to incorporate their input into its product design.

However, as companies grow in size, they often begin to insulate themselves from the customers. Instead of speaking with them directly, companies use customer support calls, marketing research, usability tests, and other forms of data. While these methods provide information, it is one-dimensional and not focused on quality.

When a company is small, they are attuned to the needs of their customers. Flexible and fast moving, a small developer maintains a close watch on their customers. They understand that their success or failure depends on their product selling.

As distance grows between a company and its customers, so does the focus of the product. The needs of the company become more important than the needs of the customers. However, the only opinions that really matter are those of the people who are buying the product. Thus, the customer has the final word on the success or failure of a product.

Beta testing is a process designed to get in touch with your customers. It allows customers to use the product, provide feedback, and deliver their perception. Using this data, a company can improve quality, prepare for release, and tune their product to meet the needs of the market.

CHAPTER 2

What Is a Beta Test?

*B**eta test* is often viewed as a "user test." While this is the essence of the definition, a wealth of information can be gained from effective beta testing. Encompassing usability, functionality, compatibility, and reliability testing, beta test provides a company with much more than a standard user perspective.

 Beta testing is the managed distribution of a product to its target market; the gathering of feedback from that market; the evaluation of the feedback into manageable data forms; and the integration of the data into the organizations it affects.

Beta testing usually solicits a company's customers to participate in a test of the product prior to its release. These testers are normally volunteers who are motivated to test for a number of different reasons. Primarily, they are interested in seeing new and innovative products. However, some also work for the prospect of free product or are looking for the product to act as a solution for an issue.

Beta testing adds value because it allows the "real" customer an opportunity to provide input into the design, functionality, and usability of a company's products. This input is not only critical to the product being tested, but is also an investment into future products when the gathered data is managed effectively.

Beta testing is not a lab environment. Often, beta will discover issues that cannot be found or even duplicated in a test lab. The eclectic and diverse nature of the beta test participants often exploits limitations in products and tests the entire product development process.

Beta testing pushes a company outside its "frame of reference." It keeps them in touch with the customer's needs and provides guidance in the design of a product. Beta testing can help improve the understanding of the impact of issues, viability of concepts, and assist in making important decisions about a product's future.

The data gathered from a properly run beta test can be instrumental to the success of a product. If understood, distributed, and managed effectively, feedback gathered from this process can provide valuable data about everything that touches the product.

Utilization of Beta Test

There are many effective ways to use a beta test to ensure a successful product. When properly used, beta can provide a wealth of data for the entire organization. The following explores aspects of the testing and how it benefits different organizations within a typical corporate infrastructure.

Engineering

The primary application of a beta test process is a development or engineering product design evaluation. Product is distributed to customers to prove concepts, ensure technical compatibility, and test features. This application acts as a final phase of quality assurance testing and is focused on looking for anomalous behavior. In most cases, the product must pass certain functional criteria prior to entering and leaving the beta phase of testing.

Engineers and designers often focus the efforts of beta testing on ensuring that each product feature and the core functionality are performing as designed. In addition, they want to see that the product works well within the specified operating environment. However, the anomalous nature of beta testing allows an engineering group to discover issues that might not exist within its limited testing capacity.

Within the engineering organization, each component of the product will have an owner, and that owner will have specific interest in his or her piece. Beta can effectively test each aspect of the product and provide specific data to each owner. This data can range from cosmetic issues to code-level problems. Using beta provides a wealth of information to an engineering team and all its members.

Marketing

Beta is also used in a similar capacity by the marketing organization. Gathering useful customer feedback provides "proof of concept" data. However, this data is used to compare to market research rather than technical specifications. In addition, customers review materials owned by the marketing organization, such as manuals, packaging, features, and sometimes product materials.

Marketing, typically the driving force behind a product, will also attempt to gather customer opinions and material suitable for promotion of the product. Beta provides this data in many different forms. Often, quotations about the product or comparative data to similar products are used. In addition, test participants act as customer referrals for the press.

The marketing organization can also derive competitive information, as beta test participants are usually selected based on their understanding of the product. That usually equates to experience with competitive products. Marketing can derive a lot of valuable market data from the test participants and the test itself.

Customer Support

The customer support organization also has a vested interest in the performance of a beta test. As the only time the customer sees the product prior to its release, beta can provide support with a lot of valuable data. It points out potential support issues, provides a customer's input into the design, and allows customer support to be more effectively prepared for the product when it enters the marketplace.

Customer support will often use the beta test period to test their infrastructure. Offering support to the test participants, support will ensure that its staff understands the test product and that it has sufficient resources and information to support the product. This participation benefits both the beta test process and the support program alike.

On a general level, beta can also be used to promote or terminate a product depending on the focus. Nothing is more invigorating to a development team than to hear that the first customers to look at their product have positive things to say about it. In the same instance, nothing is more effective for stopping a potential risk product than customer data showing negative feedback.

Caveats of Beta Test

Broken down, there are three requirements that all beta tests must enlist to be a true beta test. Following these caveats does not necessarily imply success—it isn't that simple. However, they will prevent a test from being a complete failure. Any one of these three items will destroy any value a beta test might have had.

Target Market

First, all beta tests need to use the target customer of the product to test. As simple as this concept is, there are often attempts to do something called an "internal" beta where the product is distributed to employees for their review. As large as the company might be, the objectivity of that situation is gone—the employees' viewpoint is tainted by their employment.

Beta tests need people who have no vested interest in the product's success or failure. They need to be people who want to participate because they are interested in the technology or product. They might even be experts in the product's industry. However, if they are people who want to see a particular outcome for the product, it invalidates their test data.

 Internal beta tests are not without merit. They can provide some useful data. However, it is important to remember that they are *not* your customers. Therefore, an internal beta test is only useful for quality testing.

MEDIA AS TESTERS? (PC WEEKLY)

Real beta tests ensure that all evaluators are part of the target market and are only there to assess the quality, performance, and design of the product. These candidates need to be people who are most likely going to buy the product. It is critical to find "real" users and test the product in a real environment.

Usable Test Product

The second requirement is that the product be in a usable form. The viability of the product must be assessed before the product is distributed to the customer. If a product is in a stage that makes it exceptionally difficult to use, the beta will serve no purpose other than to reinforce that the product has problems.

It is not extraordinary to use a beta test to assess a particular concept or idea. However, these still need to be complete ideas that a user will not have to jump through hoops to use. Often, test participants understand when a product has problems. However, when those problems are overwhelming and directly inhibit the ability of the customer to test the product, it effectively invalidates the test.

Want Test Results

The third and final rule for a beta test is that the company or organization performing the test must "want" the results. In other words, when a company sends products out to customers, it needs to understand that customers will have opinions and issues. The company must want to hear this information, and it is part of their quality strategy to listen.

Strange as it might seem, some companies walk through the development process and handle each step as if it is a hurdle to release. Nothing is more damaging to a beta test than sending a product out and then ignoring the results. The customers participating in the test will regard the act as disingenuous and stop working on the product. In addition, the results coming from test will almost certainly exhibit themselves in the shipping product.

A company making the effort to perform a beta test must be interested in listening to the customer and using that data to improve the product and potentially future products. Effectively, the test should not be treated as an obligatory gesture, but as a quality process determined to find product issues and gather customer feedback.

Nontraditional Beta Tests

The traditional beta test, which is the most widely used form, is the focus of the remainder of this book. However, there are instances when other types of beta tests are sometimes appropriate. These use many of the same principles in test operation, but they vary in their application. Among these nontraditional tests are the five examples discussed next.

Beta testing as a category of testing adheres to the aforementioned definition, but there are many different ways to approach this test to get the best results. The following examines many of the different types of nontraditional tests and the goal for each of them.

Never **use a nontraditional beta test on an entirely new product. Only consider it for revisions or derivative products.**

Post-Release Beta Test

The normal design of a beta test focuses on the product being pre-released. The whole idea is to find issues with the product prior to its release. However, in some cases, companies might decide to release the product and then conduct the beta test as the product starts to get into the stores.

The rationale behind this decision usually is based on the product's tenure, complexity, and overall quality. For example, a good candidate for this type of test would be a product that is in its third revision and straightforward in design. It went through the quality process with only minor issues. More often than not, the timeline on the product is critical for its success.

By performing a post-release beta test, the company is accepting the risk that some terrible issue might exhibit itself. The performance of this test does not differ from a traditional beta in process. However, it is important to notify test participants that the product is released and that this test can still impact the quality of the product.

Beta test managers might be apprehensive to perform this type of test, as it is in direct conflict with the normal philosophy of beta testing. However, there is the belief that if you find a huge issue before release, you are doing your job. If you find the issue after release, you are the hero.

Performing a beta test is a necessary part of the product quality process. However, the financial well being of the company needs to be balanced properly with the need for quality. The post-release beta test is always a better answer than no test at all.

Public Beta Test

A "public beta" is almost a contradiction by design. A beta test is normally focused on preparing the product for its release. However, there are instances when demand for a particular product or the need for large-scale testing outweighs the concern for public release.

In a public beta, the product is unofficially released to a public location for use by anyone who is interested in testing. In most cases, this will usually be software that is small or simple. However, public beta tests can be performed on large applications. Customers who choose to use the product are forewarned that the product is unsupported and could potentially have issues.

The benefits of this test are excellent when the impact of the product's distribution is low risk and well tested prior to its distribution. There will be an enormous number of test participants and almost every potential issue will usually be reported. This test also can address support-related issues by providing answers to commonly reported problems.

When a public beta is inappropriately used, the results can be catastrophic. The following case study examines when this happens.

Case Study: Broken Promises

General Optical, a producer of high-end scanning software, recently released new Optical Character Recognition (OCR) scanner software. This software takes advantage of the different types and brands of scanners by installing a proprietary driver that accelerates the recognition speed.

To ensure they would hit their market window, General Optical made the decision to release the product without the best drivers to support the FireWire port some scanners use. While the product has parallel and USB support available, the speed and connectivity of FireWire is what separates some scanners from their competitors.

In this effort to ship, the development team estimated that it would only be a week or two before the fixes would be complete. As the product reaches the shelves, the plan is to roll the new driver into the production software and post the new code on their Internet site for those who have already purchased the application. However, things are not going as planned, and it has been over a month since the product was released. The driver in development still acts up in certain scenarios and there is a lack of confidence in its stability.

Lauren Kumar is the lead driver developer on the product. She thinks the issues are related to different versions of the operating system and its support for FireWire. However, in her tests, the problems are sporadic and frustrating. She is confident that this is the best driver they have until they can get some more FireWire equipment to debug the issues. She feels her latest build should be released.

Steve O'Neil disagrees. He is the product manager, and while he is desperate for the driver to be available, he is already frustrated that the product shipped without proper support for every FireWire scanner. The press is criticizing them and the support team is screaming for a solution. Even with that pressure, Steve knows it will get a lot worse if they release with a problematic solution.

Steve and Lauren approach Randy Ascot, the customer support manager, and ask if he could post a "public beta" version of this driver on one of their support servers. Randy is uncomfortable with this, as General Optics' support is already getting many calls and he thinks this will cause an increase. However, he is also desperate for the driver and knows that some solution will help abate the onslaught of angry customers. He hesitantly agrees.

The next morning, the driver is posted with stern warnings that it is a "beta" release and unsupported. Customers are walked through several pages explaining the status of the driver and that there is inherent risk in using it. Nonetheless, within an hour, the server receives over 224,000 hits. Customers bury the company's Internet connection trying to get the file downloaded.

Not only are complaints coming in that the site is unavailable, the server is unable to handle the sudden heavy traffic. Eventually, the machine crashes and Randy is left with even more angry customers than before, a crashed support server, and a driver that they soon discover isn't ready for release.

A beta test is a controlled environment. Following the normal beta test process makes certain the product is viable before distribution. In this example, Steve and Lauren have circumvented normal processes to get something to customers before it is ready.

With this action, they have created a support nightmare and set poor expectations for their customers.

An effective public beta still means the product is ready for release. Public beta tests are not supposed to be a proving ground for incomplete software. The software must be ready for release before it is distributed. In addition, when performing a public beta, it should be focused on assessing the product's quality, not providing a support solution. It is not designed to act as a customer support program or to be used for open file distribution.

Mini-Beta Test

Often viewed as a "quick and dirty" test, the mini-beta is focused on getting results immediately. This usually involves a very small number of testers or a very short test period. Companies deciding to perform the mini-beta see the value of a beta test in their process, but don't have a lot of time or people to perform a test.

There are a number of valid reasons to perform a mini-beta over the traditional test. Companies make a decision to switch to this style of test because they need results quickly. The smaller group or time frame can allow a quick response and ensure that no critical issues exist in the product.

Of course, going smaller can potentially create a greater risk of issues getting through to the released product. To ensure that this does not happen, there are two ways to make this test work. First, if you reduce the number of test participants, make certain they are experienced beta testers. You need test participants who know the product and know how to find issues.

Second, the company must establish clear goals for the test. In a mini-test, there is not enough time or enough people to perform a comprehensive test. Therefore, extra control needs to be exhibited on the test and to make certain it serves its purpose. The mini-beta can achieve the desired result with the right people and proper management.

Focused Beta Test Fu NCTIONALITY

The "focused" test is exactly as the name states. The beta test takes a portion of the product and pushes all the energy of the test team toward that focus. Often, this test is used to prove a concept, verify an issue, or emphasize the testing of a feature. Generally, this type of beta test is very effective but loses its energy quickly. With all the emphasis on a particular issue, the focused test steers the site to a single goal. Once that has been reached, the test site sits and waits for more direction.

One of the primary disadvantages of this test is that participants are unlikely to keep this "focus" very long. They will perform the test and exhaust all avenues of testing within a very short period of time. If their interest is not maintained, they will stop testing. The focused test is designed to get limited results on a small portion of a product. It works exceptionally well on veteran products that are being updated.

Therefore, it might be more advantageous to use this form as a subset of a traditional beta rather than as a single test. Its short life makes it expensive. All the resources required to perform a beta test are wasted when the focused test is complete. Taking some of the more communicative testers from the traditional test and giving them a focus can achieve the same result.

Internal Beta Test

When companies get desperate to release a product, they sometimes take desperate measures. In these cases, the company decides that the best way to perform a beta test is to distribute the product to its own employees, have them simulate a customer environment, and then report test results. However, employees are not the target market but rather biased people who have a tainted view of the product.

An internal beta test is almost a contradiction in terms as it really isn't a beta test at all. When a company decides that an internal test will suffice for a beta test, they are doing more damage to their quality than good.

In a very few cases, an internal test is appropriate. If the population of the company is in the thousands, it might be possible to get some satisfactory feedback from those employees who are not directly involved in the development of the product.

Another instance is for the security and success of the product. In these cases, where the product is so secret, it might be necessary to use internal sites to ensure that no information about the product is released to the public. However, an internal beta should rarely be used alone; it works best when it compliments a traditional test.

Nontraditional beta tests offer companies alternative methods to performing beta testing. While they do not provide the extensive data of a traditional test, they are a viable alternative for ensuring that the customer can provide feedback into the product design.

Sounds like "Beta"

During the development of a product, there are a few different processes and functions that have similar characteristics to a beta test. These tests might make a team consider the whole process of beta testing redundant. While some of these are certainly similar, a beta test is distinctive and important; it cannot be equaled by any of these other functions.

Market Research and Focus Groups

There are instances where the marketing department will distribute a pre-released product to customers to get feedback. While it sounds similar to a beta, the comparison is superficial at best. Market research is focused on gathering marketing data—there is no interest in the technical aspects of a product. Moreover, a marketing research project is designed to discover a particular type of data. Whether it is demographic, sales, or usability data, the environment is controlled and not focused on quality.

Focus groups bring groups of people to a location and ask the participants a series of questions about a product or a technology. This process is also designed to gather "real world" feedback. However, a focus group is also a marketing function and is designed to gather specific types of information. Often, the other members can influence participants in a focus group. In addition, focus groups last only a few hours, while beta tests last several weeks.

Beta addresses these two functions in an entirely different manner. First, marketing data is readily available during the test, and test participants can be focused on a particular part of a product. However, beta covers all aspects of the product. In addition, beta is focused on individual users testing the product in a "real world" environment. Although they function as a group, they perform their work isolated from the other testers.

When a beta test is properly administrated, it can gather much of the same data that both of these two functions perform. Additionally, beta testing provides other useful data that these programs don't. Beta testing can compliment the focus group and market research processes by providing confirmation or denial of the data they gather.

Usability Testing

Usability testing does often cross over into the realm of beta, and vice versa. However, it is the focus of this testing and its controlled environment that make it different. A usability test will focus on the ease of use of a product. While it might actually reveal technical issues during a test, the program is not interested in those issues. The usability test is very limited in its scope, timing, and testing population.

Usability tests are often performed in a lab and watched by the development team to see how the customer reacts to the product through the process of using it. The company gives the product to the customer, and he or she steps through all aspects of its use. Without direction or involvement, the customer is expected to use the product alone in a limited amount of time.

The usability test uses a single clean system to test the software and then focuses its effort on the user experience. In contrast, beta testing emphasizes using the customer's hardware and software, and measures the user experience in the real world. Usability is advantageous because it provides a company an opportunity to watch the customer use the product. However, its relation to reality is limited.

Beta tests address usability issues by incident. As customers use the product, they discover usability problems and report them. Beta test is much more expansive and can miss some of the ease-of-use details that a good usability test can discover. However, beta testing is flexible enough to take on this focus if necessary.

Quality Assurance Testing

Quality assurance testing (also called "alpha testing") is performed by an engineering test group using automated and regimented testing. The focus of the quality assurance test is to completely exercise every part of the product in the most common potential environments. This is normally performed in a controlled lab environment.

Often, quality assurance departments believe that if their program is effective and properly designed, beta testing is not necessary. They feel that a good quality assurance program is all inclusive and addresses all of the needs of testing. This is not arrogance, but rather the goal of any good test program. If a quality assurance department is not aspiring to find every issue possible, there is a problem with that department.

Beta testing compliments a quality assurance test phase; it doesn't compete with it. It is unrealistic to believe that a quality assurance team can find every problem. Whether it is anomalous issues or oversights, beta testing only enhances the testing a quality assurance program performs.

There are even cases where quality assurance programs will bring in real customers to test a product. This is still significantly limited when compared to the testing a beta process can cover. A lab, even with outside testers, is still a lab. In addition, beta testing adds value to other organizations, while quality assurance is focused as an engineering test.

Quality assurance departments need to find as many issues as possible, but even more importantly, they should use beta testing to assist in that effort. When properly paired together, beta testing closes the gap on risk items getting out to customers.

 In many companies, the beta test program is part of the quality assurance department and its test process.

Field Trials

Often used synonymously with beta test, a field trial is actually a slightly different type of test. Field trials are much more focused on assessing a particular aspect of a product. While specific in their nature, they take the same approach to the test. The product is distributed into the real world, and test participants do provide feedback on the product.

However, in a field trial, distribution of the product is usually set up in a more scientific fashion with control groups and specific agendas. Beta testing is usually less formal and more comprehensive in its approach. A good field trial might neglect a lot of relevant information because of its focus.

In general, field trials are typically used in the scientific and medical communities. Beta is used more widely in the computer and information technology industry. Keep in mind that if a person mentions field trials, there is a distinct possibility that he or she is actually referring to a beta test.

Opening Up Beta Testing

In contrast to the previous section, beta testing is much more than just a simple quality test. One of the most powerful aspects of beta testing is its tremendous flexibility.

This test is designed to be an assessment tool. It is focused on gathering feedback from your customer, while providing valuable quality test data.

Being that type of tool means that it must have the ability to "assess" many different parts of the product in many different ways. Beta testing can serve many different purposes and is flexible enough to accommodate the needs of many organizations. By exploring the flexibility of this test, this becomes a powerful tool in the product development process.

Feedback from beta testing is very open. It can come in the form of surveys, issues, submissions, quotations, feature requests, email, telephone calls, faxes, forum posts, or any other response to an inquiry from the test manager. Because of this flexibility, it allows a company to gather data that is critical to the success of the product.

Unlike other processes, beta test has a well-structured process but completely flexible application. It can be used for documentation review, testing support infrastructure, to verify quality assurance issues, marketing research, and much more. Using this flexibility can allow a company to eliminate redundant processes and use beta testing to its full potential.

The Value of Beta Test

E very process has a purpose. This purpose can be narrowly focused, or cover a broad spectrum of items. Beta test has the ability to do both. It is an exceptionally flexible process with wide-ranging value and application.

Beta testing provides a company with a valuable tool to get the best product to market. From its quality assessment focus to its interaction with customers, a beta test is essentially focused on helping companies produce better products.

Here we begin to explore the value of beta test and its various applications. As you will read, this test, when used to its full potential, is a very valuable tool to ensure that the product is successful, and provides valuable assistance to the product development process.

Quality Verification

Of all its applications, assessing the quality of a product is by far beta test's most valuable asset. It is an effective tool for several reasons. First, beta testing provides feedback from the target market on quality. It reveals limitations and provides honest and untainted feedback from people who are actually using the product.

In addition to opinions about the various aspects of the product, beta test participants report problems they discover while using it. Compatibility issues are quickly revealed during a beta test. Because of the variable nature of their environment, test participants are susceptible to issues that a quality assurance lab might not see or be able to duplicate easily.

Beta testing has the unique ability to capture results from a wide variety of hardware and software for testing purposes. It is especially beneficial when testing with legacy equipment. A test lab cannot possibly build every scenario of hardware and software that a product might encounter in the field. Beta testing helps effectively reduce the number of potential risk combinations.

In addition to the random elements, beta can also be a focused quality tool. By establishing testers who meet a certain criteria for a product, you can effectively increase the number of people looking at a specific issue. In the following case study (see page 25), we see how a beta test can focus the effort of the test participants on an issue and confirm the validity of that issue.

By using beta test participants as a resource, Rick was able to quickly solve a potentially disastrous problem. Focusing the attention of the test participants, he had 30 people working with him to determine the source of the issue.

Beta testing is flexible enough to expand or narrow the scope during a project. This flexibility allows issues discovered during test to be quickly verified by the test participants. This is especially useful when quality assurance testing coincides with beta testing.

Another benefit of beta is its ability to verify its own issues. Unlike in a lab, where a machine might be testing a single scenario and another might be working on a different part of the product, beta testers all have a similar test goal. Multiple reports of the same issue immediately reveal problems and accelerate the ability for a team to discover a problem.

 In companies in which the quality assurance program is small or has limited resources, it might make sense to start the beta test process earlier in the development process to assist in verifying issues.

Using beta testers as a quality verification tool, a company can effectively reduce the overhead cost of building a comprehensive test lab, verify issues that occur in the field more effectively, and establish a process for ensuring that products meet the customer's perspective of "quality."

Design Analysis

When you hand a product to an end user and ask her to use it as it is designed, limitations will inevitably be revealed. All of us often take on tasks and make assumptions on how things should work. Confirmation or denial of these assumptions is revealed in a beta test immediately.

A software designer makes design decisions that regularly that impact the customer. Often, the designer will come to conclusions based on his or her own experience and notions about usability. However, the immense nature of developing a software application creates a huge potential for inconsistency. In addition, the subjective nature of these decisions makes them untested and potentially damaging.

Case Study: Same Difference

Wildflower Software Corporation is about to release new sound-editing software. This ultra-powerful software has the ability to manipulate every known published sound format. In addition, it comes with a completely new compression algorithm that reduces the size of sound files by nearly 20 to 1.

The product is in its first week of beta testing and there appears to be a problem that will prevent the product from being released. Twenty of the 30 testers are experiencing garbled sound when using the new algorithm. In some cases, the problem appears to be intermittent, while others have heard it since they installed it.

Rick Sanger, lead software engineer on the project, has been unable to duplicate the issue. He has attempted everything he can think of and still cannot get the software to produce the garbled noise. He has narrowed his focus to different sound cards and brands of systems.

Wildflower is a small company and cannot afford to purchase every brand of sound card and computer system. Therefore, his initial approach is to use the beta test participants to test each of the potential risk items. Working with Jared Roseland, the beta test manager, they slowly eliminate the potential causes of this problem.

Jared has testers try the software on different computers. Using data from his database, he tests the different operating systems. In desperation, he asks each tester to take out the sound card and reinstall the hardware to see if the problem disappears. Amazingly, some no longer hear the problem, while others do.

Rick and Jared are initially dumbfounded—it makes no sense. Then it occurs to them that the installation updates the sound card driver so it can support their new algorithm. Some of these computers have sound devices on the motherboard. They theorize that this issue is related to a driver conflict. The installation of the software detects each sound device on the system and is possibly updating the wrong set of drivers.

They ask all the testers to remove the after-market sound card and see if anything changes. Immediately, many of those who had the issue no longer see problems. They follow up and ask the testers to ensure that the motherboard-based sound card is disabled in the system BIOS and that all the drivers are removed. The testers respond immediately, and suddenly, they no longer have a problem.

Rick is perplexed. He wonders why the problem does not exhibit itself in the Wildflower lab. He then discovers that the test machines in the lab do not have mixed configurations. Either they have a separate sound card, or one embedded on the motherboard.

He asks the quality team to put a sound card into a machine with an onboard sound card, and immediately, the "garbled" files come through loud and clear. He is able to isolate the problem in the installation software and correct it.

The hands-on method of beta testing is exceptionally efficient for discovering issues and revealing limitations. Beta testing is focused on gathering user experience, from both a simple user reaction to a deeply technical evaluation of the product. Beta test participants challenge assumptions by using the product in the manner that appears logical to them.

Very often, what might have appeared to be a logical and natural method for using a product will reveal it to be the contrary. Beta test participants are real people and attempt to use the product as it is designed. If the design is faulty or misconceived, the testers become confused and frustrated.

This design analysis is an effective way to determine standards for implementation in future products. Using the data properly, a software engineer can remove the subjectivity from his or her design and ensure that the concepts implemented are proven.

Feature Evaluation *Late Cycle Func Assesment*

Features differentiate a product from its competitors. While some are standard, others are distinctive and critical to a product's success. Beta testing can test this aspect of the design while offering comparative data to other similar products, including those of a competitor.

One product is the same as another if the features do not stand out as different. A product loses its competitive edge when its features fail to meet the expectation of the customer. Because beta test participants are real customers, they normally have experience with similar products.

Selection of beta test participants should be focused to reflect the target market. Part of the selection criteria should also include people who have used similar products. With this experience in hand, the beta tester provides reference data to see if a feature has value, works properly, and improves his or her opinion of the product.

Proof of Concepts *Market /Func Assessment*

Concepts are purely speculation unless they have factual data to back them up. If a concept is proposed, it should have some foundation in real-world data to ensure that it is valuable. Taking the time to gather this data often slows development and causes companies to take risks. Using beta testing, a company can lessen the impact to a schedule and prove concepts more efficiently.

In the following case study (see page 27), beta test data is used to support a change to a product. Some concepts will meet resistance. This is especially true when the wheels of product development are set into motion. Nevertheless, when data is proven, it is nearly impossible to argue against.

Bart is forced to take action to support his claim. By using information gathered during beta test, he is able to establish valid criteria for change. Beta test data, when properly gathered, provides a valuable untainted resource to prove concepts. The customer's voice is the loudest when an issue needs attention.

Revision Management

The process of developing software is continuous. Enhancements, improvements, repairs, and revisions comprise the updates that software developers provide. Cus-

Case Study: Show Me the Data

Bart Carmichael, an expert in help file design, has been assigned the task of writing the help files for the latest version of Maxcash's personal accounting software. He has been reviewing the previous versions of the software and, in his opinion, it lacks severely in this area.

In the team meeting, Bart gives a comprehensive presentation of the new help files and how he feels they should be implemented. This is not a small task. Modifying the existing help infrastructure will require significant changes to the software's layout. To accommodate the new help icons, the code will need to be changed as well. In addition, it will also require a lot of new code to ensure that all the help integrates properly with the software.

He also elaborates on how poor the old version of the software was in this capacity and states that the product is not able to compete in this market without improvement. He emphasizes how it will help reduce support calls and save the company money.

Once completed, he asks the team if there are any questions. Jim O'Neill, the engineering manager raises his hand and asks one question. "Where is your data?"

Bart is a bit frustrated. He is the expert in this area and he feels that should be a sufficient reason to make the update. Jim senses this and elaborates: "You are expecting us to make considerable changes to the software and add a few weeks to the development schedule. I don't make decisions like this without some data."

This seems like a reasonable request. The obvious poor quality of the help files should have shown itself during the beta test. Bart tells Jim he will get back to him. Contacting Sarah Parson in beta test, he asks her if she has any legacy data on the Maxcash Finance Pro version 1.0 help files.

Sarah goes into her database and discovers that there were numerous complaints about the quality of the help files. In fact, she logged numerous issues, but they were deferred to get the release to market. Sarah suggests to Bart that he contact Customer Support to see if they also are seeing complaints. A quick call shows that the help files are a common customer complaint.

Bart gathers the supporting data and brings it to the next team meeting. After reviewing the information, Jim offers support for Bart's proposal and he assigns a software engineer to help with the implementation. In addition, Jim requests that Sarah solicit the beta testers to see if they might offer suggestions on where improvement in the help files is needed. Jim expects management to reject a slip in the schedule and he wants to ensure that he has the best data to support the change.

tomers have come to expect that products will be revised and newer versions will be available after they purchase a software product. Their purchase is not a one-time investment, but a long-term relationship that needs to be properly managed.

Using a beta test, companies can refine a path for properly revising their software and determine a successful road map. Validation of the material being selected for the different revisions comes from the customer and helps accelerate the decision-making process. Issues produced during a beta test phase can help determine whether an issue needs inclusion in a revision.

In addition, new features and developments can be properly assessed to determine their value when a company charges for its upgrades. During the beta testing, it is easy to see what issues customers see as improvements and what they view as repairs. Using this data, a company can establish a clear path for upgrades.

Market Research

Requirements come in many different forms. There are requirements provided by the government to ensure that a product is safe and legal. There are requirements made by standards groups that allow a particular product to carry the moniker of that organization. However, the requirements that have the greatest impact to a product are those provided by the marketing organization.

Typically, marketing is focused on understanding a company's "market." This market is a place where the company's software is offered for sale. Marketing must assess who wants to buy the product and what they want from it. To get to these conclusions, marketing uses a tool called "market research."

Market research gathers and evaluates data regarding consumers' preferences for products and services. It attempts to assess the needs of the customer and establish design requirements for engineering teams. With market research, the data comes prior to the evolution of a product. In contrast, beta testing comes after the product is complete. However, the data these two functions gather can compliment each other in many ways.

One aspect of beta testing serves the same purpose as market research: it also gathers customer preferences. However, at the point it enters the process, it is used as a confirmation or rejection of the data that was gathered in the original market research. Yet, beta test data is not restricted to the confines of the research data.

Before beginning the beta test, integrate the results of any market research as part of a beta test plan. Once the test begins, gather the beta test information and use it for the foundation of market research. This cycle of information gathered during a beta test explores customer's ideas and opinions about the product as they use it, and helps perpetuate the customer's input into the product.

Market research is limited in its potential, as it is solely information gathered through inquiries. Beta test bases its data on people who have experience with the product and who understand what need the product is supposed to fulfill. With this understanding, the information has a better chance of improving the conception of the product.

Beta test provides a much wider scope of information about the needs of the customer. By taking the data gathered in beta, a marketing team will get data to help drive revisions of the tested product, measure the needs of the market, and potentially establish criteria for new products. In addition, the data gathered in test can help plan and refine future market research.

Infrastructure Preparation

Every company wants to have better visibility into the future. The better a company can forecast its costs, the better it can manage the bottom line. Infrastructure is one of those areas in which the cost does not contribute to the profitability of the company but is a necessary part of doing business. Using the data from a beta test, a company can target a number of areas to estimate costs, establish processes, and create predictability for the business.

Beta test simulates the actual release of a product. When properly executed, the test allows a company to experience potential issues on a small scale and prepare to handle those situations. In the following sections, we examine how beta testing can help implement proper infrastructure for a product's release.

Customer Support

As beta test participants are real customers, they encounter real issues and have real questions. Depending on the size of the beta team, the issues generated from a beta test can be more effectively handled by the customer support organization.

There are several key advantages to using the customer support infrastructure to support the testers. It allows them to gain insight into potential issues customers might experience when the product is released. It provides an opportunity to get early training on the product. Last, it helps them to establish their infrastructure to handle the different methods of support.

The customer support organization is usually very interested in assisting in the beta test process, as they understand its value and how it assists in a product's preparation for release. This can provide valuable assistance to the beta test process and ensures that the beta test team can focus on addressing issues rather than dealing with support-related problems.

Internet Infrastructure

When software is released, an assortment of Internet-related processes interface with the product. From Web registration and software updates, to hyperlinks and support files, the beta process can ensure that these exterior parts of the product are properly tested.

While the scale is not the same as an actual product release, beta testing ensures that the functionality is effectively tested. In addition, beta testers can provide feedback on their experiences. Web-related material often does not get a proper beta test. This added benefit allows the beta tester to get the full product experience and provides the company with valuable data about the "whole" product.

Process Evaluation

Companies are comprised of many different departments and people. Each owns a part of the product, but not the entire thing. Thus, there is a huge potential for communication errors once a product is released. During the development phase, teams usually work together, driving the product toward a release. However, this team usually disbands once the product is shipped. The communication channels become unclear, and soon, issues arise.

The beta test process is focused on exercising all aspects of the product and the related processes. When an issue appears, it very often reveals limitations in the communication process. In addition, beta testing can check to ensure that some mechanism exists to get the setback resolved.

Quality processes are flexible and documented. Beta testing allows companies to test these procedures to make certain they work efficiently. As mentioned, customer support is one example of a process test. However, items ranging from the bug tracking system to the marketing data distribution can be tested. Once a process error is revealed, beta test can also be used to ensure it is corrected.

 If you have a process that is failing, have the beta test team incorporate it as part of a product test plan.

Documentation Review

One of the most arduous and painful parts of the development process is the creation of the user documentation. While it is a necessity, review of the documentation is a time-consuming enterprise, and few have the time to dedicate to it. Beta test participants are the most effective reviewers and can be used to improve this process.

Distributing documentation to beta test participants provides many advantages over traditional methods of review. First, beta testers are the audience for the material being written. Therefore, as customers, their input into the documentation is directly relevant to the final output. It is by far the most valuable feedback you can receive about the documentation.

Second, beta test participants use the documentation. Most people who will review within a company read the documentation as a book and don't test the text. Beta test participants have a sample product to use with the documentation. They use it as it is intended, and have a better chance at catching important errors.

Last, beta test participants are usually traditional end users and can determine if the documentation is usable, reliable, informative, and necessary. Too often, documentation is either too comprehensive or lacks critical information. Technical writers looking to refine the product documentation need only ask the testers what they used.

Localization

Shifting a product from a domestic market to a global one has multiple challenges. *Localization* is the process that takes a product and makes it "local" for an international location. Changing the manuals, software, and even the design of the marketing materials, localization attempts to make the product jump a cultural barrier.

This task is an expensive and difficult operation. There are innumerable factors to be considered to move a product to the global market. Apart from the tremendous amount of government and technical challenges, the cultural and language hurdles are probably the most difficult of these tasks.

Products need to be properly translated and reviewed on systems configured to operate in the specific language. Beta testing is the most cost-effective and efficient method for testing products internationally. The product itself and the shipping are the small costs that ensure that it really feels "local."

By locating beta test participants within the target country, using the country-specific version of the software and having it reviewed by native speakers, a company can ensure a properly localized product.

Beta testers can make certain translations properly convey the intended message. They can test that other localized software properly operates together and that the infinite buttons, message boxes, icons, and text all work collectively and maintain the "local" impression.

Better Preparation

Beta testing normally sits at the end of the development process. As managers wait impatiently for the results of the test, beta holds the key on whether a product is ready to ship. Tragically, this sometimes causes companies to reduce or eliminate the beta test. Analogous to the ostrich with its head in the sand, these companies attempt to hide from the potential issues the product might experience.

Ignoring the results of beta test does not make them go away. In fact, without an effective beta test, a company positions itself to see the issues once its customers purchase the product. Thus, it damages the relationship with its customers and the company's reputation. Ignoring or removing beta testing from the development process sets a product up for failure.

By viewing beta test as a phase for preparation rather than confirmation, the results are more of a rehearsal for release than a hindrance. With this motivation, a company establishes a positive reason to perform beta testing and looks forward to hearing the results. Beta testing becomes a confirmation of their process and the product.

Better Products

The objective of any testing is to ensure that a company produces better products. In this chapter, we examined the value of beta testing. However, this list is only a sample of some of the larger profits to be gained. Beta testing can provide a multitude of smaller but still significant benefits to a company.

Companies might even see greater benefits from testing in the form of good will. The user community views beta testing positively. Many customers see beta testing as the company's commitment to quality and that it values the customer's feedback about the product. By performing a beta test, a company tells users that it "cares" about them and their opinion.

Beta testing also demonstrates to the public that a company has confidence in its market position and is not rushing a product to market. It enforces that the company is taking the time in the quality phase of its testing to ensure no critical issues hit the street. This faith in the customer and the marketplace translates into customer loyalty.

The sum of all these different benefits is better products. The fact is that any step a company can take to reduce product issues and increase customer involvement in the development process benefits the product. This alone demonstrates that beta test has value and is sufficient justification for ensuring that a test is performed on every product.

The Cost of Beta Test to Your Organization

This chapter could begin with a laundry list of equipment, paperwork, and other items that you need, or it could throw out a single figure designed to establish the entire cost of test. However, this is not realistic, as every company is different and the beta test process costs vary tremendously depending on the product and the program.

Beta test programs, when compared to other entities within a company, are very inexpensive. Many of the costs associated with its operation can be controlled easily, and there are many effective ways to manage some of the more expensive items. This chapter appraises these costs and offers suggestions on how to manage them effectively.

Return on Investment

Any program must produce something to make it valuable. In the case of *return on investment* (ROI), the value that the program provides must exceed the cost of operating the program. In the case of beta test, much of the value is real but intangible. The return comes in the form of abstract items such as quality, customer satisfaction, product issues, and feedback.

While this information is exceptionally valuable and useful, it is hard to put a specific value on it. For example, how much does one bug cost a company? How much value does one place on an excellent customer testimonial or quote? These things are not bought or sold, but have real usefulness to a company.

A beta test program should be measured on a number of factors. However, the most important is the feedback it produces. To calculate an actual return on investment, a company will need to determine what *not* testing would cost. Whether it is the risk of sending a product to market with potentially serious issues, or the loss of valuable feedback, neglecting to beta test a product costs much more than the beta program itself.

 ## Case Study: What You See Isn't What You Get

Blue Fire Productions has begun beta testing their latest application. Blue Fire's "Wwwow!" software is a WYSIWYG (What You See Is What You Get) application designed to make Web programming a breeze. Included in the application are hundreds of pre-built templates to which a user can simply add text and generate the HTML page. The application also includes graphics and some other simple material to get the site online quickly.

Edward Lowe is the beta test manager for Blue Fire and has distributed the first version of Wwwow! to the beta test participants. The software is getting terrible reviews from some of the sites. Their beta test data indicates that the templates do not generate the HTML pages properly, resulting in differences between the application and the output.

Denise Golan is the product manager for the product and she is perplexed. QA testing did not see any issues. However, almost every site is seeing the problem. This issue is critical, as it is in direct conflict with the design of the application. She calls an emergency meeting of the development team to discuss the issue.

At the team meeting, Edward discusses the problem with the development team. He is unable to duplicate the issue in his test lab, yet the sites have sent in screen shots showing the problem. In the application, the Web page appears one way; on the Web, it appears another.

Denise enforces the importance of resolving this issue by informing the team that every day the project is delayed costs the company thousands of dollars. The orders for Wwwow! are coming in, and every delay impacts the shipment date. Denise also explains that the company desperately needs to get evaluation copies out to the press and to key buyers so that they can get the product into the channel before the back-to-school sales.

Working with the beta sites, the developers generate several new versions to fix the application. In three short days, the test participants experiencing the problems are able to test until the problem is resolved. The issue appeared when customers selected fonts that were installed on their system but not supported by Wwwow! The developers addressed the issue by adding 20 fonts and ignoring those not installed with the application.

The reason the QA department and others did not see the issue was because everyone was using the default fonts included in the package. With over 60 choices available in the application, nobody considered that there would be a need for more. In addition, the application itself showed the unsupported fonts during design, but when it went to generate the Web code, it ignored them and used the default.

Denise is pleased that the solution was found and that the product is back on track to release. By her estimation, the discovery of this issue saved the company thousands of dollars in support calls and revisions, and made the company even more money because the product was back on schedule for its original release date.

In this example, the return is huge. The beta test discovered a critical issue and used the test participants to resolve it quickly. The cost in this instance is some free copies of the software to the sites, the operation of the program, and the resources to address the issues. The return is a successful product, which is an ideal return on investment.

Infrastructure

The infrastructure of a beta program is its inner workings. It is a combination of the people, the equipment, and all the associated material required to operate the beta program. Depending on the size of a company, resources vary tremendously. In the following sections, an analysis of the beta test infrastructure is presented in relation to the size of the organization.

Keep in mind that the size of a company does not always correspond to the number of projects. If a company is small but produces a large number of products, the model for a large company might be necessary. Conversely, a large company with a single product might need to use the model of a small company.

Small Company

The small company has many challenges in developing a beta program. While it has the same quality goals as a large corporation, it normally does not have the same resources. Because of this, it makes sense for the small company to share equipment, space, and sometimes people within its own organization.

Headcount

The headcount of a small company needs to be correlated to the number of products a company produces. While this factor is applicable for any size company, it has the most impact on the small company. If there are only a few products a year, the company's quality assurance program might be able to spare a resource for this purpose.

If the company is continuously developing products throughout the year, it makes sense to dedicate one or two people to the program. These people should be very technical and be able to understand the product in detail.

Beta testing is very labor intensive, with product distribution, issue communication, and other time-consuming tasks. Therefore, it might be necessary to pull in the assistance of an administrative assistant to help with product distribution. In addition, if the company has a technical support department, it might be able to lend a hand in communicating with the test sites.

In this sized company, the need for a beta test manager is superfluous. More appropriate would be a single beta test engineer focused on administration of the test. There is not much need for a beta test coordinator, as a department administrator can help with these tasks.

In general, dedicated resources are best for a beta test program, but should be balanced with workload and the budgetary constraints of a small company. The best scenario leverages the different organizations within the company, and everyone offers a helping hand.

Equipment

Much like the headcount solution, the equipment in a small company might need to be shared to best use the resource and get the most savings. New equipment is costly, and because of the variable nature of beta test participants, it will be very difficult to duplicate multiple test scenarios.

Sharing servers, software, and equipment, the small company must combine efforts to provide the beta program sufficient resources to perform the test. The greatest concern will be enabling mechanisms to get feedback into the beta program. For a beta test to be effective, the test participants need to have simple methods for returning comments. An analysis of available company resources should be performed, and there should be some method to help the beta program.

Space

Using existing lab space, a beta program in a small company should try to do its best to share space. In a typical lab, a beta program will only need a small bench or cubicle to set up test systems for duplicating bugs. There is no real need for a separate beta test lab, but some designated space is necessary.

Beta test programs also need a decent-sized area for storage. Packaging materials, shipping materials, sample product, additional hardware, test incentives, and other items are some of the many things a beta program needs to keep stored. This storage needs to be secure, yet regularly accessible.

Medium Company

Companies that have grown to a fairly decent size usually have a correlating number of projects to justify a larger beta program. With this growth in size, a company does expend more financial resources to maintain the program, but also has a larger return on that investment. With this size of company, the sharing of resources is still valuable in some cases.

Headcount

In a medium-sized company, projects start to enter beta testing on a consistent basis. Because of the nature of this workflow, there is a need to build a beta test team. A company this size produces between two and four products a quarter, which justifies full-time beta test personnel.

Beta test preparation, test operation, and closure consume a lot of time. With multiple projects consistently coming and going, it is impossible for someone to have other duties besides the operation of the beta tests. In fact, any more than two or three beta tests being managed at once is a tremendous workload.

At a minimum, there needs to be at least a few beta test engineers and perhaps a working beta test manager. The need for a coordinator could be delegated to a department administrator if he or she has enough time. However, there is a lot of work involved with shipping that many projects.

Equipment

For the gathering of test data, a beta program this size has too much information coming in to use email solely for communication. There will be a need to develop some form of Web-based operations. It might make sense to collocate the beta test Web interface on an existing server. It requires a lot of time and resources to properly maintain a Web server and an underlying database.

The beta program will need some dedicated hardware for the qualification and duplication of issues. Depending on the product, there might be a need for multiple systems, as well as some extra equipment used for storing data. Additionally, dedicated equipment for the duplication of discs is probably necessary, but could be shared.

Promoting sharing of resources is still valuable. Yet, when consistent workflow interrupts the ability to share properly, it means it is time to dedicate the equipment to the beta program. Monitor hardware activity closely, and if complaints arise about availability, it might be time to put money into beta test specific hardware.

Space

In the medium-sized company, there does need to be a dedicated space for the beta program, but it can still reside in the same lab as another test organization. A couple of benches or a few cubicles will suffice. Beta testing does not typically take a lot of space in a lab, but the area is constantly used just prior to and during a test.

There is a definite need for storage space with a beta test program of this size. The abundant packaging material, shipping materials, and test incentives take up a lot of room. In addition, depending on the lab equipment and software used to test, a dedicated storeroom will be necessary.

Large Company VERITAS

The large company can efficiently run a beta program with a moderate-sized but well-managed team. However, large companies typically run bigger tests, and thus require more resources to effectively administrate them. The sizeable number of beta test projects as well as a greater number of test participants means that a beta program for a large company is challenging to create and maintain.

Headcount

A complete beta test team is necessary to support a large company. Normally, the number of projects going through the beta test process is constant and complex. They often have multiple projects simultaneously running, and the need for a complete beta test resource is definite.

In most cases, there are multiple beta test engineers, a beta test manager, and beta test coordinator. In addition, there might be a need for a network administrator and potentially a lab manager. These people make up a team that will support five or more projects a quarter.

The workload is broken up among the multiple team members. Beta test engineers focus on performing the beta tests, the manager focuses on running the program, and the coordinator keeps the test product going in and out to customers. The additional people are there to simplify the support for the infrastructure and to help keep the beta test engineers focused on performing beta tests.

Equipment

When a large company dedicates itself to performing beta testing, it needs to focus on providing all the necessary tools to perform the testing effectively. The size of the program justifies the need for dedicated equipment to ensure that testing is performed efficiently. In some cases, sharing of resources might be appropriate, but that needs to be at the discretion of the beta test team.

The beta test program will need to maintain its own communication infrastructure, including Web servers, mail servers, fax machines, and so forth. The constant use of this equipment makes sharing difficult, if not impossible. More than likely, these resources will need good backup and security measures in place. Additionally, large companies have strict information technology requirements to which this equipment will need to adhere.

There also must be dedicated resources for the testing and verification of issues. Even for a program only doing issue qualification, a large company's program needs its own test hardware and software. Depending on the project load, beta test engineers might be able to share test systems within the department. However, that equipment must be able to be reconfigured very quickly to meet the needs of a new test.

Space

A beta test program for a large company should have a dedicated lab to make certain there is excellent security and efficiency. Sharing space becomes impractical because the beta program's resources are in constant use. The space does not need to be exceptionally large, but it should be separate from other test departments.

In addition, space will be needed for the communication tools such as servers, fax machines, and so forth. This space often requires special power and cooling to ensure reliability. In many companies, there might be strict corporate requirements on the location of this equipment.

Storage space is also critical for a large beta test program. All the materials needed to run a beta program consume a lot of space. Just as in a smaller program, incentives, shipping materials, packaging materials, additional test hardware, and test software will need a secure yet accessible location. In some cases, it might make sense to locate the storage near the shipping dock to avoid an inordinate number of trips back and forth.

Outsourcing

The benefit of outsourcing is its ability to allow any sized company to use minimal internal resources to operate a beta test program. Depending on the level of support the outsource company can provide, it might only require one part-time person, with no equipment and negligible space.

This allows a company to free up any resources dedicated to beta testing while producing the same results. Only a limited number of people actually need to be involved in the beta test process, and these people are mainly focused on evaluating user data.

Additionally, outsourcing can insulate a company from the customer. Outsource companies host the test and subsequently act as an interface between the client and the customer. This can have positive effects on the beta test. Customers see the test as owned by the outsource company, and will not direct their frustration about a beta product toward the developer.

Another added benefit is the flexibility an outsource company provides. Internal test resources typically require significant time to prepare for a beta test. However, outsource companies are in the business of doing testing and are focused on being ready for their customers. With a limited amount of time, the outsource company can be ready to test a product.

Outsourcing also offers a company an opportunity to supplement an existing test infrastructure. If a smaller internal beta program exists and is getting overloaded, the outsourcing company can help pick up the additional work.

The use of an outsource company needs to be considered carefully based on the project workload and the availability of internal resources. Outsourcing is viable when communication is extremely effective inside and outside the company. The outsource company must have a clear understanding of the needs and goals of the beta test and of the developer.

Headcount

If a company is using outsourcing as a solution for beta testing, there doesn't necessarily need to be a person dedicated to beta testing. Any person coordinating testing in the company can potentially interface. A quality assurance person, marketing manager, or customer support representative could all capably handle the communication.

In some ways, it might be useful to have a single person dedicated to managing the beta process and handling all communication between the outsource company. This person could ensure that all the related communication and resource management required to effectively using an outsourced solution happens.

A single dedicated point of contact makes managing an outsource solution much more efficient. Depending on the number of projects, this person might need to spend a lot of time working to schedule tests, gather data, and distribute product with the outsource company. This person can ensure that the needs of the company are being met by the outsource company and keep a close tab on their performance.

Equipment

There is little if any equipment needed to support an outsourced effort. If a company chooses to outsource a project, it might still want to have an internal bug evaluation process in place. In this case, existing hardware would be used. This decision is based on the level of commitment the outsource company is taking on.

Additionally, there might be a need to have a server or some form of storage to keep the data that is delivered from test. In most cases, the company will send the results in a format that can be easily reviewed by the developer. Alternatively, they will have an on-demand method for evaluating the data when the development team deems necessary.

Space

Of course, using an outsource company requires little or no space. However, depending on the scope of the test, there might be a need to use some internal resources to assist the outsourcing company with the debugging. However, that entirely depends on the relationship and contract established.

There might be interest in letting the outsource company collocate during the test period to ensure that the needs of the project are appropriately met. Then again, that scenario would only make sense on a critical or extremely large project. Regardless, space will be a minimal issue if the decision to outsource the beta test is made.

Test Cost

The previous section examined the cost of developing a beta test program. It was provided to help understand what expenses will be incurred as a company builds the program from the ground up. In this section, an analysis of the components for an individual beta test is provided.

Like the previous section, this information varies tremendously from company to company and project to project. However, there are certain basic materials necessary to conduct a beta test. In order to establish a definitive cost of a single beta test, a company will need to determine a number of variables.

Factors such as the duration of the test and the demographic coverage often appear simple at first, and then gradually grow more complex as the scope of the product changes. Using the following as a guideline, a management team will have a good basis for establishing a cost for a single beta test.

Number of Test Participants

The number of testers impacts the project budget based on the cost of the product. The company will need to determine how many test participants will be needed to appropriately test the product, and from that information, there is a method to determine many of the remaining costs of running the test.

Determining this number is not always easy. Often, the number of testers correlates to the resources available to administrate the test. However, that is only one factor. The complexity, geographic and demographic distribution, and existing number of users of the application are all factors considered in this decision. Early on, a development team needs to determine this number.

Once the quantity of test participants has been established, there are a number of additional costs that can be established. From this, a management team can successfully build a model to determine the cost of running the individual test.

Shipping

Distribution of the product can be a huge investment. Overnight shipping costs add up very quickly when you have a large group of test participants. Prior to beginning the test, a clearly defined budget for the project should be established. Once this figure has been determined, keep to it—it can get out of hand very quickly.

A company can reduce this cost through a number of effective methods. First, set up a contract with a shipping company in order to get a reduced special rate. Most major carriers will be happy to set up an account and offer a lower rate depending on volume. An added benefit of this is detailed billing reports.

Second, establish weight and size restrictions. Shipping companies determine the price of a package based on its gross weight and size. Most software can be simply slipped into a small envelope. If you have weighty documentation, determine if you can send an electronic version instead.

Depending on the schedule of the test, shipping costs directly correlate. If the product is on a tight release schedule, overnight shipping will be necessary. Conversely, if the test period is long and time is available, it might make more sense to choose a slower method and gain significant savings.

As an added concern, the duration of test must be considered. Depending on the number of revisions and the size of the application, it might be necessary to send multiple versions of the application. Multiple versions equate to multiple shipments. Regulating these will help keep a control on this cost.

Duration of Test

The length of the test period has a lot to do with the cost of the program. The longer the duration, the greater the cost. The reason for the larger cost is not necessarily tied to the time involved managing the product, but the material needed to keep the project running.

There might be a need for multiple shipments if the product is being distributed on CD-ROM. More cost might be incurred if the test participants begin to lose interest. If the duration of the test becomes excessive, there might be a need to add incentives for those who see it through.

Try to establish a clearly defined test duration before the beginning of the test. If possible, keep within those parameters and consider a second test if it cannot be completed during that time frame. This will keep the productivity on the test high and the cost low.

Incentives

Nice —
Theory

Incentives have a relative cost to the value of the product. If the product is very expensive, the need for incentives is small. Conversely, if the product is low cost, there needs to be sufficient value added to the cost of the application to make the product worthwhile to test.

Companies looking to add value do not have to budget a lot to increase the value of their product. The incentive does not necessarily have to be expensive—it is all about perception. If the customer is excited or motivated by the incentive, the price is irrelevant. Invest time in finding what might excite and motivate the test participants, and budget for those items that work. Plan on every tester earning the incentive. In actuality, only one-third to one-half will actually meet the criteria for the test. Yet, that incentive must be there to motivate the test participant.

 Check around the office. T-shirts, coffee mugs, or some other marketing material are often great incentives.

The "Beta" Product

Before beginning test, companies should determine a single-unit cost of the product. Depending on the type of product, this cost can range from negligible to expensive. However, understanding this cost is critical to establish a baseline cost for the beta test process.

Determining the value of the beta product can often be confusing and complex. The fact is that people seem to devalue software because it lacks tangible characteristics. Because they cannot touch it, hold it, or use the media it is delivered on for anything but its application, there is a perception that it has less value. Because of this, there needs to be a method to increase its worth.

Even within a company, people are willing to send out software immediately without regard to its value or what it costs. Because of this, the perception conveyed is that the software has no real value. However, nothing could be further from the truth.

To increase the value of the product, there needs to be a method for instilling how much the application is worth prior to the test. Two types of values need to be considered: the first is the perceived value, and the second is the actual value.

The perceived value is critical to recognize, as this is the cost you need to tie to an inactive test participant. Beta test product can often lose its perceived value as issues appear. While it might not be the actual cost of the product, inactive beta test participants cost company money and need to be looked at as a financial cost.

MAX Customers

PERCEIVED VALUE

The *perceived value* is the *manufacturer's suggested retail price* (MSRP) or *list price*. This is what you will convey to the beta test participants and the general public.

In contrast, active participants are returning the value of the product with their work. The effort they put forth is compensated by the value of the product. If the test participant meets the expectations of the test, then the perceived value of the software is equitable.

ACTUAL VALUE

The *actual value* is the estimated cost based on all the material that comprises the product. This is the commonly referred to as the "cost" of the product.

The actual value can usually be assessed from a *bill of m*aterials. The bill of materials is a categorical list of every part of a product. This list is assembled during the product development process. It is fairly comprehensive, but constantly changing.

Nonetheless, it is important to include all of the materials that will be distributed to the customer that are part of the product. This includes items such as CD-ROM, manuals, packaging, or accompanying third-party software. While the sum of these materials might not be much, they help in keeping the cost of the project in focus.

There usually is a significant cost difference for a software test than for a hardware test, and many times, it is easy to look at software as a non-cost item. However, it is critical to determine the cost of the product being tested, even if it might seem intangible initially. By determining all the materials on a per-unit basis, there are grounds for establishing a cost for the test.

Communication

Communication is a critical component of a successful beta test. Keep in mind that test participants are out in the field and are being asked to communicate with you. Thus, it is essential to provide every possible avenue of communication to get effective feedback. Directing people to use low- or no-cost solutions can manage this cost. However, there are times where expensive methods are necessary.

In Table 4.1, different communication methods have been broken out and where they fit into the cost. Higher price does not necessarily equate with greater efficiency. However, depending on the investment and how they are used, each can produce an equitable ROI.

Communication is the most critical aspect of performing a beta test. Without good communication tools, a project is doomed to failure. A company must plan on investing in effective tools relative to the size of its organization and the systems available. In many cases, there might be ways to share existing resources and leverage these costs.

Dispatch model

Table 4.1   Communication Cost

NEGLIGIBLE	LOW	MEDIUM	HIGH
Email	Public mailing lists	Standard telephones	Private mailing lists
USENET	Traditional mail	Fax	Cellular telephones
IRC	Chat applications	Toll-free numbers	Private forums Web-based system Private bulletin boards

Additional Costs

Not everything falls under the infrastructure or the individual projects. In some cases, there might be additional costs that need to be budgeted. These costs are inconsistent and vary in size. However, they do have an impact on a beta test budget and need to be considered.

When addressing the following issues, try to reference some historical data or discuss the cost with the responsible party. This way, a tangible number can be added to a budget in case it becomes necessary to use.

Legal

The tragic and difficult part of the beta process is the amount of time that needs to be dedicated to legal concerns. Beta tests need non-disclosure agreements (NDAs) created, contracts reviewed, and sometimes, take legal recourse for collections. These costs are infrequent and sporadic. However, they are an expenditure that needs to be anticipated.

Contact the company lawyer or legal department and determine a bill rate for the work that is performed. When a task comes up, try to determine the number of hours that will be needed to perform the task. Once that has been determined, establish a budget for this cost. In some cases, it might be difficult to get an exact cost.

Interdepartmental

With all this discussion about the benefits of sharing resources, there also might be a need to share the cost. If the beta program is borrowing equipment or using space to conduct beta tests, some departments might want to bill back the cost to the program's budget.

If the beta program is using another department's resource, it makes sense to share the expense. Calculate the amount of time the resource is being used and appraise the value of that resource to determine a percentage that is satisfactory to both the beta program and the department.

Incidental Costs

Everything from office supplies to the occasional team event, there are numerous expenses associated with the day-to-day operation of running a beta program. While these costs might seem mundane to manage, they do add to the operational expenses and can add up very quickly if left unchecked.

Establish a budget for the department and determine what those costs should be. In addition, accommodate for growth and project needs. In this budget, anticipate updates and changes to the beta test equipment. Overall, the expenditures to run a beta program are small. However, keeping a close watch on these costs will ensure an efficient and cost-effective program.

CHAPTER 5

Reducing Costs through Beta Test

The cost to develop a product directly correlates to the profit margin of the product when it is completed. The lower the development cost, the higher the profit. Thus, all businesses are looking for ways to reduce this cost. By providing companies with many ways to save money, a beta test compliments the product quality as much as the bottom line.

Through the use of beta test, a company can earn significant savings and increase product quality. In the following case study (see page 48), consider the true beneficiary of the beta test process, the customer who receives a free product, or the company that gets the feedback.

This example demonstrates cost savings in many manners. Initially, it looks like the savings come to Jim—he is the one getting the free software. However, Jim's benefit is small compared to the benefit Peronta is receiving. They are getting a real-world test system, QA engineer, marketing resource, and customer support trainer.

The Tools

When a company decides to perform a beta test, it is usually to ensure product quality. However, with a little creative thinking and some effort, a beta program can be used for many other purposes. By establishing a strong beta test program, a company can take advantage of the enthusiasm of its customers and impact the cost of a product.

All the tools that are necessary to drive down cost are provided through a beta test. It is simply using them properly and getting the most from the program. In a typical beta test, a company has anywhere from 30 to 50 people motivated to test a product. With a

Case Study: 100 Pennies Make a Dollar

Jim Washington has been beta testing for Peronta Corporation for the past three weeks. He is a world-class beta tester and has reported more than 100 distinctive and critical issues. He has been testing their small business software called EZBIZ.

Jim has a vested interest in the success of this product, as he is a small business owner and has been using the software for nearly three years. He volunteered to test the latest version of the software, as he recently updated his point-of-sale (POS) system and EZBIZ's earlier version no longer worked.

Investing hours of time, Jim is focused on exercising the software as much as possible. He quickly responds to Peronta's inquires and is focused on giving accurate feedback. EZBIZ is an expensive piece of software, and Jim knows his effort will be rewarded with a complimentary copy. His hard work is paying off, as he is quickly becoming an expert on every aspect of the product.

What Jim doesn't know is that the entire Peronta development team is keying in on his feedback and discussing his issues intensely. Behind the scenes, engineers are assembling special builds to address his needs and working on his issues before all others. Jim's configuration is one of the most common scenarios in the retail world and if it works for him, Peronta can confidently ship the product.

Peronta wants to build a lab environment similar to Jim's business so they can ensure they simulate issues and work on further revisions. However, it is taking a tremendous amount of time to populate the POS system with data. In addition, Jims' work compliments the QA process and provides emotional feedback about the interface.

Through this beta partnership, both Jim and Peronta benefit. Jim gets the valuable fixes he needs, a free copy of the software, and improves his understanding of a product that is critical to his success. Peronta gets valuable real-world feedback, a system to verify issues, and a loyal customer who will promote their software.

little push, they can also produce marketing data, competitive analysis, training material, and other material.

Getting the most from the beta test process requires an efficiently run program and an involved development team. There is nothing wrong with focusing a program exclusively on product quality. Yet, the resources are there to get much more from the test, and it seems tragic not to use them.

Product Quality Assurance

Most companies try to duplicate the "real world" by acquiring as much of the hardware, software, and other variables that are possible to obtain. While this effort has good intentions, it is literally impossible to match the factors that exist in the real world. The variables are innumerable, and few companies have the financial resources to accomplish this task.

Beta testing is the most effective way to ensure product quality and cover this variability. By focusing the quality assurance testing on the most realistic and common profiles, beta can be used to cover those that are less than common but are risks. By effectively selecting test participants, a beta test can compensate for holes in a test infrastructure and provide other valuable data.

In addition, quality assurance programs can take beta test data to help refine their lab infrastructure. Beta testing often explores areas that are overlooked, forgotten, or ignored in even the most comprehensive test plans. By using beta to refine quality programs and cover secondary areas of concern, a better-managed and more effective quality assurance program emerges.

Companies using this method for process improvement can see significant savings in an area that typically consumes large amounts of financial resources. By balancing the test duties of the quality assurance program and the beta test program, a company achieves a more comprehensive and less expensive test program.

Customer Support Cost Reductions

Customer support can be one of the most expensive aspects of releasing a product. If a company presses to distribute something that has not been adequately tested for the market, the impact can be devastating. Customer support costs are difficult to manage, as they are unpredictable.

Beta test provides three ways for company to save significant cost in the support area: training, forecasting, and evaluation. Each enhances the ability for support to handle incoming issues and effectively reduces the cost of operating a customer support department.

By using the support infrastructure during the beta test, the support team will be able to be properly trained on how to handle calls. Rather than arranging expensive training sessions for a product, the support personnel get first-hand experience with real customers using the real product, and thus are properly educated and trained.

This training also acts as a forecasting system for the support staff. During the test, customer service can adequately assess what type of effort it will take to support the product after release. As issues are revealed, the support program can establish which issues will become problematic after release and set up their infrastructure to handle it. With effective forecasts, costs are more efficiently budgeted and managed.

Last, the beta provides valuable evaluation data from the customer. Test participants are able give support important feedback on the level of quality the support team provides. This feedback can, in turn, help drive a more effective program and reduce cost of operation. Items such as hold times, responsiveness, knowledge, and resolution can also be measured.

Understanding and anticipating the risk of a new product, customer service teams are usually eager to assist in the beta effort. This assistance can be used to reduce the overall cost of administrating the test. By involving support, a beta test manager can ensure that the test participants are getting the help they need while helping themselves. It is an effective symbiotic relationship that should be explored.

Cost Savings from Testing

What is the cost of a bug? It is a question that is small but very important. Companies measure many different factors when attempting to determine the cost of a single issue. Items such as support calls, replacement product, bad press, and so forth are hard to place tangible figures on. Regardless, there is one fact that can be ascertained from this: a bug in a released product has a significant cost.

Considering this cost, it is only logical to assume that any effort designed to reduce the number of issues prior to shipping is a way to reduce the cost of the product. In addition, it is important to remember that the time and cost of this effort should not exceed its benefit.

In Table 5.1, Microsoft Corporation demonstrates the effective cost savings by sending a pre-released product to their Windows Development Labs. They are conveying the importance of discovering issues prior to release. The return on investment (ROI) is significant.

Experience indicates a high return on investment for manufacturers who send hardware to Microsoft Labs. These estimates are based on actual experience with Windows 2000.

Effectively, Table 5.1 shows how much one bug can cost a company to support. In the scenario presented, one issue can cost a company millions of dollars and virtually thousands of support calls. Even on a smaller scale, these issues are still costly to any company that does not invest in effective testing.

Beta testing provides a cost-effective additional form of quality assessment to a development program. As noted in Table 5.1, the cost of a single issue can be huge. While the example provided is not referencing beta testing, it reiterates the value of having outside eyes look at a product.

The significant difference between the two is that beta testing is handled internally and costs significantly less to the company. Outsourced test labs certainly add value, but are often redundant to the internal process, while beta testing adds a completely new and expanded view on the product: the customer's.

Both Microsoft Labs and beta testing provide an external opinion on a product. Both establish static test criteria and measure products against that criteria. Most important, both add value by providing more testing to a product. However, a beta test program provides a company with real-world customer feedback.

Issue Verification

Often, companies make a large investment in their testing infrastructure to be able to duplicate issues that come through quality assurance testing and from support. Beta

Table 5.1 ROI for Placing OEM Systems in Windows Development Labs

ASSUMPTIONS	ESTIMATE
Average support call cost	$20
Number of support calls generated for one hardware bug per 100 upgrades	10
Number of systems upgraded per model type	250,000
Number of units sent to Windows labs	50
Number of different model types at Microsoft	10
Average cost per system	$2,000
Fix rate on hardware bugs	65%
Incremental engineering cost to spin BIOSes	$100,000
Number of bugs per system submitted	1
Economic impact	
Investment in systems	$100,000
Investment in systems and engineering	$200,000
Number of support calls	250,000
Cost of support calls	$5,000,000
Support cost savings	$3,150,000
Systems ROI	3150%
Systems and engineering ROI	1575%

Microsoft Hardware Newsletter
Special Edition
Testing for Success
©2001 Microsoft Corporation.
All rights reserved.

test can provide a more accurate and realistic duplication scenario than a lab can. Instead of investing resources to duplicate systems in-house, beta can locate test participants with similar equipment and test an issue.

For example, if a product issue appears in the field, rather than invest money in trying to duplicate the issue, beta can go back to the field and find additional people to verify and duplicate the problem. In contrast, if an issue comes from an internal source, beta test programs can go out to the field and find test candidates to confirm or deny the existence of an issue.

This is not to suggest that beta testing replaces quality assurance testing. On the contrary, the focus of issue verification is when abnormal issues are exhibited and the quality assurance program does not have the equipment or software to duplicate the issue. Rather than spend the money on equipment to duplicate the issue, a beta test program can achieve the same result.

Beta testing can provide unlimited varying scenarios against which to test. The extensive cost of duplicating issues in a lab environment prevent internal systems of issue verification from being totally effective. In addition, the time it takes a beta program to bring these test participants online is considerably faster than an internal system. In all, a beta test program can verify issues at little or no cost to the company and do it faster.

Documentation

In order to effectively reduce the cost of producing documentation, a company needs to have an effective review process. The fact is, very few people have the time or the inclination to review documents prior to release. However, without proper review, manuals could be thrown away or require addenda.

Using beta test participants to review documentation is an effective way to improve the documentation and reduce the number of revisions, thereby effectively reducing cost. Beta testing also allows a company to experiment with innovations and determine the least expensive way to produce high-quality and low-cost documentation.

Geographic Savings

Localization is the transformation of a domestic product to meet an international market. From translation to compliance to local laws, localization is an expensive process. By using international beta test participants, you can verify that your investment has not been wasted.

A beta test program can locate people in these new markets and get them to verify the quality of the localized material. These native speakers are the most effective reviewers of translated documentation. In some cases, companies have foreign nationals who can perform the review. However, these people have other jobs and often do not have the time to review.

Additionally, international test sites will more than likely be using international hardware and software. This saves the company significant amounts of time and money. A company, with a small amount of research, can make the beta test participants match the necessary demographics their product requires for the international markets. Rather than investing in equipment overseas, the test sites can provide the necessary test platform.

It is also significantly less expensive for a company to distribute test product than to send engineers to each global location to test. Often, companies have to hire outside resources to test inside each country. By using beta test participants, a company achieves the same goal for a much-reduced cost.

Marketing Data Analysis

Data gathered during a beta test comes in many forms. Much of what is received can be used directly by the marketing department. Beta tests do not send in their feedback in scientific reports, but as incidents, comments, and quotes. This material has multiple applications for marketing. Best of all, the data is free.

Beta test can cover excellent demographic representation for the target market of a product. Companies can gather information from test participants about their demographics as part of the test participation. Rather than spend large amounts of money on performing market research, beta test participants can represent a sample of the product's user population.

Another notable aspect of the marketing data is quotations that come from beta test participants. A good quote from a customer can be exceptionally valuable. Beta test participants are real customers, and the testimonial element of a quote says a lot about a product. When a product is successful, good quotes can help with public relations, advertising, and press-related material.

Aside from the data being free, marketing can also use the program to assess concepts. Through surveys and questionnaires, beta test participants can often provide valuable market research that would normally be obtained through expensive market research firms. Large investment into focus groups is no longer necessary.

Finally, marketing is often interested in gathering competitive information. As beta testers are usually expected to have experience with the technology being tested, they often have experience with competitor products. Rather than invest in these products, it is possible to have the testers perform comparative testing and share the results.

Twenty Ways that Beta Test Saves

Beta testing is a powerful tool to assist in the reduction of development cost. Some of the savings are obvious, while others are more elusive. Either way, properly executed tests can promote cost savings and quality at the same time. To reiterate, the following 20 items show areas for potential savings and process improvements, which result in lower cost:

- Early and preventative issue resolution
- Elimination of redundant testing
- Reduced customer support calls
- Reduced regression and version tests
- Reduction of quality assurance test time
- Improvements in documentation
- Additional marketing data
- Material for advertisement and PR
- Preparation for support
- Prior understanding of potential customer issues
- Reduced risk of refunds and recalls
- Reduced risk of interim releases

- Promotion of customer input into design
- Reduced cost of quality assurance effort
- Lower geographic and demographic distribution costs
- Improved customer relations
- Valuable usability and design feedback.
- Potentially reduced warranty costs and liability costs
- Low-cost promotion of the product
- Alternative uses for test participants

Putting Beta Test into Your Organization

There are few departments within a company where a beta test program can't reside. The broad application and appeal of the program make a number of different teams well suited to run it. Selecting the appropriate location to put beta test is critical to the success of the program and the company.

Additionally, not only is "where" significant, "when" is also exceptionally important. Determining the best time to perform a beta test depends solely on how it fits into a company's development process and its products. Focusing on the proper project scheduling, readiness, and the viability of the product, each of these factors must be considered when making this decision.

To successfully implement a beta program, both of these decisions need careful scrutiny. Examining the varied departments with a typical corporate infrastructure, this chapter discusses the advantages and disadvantages of each location. In addition, there is an analysis of when beta testing should occur.

Where?

Where should a company place its beta program? This simple question holds complex problems and difficult answers. Before going forward, you need to understand that there is no single correct answer. The decision depends on a company's culture, competencies, and the ability to support beta testing. The following case study examines the complexity of the problem.

Case Study: Lost Cause

Heartlife Medical's software division is launching new inventory control software for pharmacies. This innovative program allows pharmacies to keep close control on their inventory and keep a handle on their budget. In addition, it has Internet connectivity for accelerated ordering, which a separate division of Heartlife controls.

Jack Greenberg is the general manager of the division and has decided that with the new ordering system, a beta test will be critical. Their first few software packages were met with mixed reviews, and this one must be successful if Heartlife will continue funding this division.

Gathering together all of his direct reports, Jack tells the team that he has decided they want to have real pharmacist input into the design of the product, and he wants someone to take ownership of a beta test. He explains that this is a critical project and that the division needs a "home run." He elaborates that this test will be the crucial element for a successful product.

Mary Cannon, director of engineering, offers to take on the task of beta testing. She states that the quality assurance team can manage the task, and it will just be another facet of the quality process. In addition, she feels that this will require an engineer to evaluate the data.

Oscar Montoya, marketing director, has a different view. He sees beta testing as something his team should handle. He has a lot of potentially qualified test candidates; his marketing engineers are much more experienced with using Heartlife's products. Last, he sees this as a great way to get some excellent reference material for press releases and the marketing campaign once the product is released.

Geoff Taylor has a completely different stance. As director of customer service, he feels that his department naturally owns beta testing. They are responsible for supporting the customer, and beta testing is a customer test. He insists that his team already has the infrastructure to support the test, and he will keep the focus of the test on quality.

Jack sees each person's viewpoint and needs to find an answer. Each team has valid concerns and each will certainly do an excellent job. Taking sides with one might offend another, but he has to make a decision. He is committed to getting a test performed. The question is, who should own the test?

Jack decides to set up the program in the engineering department under the QA organization. His decision is based on the competencies of that group and their ability to handle the technical data from a beta test. He asks Oscar and Geoff to each provide a resource that will work with the beta team to ensure their needs are met. Everyone is satisfied with this solution.

Jack takes on this decision with as much diplomacy as one can offer. However, in the end, common sense and his available resources dictate where the beta test program will reside. Because these decisions often have political and emotional ties, all factors should be considered before a pronouncement is made.

As the case study demonstrates, this is not a simple choice. Some locations have excellent benefit to the product, while others provide benefits to the customer. Thus, there is really no correct answer as to where the beta program belongs. A company must look at itself and decide what best suits its infrastructure and personnel.

Self Examination

Finding a home for a beta test team requires examining a company and its composition. Some are more engineering driven, while others maintain a marketing focus. Sales and support often demand attention, and in many cases have a viable reason to own the process. Regardless of the location, a company must determine who is best suited to support the program and ensure that resources will be available for its operation.

Beta testing touches most aspects of the product. In considering different organizations, it makes sense to analyze what each organization brings to the table. Some might not want ownership of the process. Some might want to own the process, but have selfish motivations. Others still might have genuine desire to own it, but not the resources to run it. Whatever the reason, the decision needs to be based on the needs of the company.

Beta testing touches every part of the product. No matter what decision is made, it makes sense to keep every department involved in the beta test process.

Engineering

Engineering is the most logical and most common place to situate a beta test program, as it is a compliment to the quality assurance process. In many companies, beta test is part of the same department as QA or reports to the same organization. Because of this, there are many logical reasons to locate the program here.

Advantages

Beta test is a quality assessment process, a test. While it can serve many purposes, its primary focus is on ensuring the quality of the product through testing. The organization that has direct responsibility over the product's quality is usually engineering. Thus, by locating it within engineering, the results of beta test can quickly and effectively impact the product.

Issues discovered during a beta test are usually tracked in an issue-tracking software. This is something that an engineering department usually manages. Engineering has technical resources to support the issue verification process. Often, complex technical issues will arise during beta testing, and people experienced with the product need to manage this.

There are other processes within engineering that compliment beta's effort, including quality assurance, reliability, design verification test, and homologation programs. Using these functions to compliment the beta test reduces redundant testing and repetitive tasks. In addition, a more effective coordinated effort can be achieved when these programs work together.

Engineering usually has to deal with the most issues generated from a beta test. The program is designed to assess quality, and much of the material derived from the test centers on fixing problems. Keeping the beta testing close to engineering allows the program to remain in touch with the issues being addressed by the developers.

Beta test personnel are typically very technical people. In most cases, they are engineers. It makes sense to use the personnel talent within the engineering team to build a beta program. In addition, for human resources-related issues, it fits nicely with the management and development structure.

Last, engineering usually has the space and equipment to accommodate a beta test program. Rather than invest a large amount of money in building a beta program from the ground up, it might be possible to leverage existing resources.

Disadvantages

With an engineering focus, there might be a tendency to neglect the other benefits that beta testing provides. As marketing and customer support information comes in, an engineering-based group might ignore those issues and focus completely on resolving the technical matters.

Additionally, an engineer might become impatient with the novice nature of some beta test participants. Beta test participants are normally average customers with many simple questions. Thus, the mundane support aspects of a beta program might be annoying to an engineer or ignored completely in pursuit of technical issues.

Another concern is how close the engineers are to the project. Constant involvement with development might cause the engineer to overlook issues because he or she is aware of its status. Even worse, the engineer might ignore a problem because it does not seem serious enough for consideration.

Beta testing is very effective when it exists within an engineering organization. However, those who are administrating the test need to put the interests of the customer and the quality of the product before the needs of the department. Maintaining a scientific and objective approach to the beta test, the person running the test cannot be tainted by his or her association with the department.

Quality

Many companies manage quality functions through the manufacturing process. While beta test is certainly a process for determining quality, it is rarely tied to the manufacturing part of the business. Beta testing normally works on a different development path and is not in touch with the quality program. However, there are some advantages to having it located there.

Advantages

The quality department ultimately owns and manages the quality of the product. It oversees every aspect of product development and ensures that each group is following its process. Placing beta test under that organization will get excellent visibility to the entire company. In addition, in companies where the quality program is a stand-alone entity, beta test can get a more objective testing viewpoint.

Quality normally implements process improvement systems such as 1SO 9001, Six Sigma, and QS 9000. These programs are designed to ensure a quality product development process. When beta testing exists in the quality program, it can help reinforce these processes. In addition, the measurement of success for these systems is customer satisfaction. With the beta program in quality, the department has a tool to keep in touch with that measurement.

Since the quality program dictates the development process, beta testing effectively becomes a mandatory test. When partnered with the quality team, there is excellent exposure for the beta program and its goals. This exposure allows beta testing to provide data back to the development team in all stages of product development.

Disadvantages

Quality is usually not a technical group. Although they do have some technical competence, their primary focus is on ensuring that the process is successfully implemented. Because of this, the needs of a beta test program might not be properly served in this location.

Additionally, a beta test team needs to be able to keep close ties to the customer. A quality program is focused on internal operations. This focus might push the beta program into performing tasks not normally associated with its operation, including beta testing internal processes or performing tests at inappropriate times during development.

Ultimately, quality and a beta test program have similar goals but don't necessarily need to be in the same department. Yet, there should be good communication between these programs, as they both are focused on the product's level of customer satisfaction.

Marketing

Marketing offers tremendous value when it owns the beta test program. It is the driving force behind the development of products. In this capacity, marketing has a vested interest in the results of a beta test. The feedback customers provide during beta testing can impact marketing decisions, and is useful for marketing programs.

Advantages

As the leaders in releasing a product, marketing has a clear understanding of what needs to be assessed during the beta test process. In addition, marketing normally determines what features are implemented. With marketing owning the beta process, the feedback from beta testing can help drive those features.

In some companies, marketing has a strong technical aspect. Marketing engineers, usability, compatibility, or certification programs often exist under the marketing authority and are complimentary to the beta process. By using these resources, a beta test program can achieve excellent technical and marketing balance.

The valuable quotes and customer feedback gathered during a beta test are often used by marketing to promote a product. When located within the department, beta test can become more attentive to this material and ensure that this aspect of the testing is emphasized. Programs such as public relations, documentation, and product management all have uses for a beta test program.

Finally, marketing often communicates with customers and has a strong relationship with specific accounts. These associations can be leveraged to provide valuable beta test participants. Marketing manages reference accounts that have large resources to test with and are willing to assist because of this special relationship.

Disadvantages

Marketing has its own interest in the results of a beta test, which might take the focus away from its quality goals. By setting the agenda for a beta program, it might effectively reduce its impact and cause critical issues to be overlooked.

Additionally, a marketing team might not have the technical background or the customer service savvy to perform a beta test effectively. While some programs do have technical people, they are focused on the company's products and not on the engineering-level understanding that is necessary to effectively test a product.

There also might be an inclination to change the focus of the beta program to promote a product rather than test it. The marketing team might drive a beta test program to grab quotes and other marketing material rather than support the test team. This results in a test that has little meaning.

Customer Support

The closest organization to the customer is most certainly customer support. Communicating with the customer on consistent basis, they are most in touch with the customer's needs. They also understand the product issues and what needs to be corrected for pending releases. Customer support has a lot to offer a beta test program.

Advantages

The infrastructure needed to support a beta program is already in place in customer support. They might have expertise in Web services, toll-free numbers, fax systems, email, servers, and other methods of communication. By locating in customer support, a beta program has all its communication needs fulfilled.

Customer support has a large resource of qualified technical people and is motivated to provide the best quality product to the customer. They are usually involved with the issue submission and tracking process and are motivated to find new issues.

Customer support also has the greatest access to a customer database to find qualified test participants. They have a lot of excellent data available to get specific test participants to meet the needs of the test. This is especially useful when upgrades and revisions are being tested.

Finally, customer support has a vested interest in an extensive and detailed beta test process. From effective training on the new product to a reduction in the number of support calls, a beta test benefits the program tremendously. Locating beta test within customer support ensures that the test will be promoted.

Disadvantages

Customer support is usually the most expensive and highly scrutinized program in the company. Pairing a beta test within the department might make getting financial support difficult. This means it might have some excellent resources for executing test, but not for maintaining the program.

Moreover, there might be a tendency for customer support to use the beta test program as a support resource by distributing pre-release software to customers experiencing issues. This is not the purpose of a beta program and can damage its credibility as a test organization and the faith the engineering program has in distributing test software to beta test.

Last, customer support might emphasize its own agenda rather than take an objective look at a product. For example, if an issue that has been generating a lot of customer complaints, they might preempt other issues to get the issue they consider important addressed. This also can damage the credibility of the test.

Sales

A sales department is in close contact with the customer and is tuned into their needs. Thus, locating a beta program within sales has some credible reasoning. Because they drive the revenue for the company, they are a powerful organization that can help build an effective beta program. However, beta testing is not a system for distributing seed units, and sales might be inclined to use it this way.

Advantages

Sales programs are usually rich with resources and can offer a beta program a lot of support. There is normally a lot of technical staff within a sales program to handle customer issues and ensure that a product is successfully tested.

Sales has one of the closer relationships with the customer. They are in touch with their needs and are driven by them. By putting beta test into the sales organization, there is a large pool of potential test candidates. In addition, salespeople usually have detailed knowledge about the customer and can help find experts.

The sales department is also focused on winning the company business. When this focus is paired with beta test, there can be some success. However, this success can only be achieved when the beta test remains focused on product quality and not earning sales for the company

Disadvantages

Putting beta product into a sales atmosphere might not harm a beta program, but it can often seriously damage a sales relationship. Sales teams are always looking for a reason to go back to the customer. A misconception exists that providing the customer early samples will provide that opportunity. In reality, beta test products can only damage that relationship, and a company puts itself at risk of losing the business.

When a company gives a potential sales lead a product that has inherent problems, it can damage the relationship it worked hard to establish. If the beta sample is riddled with issues, this might plant a seed of doubt about the quality of the product

In addition, sales departments like the exclusivity of beta test and enjoy leveraging the relationship to get the lead onto a test. However, these candidates typically will not provide the necessary feedback. As the beta test team drives feedback from the test participants, they potentially create a division between the customer and the sales team.

Information Technology

Information Technology (IT) owning the beta test process would certainly be a different but not illogical place. IT has a lot to offer a beta test program in the way of communication tools and server infrastructure. Depending on the product, they might also have the technical expertise needed to operate a test.

Advantages

Being outside the development process, IT could bring some objectivity to the test while remaining within the framework of the company. This benefit would be especially useful in companies with multiple divisions. Using IT would allow a company to establish a single program that acts as a company-wide resource.

IT also has the work force to manage a beta program. IT departments are normally on 24-hour call. A beta program can benefit tremendously by having this level of support. In addition, the IT program has an excellent infrastructure to support the program.

Disadvantages

IT is not focused on the customer, but rather on the internal operation of the corporate network. This focus leaves it out of touch with what the customer needs. In addition, IT is usually not involved in the product development process, and thus might not be prepared to test the product effectively.

Moreover, depending on the nature of the software, there might not be any technical expertise to handle the company's beta testing. IT people are technical, but with a networking focus. If your company develops something outside this realm, there might not be enough technical competence to run the beta program.

Outsourcing

Using an outsource business is a viable alternative to locating the program within a company. The flexibility of the beta test process allows it to be located in a variety of different places and still be effective. Outsourcing permits a company to eliminate the resources needed to administrate the process, but still get the benefits of the test.

Advantages

In the case of beta testing, outsourcing can provide a company with anonymity. This is an excellent benefit when a company is trying to create excitement over a release and doesn't want to compromise the secrecy of the project. The anonymity is also excellent for testing concept products that a company might or might not pursue.

Outsourcing beta testing is also practical, as it will place the test in objective hands and let each company organization reap the benefits of the testing without tainting it with its focus. An outsourcing company has no vested interest in the success of the product; they are only interested in the success of the test.

In general, outsourcing allows a company to hand off tasks that are not its expertise to an organization that is more qualified to handle it. Thus, they use the best practices possible and achieve the greatest results.

Outsourcing also adds flexibility to a tight development schedule and permits a company to spend very little preparation time on the test. Basically, it delivers a beta test product when it considers it ready, and the outsourced resource distributes and performs the beta test.

Disadvantages

Outsourcing can be problematic because it is outside of the company. Without a full-time person involved in the process, it could become risky to rely on a third party to ensure that the test is properly executed.

Furthermore, the outsource company might not be close enough to the product to understand the specific needs of the beta test. Their expertise is not in your product, but rather in performing the testing. Because of this, they might miss critical issues during the beta test process.

Last, an outsource solution requires handing off company property and information to someone outside the company. Depending on the secrecy and the nature of the product, this might put the company and the product at risk.

When?

As important as "where" to put the beta test program is "when" to put it into the process. Beta is universally considered to be at the end of the process, but when it comes to what "end" is, there are many different opinions. Again, there is no definite answer to the question, but some significant justification for each path.

Viability

One factor must be considered prior to entering test: "Is the product ready to distribute into test?" This question attempts to assess the stability, consistency, and quality of the product prior to its entrance into beta test. This method for determining these factors is called "viability."

 A product is viable when it and all of its components are capable of successfully operating as designed and are ready to be distributed into test.

Each product is different, and it is the responsibility of the company to establish clear criteria of what it considers viable. These criteria need to be documented and remain static. Whether a product is viable is objective: either it meets the criteria, or it doesn't.

Instituting viability criteria is a complex process. While it is the responsibility of the person performing the beta test, input should be gathered from every member of the development team, as they will be measured against it.

When viability is used properly, the interests of the development team coincide with the needs of the beta test participants and an effective test is performed. To ensure a product is ready, there are three potential positions to take.

The strictest definition of the process begins a beta test after every aspect of product development is complete. All of the materials are gathered together and the focus of the development team is on the beta test results. While this is certainly ideal, it is often impractical.

First, rarely do all the components of a product come together at the end of a development schedule. More often than not, the different parts are staggered, and might or might not be ready for the beginning of the test.

Second, beta test needs to be an adaptable process. When the timeline is strictly observed, it tends to cause teams to either be frustrated or ignore the beta test all together. While it is theoretically valuable to strictly hold to a schedule, in the end it is more of an inhibitor of the product's development.

Last, depending on the criteria for viability, a product might never meet the recognized guidelines, even if they are agreed upon. Viability is designed to ensure that a beta test participant never receives a product prematurely. However, it can act as a stranglehold on the development process and keep a good product from going into beta test.

Viability is simply a guideline to ensure that the customer has a product that is ready to test. It is not a gating item, but rather a way to measure the product to ensure that it will get an effective beta test. By using viability properly, the customer will produce the best test results and the company will receive the greatest benefit.

Flexibility

A flexible interpretation of the process permits beta test to occur close to the end of the quality assurance phase. It allows for some of the components to be incomplete, and it has a more flexible view on viability. Without sacrificing quality, it emphasizes balancing the needs of the test participant with the needs of the company. This interpretation is the most successful, as it attempts to accommodate both beta test and the development team.

Keeping the program flexible is critical to meet everyone's needs. Management needs to take the needs of the beta test seriously while its needs are continuing to be met. A flexible program allows each product to be handled on its own merits. For example, a product with a history of issues might need to have strict test entrance criteria, while a simple software utility with a solid history might have very liberal criteria.

Beta test is not designed to obstruct the process, but rather to enhance it. By promoting the program through flexible yet viable test criteria, a program will earn the respect of the development team, and when future tests are about to begin, the teams will be prepared to provide a good product that is ready for test.

CHAPTER 7

Common Failures in Beta Test Implementation

The blame for a failed beta test is usually placed on the shoulders of the person executing the test. However, these accusations are normally unfounded and inaccurate. While it is certainly the responsibility of the beta test team to ensure successful results, many factors coming from a variety of sources can contribute to a failed test.

Unfortunately, company management is often the key contributor to the failure of a proficient beta test. Whether it is misuse, slow decisions, or lack of support, the program fails to produce effective results. Instead of placing blame, take every measure to get the most from the test. By identifying these potential avenues for failure and addressing them before the beta test begins, a company can ensure successful and productive projects.

Programs can also fail because they aren't properly designed or implemented. In the second section of this book, material is provided to build and operate a successful beta test program. By using the information provided in this chapter combined with an effectively designed program, a company can get the most out of its beta program.

Understanding Failure

As the progression of product development moves forward, it touches many different people, departments, functions, and processes. Each company manages these items in a different manner. However, there is one common element for all companies: a schedule.

Successfully managing a schedule results in meeting market windows, properly allocated resources, and ultimately, a successful product. Conversely, missing a schedule is effectively considered a failure. Therefore, prior to deciding on a schedule, items that could potentially cause a project to slip are identified as being on the "critical path."

In many development processes, beta test is the last phase of testing prior to product release and often lives on the "critical path." Thus, it becomes the most scrutinized and most poorly executed of all the phases of development. Beta test very often reveals problems, and most companies do not want to risk slipping their schedule unless an issue is significant.

Companies often settle for a poorly executed beta testing to ensure a successful schedule. This places them at tremendous risk. The cost of poorly executed beta can be felt throughout an organization. Depending on the issues discovered during test, everyone from the frontline customer support to the CEO could feel its impact.

Beta testing is the most effective tool to ensure a successful launch of a product into the marketplace. A successful beta test program will quickly identify risks, gather useful marketing data, determine customers' needs, provide useful product feedback, and promote quality.

Beta testing often underachieves its potential because programs are poorly designed, executed, and employed. There are many simple and common elements that cause a reduction in effectiveness. The following subjects cover many mistakes that prevent a successful test.

Poorly Managed Data

Beta testing is only effective when the data gathered from testers is properly managed and distributed to the responsible team members. Very often, development teams use poor systems to gather and distribute data. From bad issue-tracking systems to poor participation in the beta process, test programs rely on a good communication structure to ensure that issues are addressed.

Data gathered during the beta test is often time sensitive and requires the immediate attention of the responsible person. The problem lies in the fact that beta covers so many areas of a product that, often, focus turns to the issues that potentially prevent a product from shipping. Thus, a system that effectively delegates the issues to the responsible person or party is essential.

Whether it is a hand sort and delegation or a complex issues-tracking system, problems discovered during test need to get to their owners. Once the proper people have their data, ensuring that it does not get lost is essential. Providing an effective channel between the customer and the developer is a key responsibility of a person administrating a beta test.

Poor Test Candidates

Very often, participation in a beta test is an exciting and unique opportunity for a customer. However, companies often select test candidates for inappropriate reasons. Potential sales leads, good customers, friends, employees, recommended or random candidates are the easiest choices and usually the worst testers.

Adhering to the criteria designated for the selection of test participants is a key aspect of beta testing. Ineffective testers equate to a failed beta test. The person administrating a beta test program must resist the temptation to take easy candidates and focus on getting qualified applicants to participate.

In addition, people administrating the operation of the test need to ensure that they are not coerced into accepting candidates that are unqualified. If a senior person demands that a particular candidate is included in the beta test, it is best to separate that person from the qualified pool of testers and accept that the person might not do any testing.

Sometimes, including some of these unqualified people is unavoidable. When this situation arises, the beta program should be absolved of the responsibility of getting data from that person. The fact is, when candidates are forced upon the beta program it is more than likely that the reason they are being included is not to beta test but for some other purpose.

Poor Test Participant Communication

Beta test participants are customers. Often, as issues appear during the test period, the temptation to put effort into addressing these problems preempts the necessary communication a test participant expects. Once a tester feels neglected, he or she is unlikely to continue to produce test results. Recognition of the tester and his or her contribution is vital.

Simple communication is often overlooked in cases when it is most critical. A straightforward "we are looking into it" can often abate test participant frustration. Normal and regular communication with the test participants promotes trust, enthusiasm, and involvement.

Promoting communication can be most effectively accomplished using Internet-based test tools. Using mailing lists, forums, or Web-based gathering tools can ensure the customer will provide continuous feedback during the beta test period.

 Set up an email address and a toll-free number that the customers know will always work; for example: beta@yourcompany.com.

Effective communication with participants promotes good test results. Implementing tools and systems to make certain the sites are able communicate with the beta test team will also eliminate excuses from the test sites. This eliminates excuses for a lack of participation in the beta test.

Use as a Sales Tool

One of the most common reasons for failure comes when companies decide that their beta test program is better used as a seed program for the sales of the product than as a quality test. There are several fatal flaws with this practice.

First, a beta product is pre-release. By distributing this product to potential sales prospects, an inherent risk of the customer experiencing complications exists. A company will lose the sale because the customer encounters problems that are being corrected. Even worse, customers judge the product based on this sample.

Second, the customer might be a good prospect but not a good beta tester. These people are not focused on the company's need but rather on their own, which results in skewed and incomplete results. More than likely, the only data that will be reported are issues that prevent the customer from using the product that are important to him or her.

Third, there is a chance that these participants will impact the performance of the other testers. Through their lack of participation or narrow focus, the communication during test might drive the project in the wrong direction. Sales, not quality, becomes the focus of the test.

Next, including a sales prospect creates an additional communication layer. In most cases, there is a single sales contact interested in ensuring the needs of the customer who expects that all communication with the client go through him or her. This additional layer makes getting test data difficult.

Last, because the decision of this customer might impact the sales of the product, the test manager might be asked to give special consideration to the prospect. Test participants given this type of treatment often are unresponsive and ineffective as testers.

Unfocused or Too Focused Test Design

Most successful tests have a defined process behind them. Likewise, most failed tests were lost from the start because there was no definition of what needed to be tested. Without a clear and refined plan, beta tests can meander and grab a lot of derivative and often useless data. Without direction, the data gathered from the beta test might miss critical aspects of the product's design.

In contrast, placing emphasis on one aspect of a product drives the test participant to a refined focus and leaves other areas ignored. The focus might have momentary importance, but when the issue is resolved, it becomes difficult to change that customer focus back to the general testing of the product.

Aside from a well-written test plan, delineated test procedures can address this issue. However, it can also become a restrictive process. Tests that are spelled out for a test participant do not encourage experimentation in a real environment. It basically creates a test lab in the real world. Freedom to explore and experiment must be balanced with a defined plan with goals.

Promoting a program that balances the real-world test atmosphere with some concise goals will allow a beta program to produce both effective and important information about the software. A beta test should allow the customer to experience the product as if it were just purchased from the store, while providing feedback that the company needs to get the product to market.

Poorly Motivated Test Participants

Test participants are not governed by an altruistic need to ensure quality in products. They have selfish desires that necessitate proper channeling to get the best test results. If these needs are not met, the test will be a failure.

Providing sufficient motivation to test needs to be a top priority. Some form of reward needs to be waiting at the end to make certain the test gathers sufficient data from the participant. Clear paths to the reward need to be established for the test participant. In addition, recognition of achievement is also an added incentive. Test participants need to understand that their contribution is valued and that their effort will be rewarded.

It is also important to motivate in an effective manner. Setting testers against each other for competition will destroy the beta test. The top testers will produce an inordinate amount of redundant data to win, and those who realize they don't have a chance to win will stop producing feedback. Incentive needs to be individually driven and measured.

 Properly motivated test participants provide a wealth of feedback. In contrast, poorly motivated testers are useless. Details about how to properly motivate testers and get the best results are provided in Chapter 14, "Getting Results."

Premature Product Release to Beta

In the furor of getting a product released, development teams often push a product to beta test too early, thus ensuring failure of the test. Beta testers are not quality assurance engineers, but customers. Unreasonable numbers of problems cause testers to become overwhelmed and frustrated.

Some test participants can be technically savvy; thus, teams get a false sense of security about the ability of the tester to handle the problems. However, this usually leads to the tester experiencing an inordinate amount of downtime and creates an excessive amount of support time for the administration of the beta test.

Test participants are not being paid for this work; therefore, it is crucial to treat them with respect and consider the quality of the product you send them. Ensuring that the product is a viable candidate for release also ensures a viable beta test.

Under-Utilization of Test Participants

Besides the prospect of a free product, test participants are motivated to test for a variety of different reasons. Some do it for the exclusivity of seeing pre-release products before anyone else does. Others are interested in a specific technology or application the product provides. Many are just fascinated by technology. However, in a properly run test, almost all participants eventually become interested in finding issues and ensuring the quality of the product.

If test participants are not used properly, they lose interest in the process and become ineffective. This failure can exhibit itself in many different ways. Extended test periods, slow issue response, lack of responsiveness to communication, overly simplistic test procedures, and mundane tasks can drive a tester to inactivity.

Consistent and valuable work for a test participant promotes communication and test involvement. Coinciding with the test plan, a test administrator needs to understand planned product revisions and where the test participant effort should be focused.

Balancing the amount of work with the type of work throughout the duration of the test, the beta team should look for ways to keep the interest of the site. In conjunction with this effort, the development team needs to manage its revisions and ensure that the beta test team is aware of when changes will be made to the product.

Peripheral Process Failure

Beta interfaces and integrates with many different organizations within a company. Often, teams are unprepared to handle the data that comes from the test. If peripheral teams that use the beta test data are not properly informed, there is a risk that they will impact the beta test itself.

When another department provides a service or requires a service of beta test, it can be a hidden risk that will impact the test process in many different ways. If it is a service to the department, schedules can be impacted. If it is a service that beta test provides, unnecessary time might be dedicated to helping the other department. Communication between these different teams needs to be clear and consistent.

Test administrators managing deliverables should have an unambiguous understanding of what these items are and when they are due. Materials and services leverage from other corporate organizations should also be clarified prior to beginning test. The logistics of beta can often be as time consuming as the test itself. However, they are critical to the function of the test, and thus, essential for success.

Had John taken the time to communicate with the build manager earlier, the situation might have been averted. However, just prior to distributing the product into test is an exceptionally busy time. It can become overwhelming trying to assemble all the materials needed. If John had been focused on communicating with the build manager, he might have been prepared for this issue.

Beta testing is an imitation of the development process. A beta test team needs to understand the different deliverable items and their owners. It might not be the fault of the beta test manager that the product did not get into test; however, the blame will reside with him or her. As the product moves toward release, it is critical to make certain that there is effective communication with all the different component contributors. See the Case Study on page 73.

Case Study: At the Gates

Spectra Studios has completed the last phase of quality assurance testing and is about to begin the first phase of beta testing on their new game, *The Gates of Minithra*.

This multiplayer adventure game is driving toward a fall release schedule and is designed for play on most console systems. Although the development schedule has been going well, they have a very small window for testing, and John Corbett, beta test manager, has been quickly gathering material to get the product distributed.

At the team meeting, John brings to the attention of the team that the game will not be ready for beta unless he gets the latest build on his desk this afternoon. They will be distributing the product to about 60 testers and he needs time to get it duplicated and properly labeled. The software duplicator has informed John that a huge project will begin in the next couple of days, and if he doesn't get them the build, they will be unable to fit his project in for another week.

Karen Crow, project manager, states that she is waiting to get the latest build from the build manager, and as soon as she has it, John will get it. However, a sudden voice disrupts the meeting. Tanya Carlin from marketing informs Karen that the last build is experiencing problems: it does not support multiple controllers, thus making multiplayer gaming impossible.

The issue appeared when the most recent build was generated, and the build team is blaming engineering for the issue. Engineering claims that the game works fine in the lab, and obviously the source has become corrupted. Tanya feels they will get the problem resolved and the product will be ready.

John asks if they can provide another version of the source code to the build team, but no engineering representatives are in the meeting to answer his question. In addition, he has already notified testers that the game will ship tomorrow, so there is a lot of anticipation for its arrival.

Karen decides she will take the action item to ensure that John gets the build, and the meeting ends. John returns to getting the other beta materials ready. However, as the day closes, no build arrives and the test is now delayed. In addition, John has now had to inform the testers that they will not be receiving their product when they had hoped.

Insufficient Test Materials

As beta is normally the last procedure prior to release, there is a tendency by development teams to skim hardware from the beta pool. The allocation of hardware is usually done early in the product development process. Beta materials are normally the closest to resembling the release candidate. Thus, many want to get a sample for a variety of purposes.

Inevitably, there will be some loss of hardware along the process. It is logical to assume that some material will be defective. Additionally, it will be necessary to budget for failure in the field. However, if not properly managed, beta can be severely impacted by a shortage of software or hardware necessary to perform the test, Beta test managers should anticipate that some quantity of material will be confiscated for other purposes, along with anticipating the aforementioned risks.

Insufficient material is an exceptionally difficult failure to overcome. Without sufficient material, test schedules can be forced to shift, participants might need to be dropped, and eventually the quality of test results is affected. Managing the inventory of test materials and establishing a process to ensure that material is ready for test is critical to the success of a beta test.

The Impact of Beta Test Failure

Beta testing is designed to make certain a product is ready for market prior to release. When a beta test produces no test results, it is an indication that either the program or the process has failed, and there are byproducts of that failure. From rising product costs to negative customer perceptions, a failed beta test creates exponential problems for both a company and its products.

When a beta test fails, its impact can be felt in every part of a company. The impression might not be immediate or obvious, but it is there. The issues that were missed, the comments that were not heard and the information that was not gathered eventually have a devastating impact on the product's and the company's success.

The first and most prominent evidence of a failed beta program is the discovery of issues after the product has shipped. The product is in the channel and customers are purchasing it. Tragically, they are calling customer support to get resolution for a problem they are experiencing.

Like a fire, it immediately catches everyone's attention, and every effort must be made to extinguish it. These issues take the entire company's focus from development and push it toward resolving the issue. Moreover, the longer it takes to resolve these problems, the worse the impact on the company.

From these issues, customers' perspective on the product becomes tainted. They lose the perception of quality that inspired them to purchase the product in the first place, and unless the issue is handled effectively, customers are influenced negatively for future product purchases. In addition, they will influence other people about your product.

The effect extends even further as the cost to support these issues eats away at the company's bottom line. From customer calls to replacements or returns, the price tag of a failed beta test escalates with the impact of the issue. Moreover, the cost grows exponentially with more issues.

Efficiently run beta programs are designed to reduce this risk, if not eliminate it. With an investment in beta testing both financially and through program support, a company prevents the potential beta test failure and establishes a system to prevent problems getting to the customer.

PART TWO

Building a Beta Test Program

Summary

This second part is designed for people who need guidance in implementing or operating a beta test program. It focuses on providing significant detail on the different functions that are part of the entire beta test process. Every aspect of a beta test's operation is included. You will want to read this section if any of the following applies to you:

- You are currently deploying a beta test program.
- You are a manager of a beta test program.
- You are looking for a detailed explanation of different parts of the beta test process.
- You are responsible for the beta test results.
- You want to determine if your beta test program is effective.
- You have certain beta processes that need improvement.
- You want to fix a broken beta test process.
- You want to understand what the beta test process entails, and what type of work will be required to perform the test.
- You don't know how a beta test is run and you want to understand the process in detail.
- You are training someone on a beta test program.

This part of the book provides extensive details on the process of doing beta testing. Part One, "Understanding Beta," provides a general overview of the program while exploring its benefits to an organization, and Part Three, "Making the Results Work," examines how to use the test results effectively.

CHAPTER 8

Building a Test Team

A beta program can consist of a one-person operation or a large and complex group of engineers and marketing people. Often, the size and complexity of the organization directly correlates to the number of products being tested. However, it can also correlate to the size and complicated nature of the beta tests being performed.

The following sections describe the potential personnel in a beta test team and their roles. Because of the sporadic nature and relatively short duration of these tests, some companies might opt to have an existing person handle the program while a project is in test. These positions are described in the context of a dedicated person whose focus is to support a beta test program. However, each could be potentially handed off to a person with similar qualifications.

Beta Test Manager

The beta test manager develops and fully implements a beta test program. In a small company, this person could be the entire program. In a larger corporation, the beta test manager oversees the operation of multiple tests, people, and projects. The beta test manager ultimately owns the responsibility for a successful test.

Responsibilities

The beta test manager is focused on developing and continuously improving the policies and procedures that comprise the total beta test program. He or she will supervise and manage the different people, resources, and budget to maintain a fully functional beta test operation.

Working directly with different people within the company, the beta test manager's goal is to define the needs, requirements, and expectations that are needed to perform each beta test. These items are varied and often complex. The beta test manager should have a good rapport with the many people who are involved with the development of a product.

This is especially important when working with the marketing and legal departments to develop and periodically update applications and agreements for use in selecting and contracting with beta test participants.

The beta test manager is expected to train each beta test employee on the purpose, policies, and procedures of the beta test program, and to make sure that the overall operational quality of the program is exceptional. In addition, the beta test manager should be clear on each person's responsibilities and delegate work appropriately.

With the numerous projects that come and go through a beta test program, it is crucial that the beta test manager understand what each of these are and their key components. While it is not the goal to micromanage each team member, the manager should monitor who has access to pre-release software and ensure that distribution is being carefully controlled.

The beta test manager should take leadership on all beta test issues. From the scheduling of tests to the deployment of new technologies into the infrastructure, this manager's role is critical to the success of each project. Providing guidance, the beta test manager guides the program to guarantee a low-cost, highly efficient service.

As with any manager, it should be his or her goal to establish a clear, long-term strategy for beta test. These goals should focus on quality and efficiency while involving some aspect of the company's overall mission. By establishing a strategy, a beta test manager can successfully adapt to growth and maintain focus on the program.

A beta test manager needs to have comprehensive knowledge of the complete development process. Beta testing evaluates an entire product. When a beta test manager brings a project into test, he or she needs to understand how the issues discovered in test will impact the different organizations and provide guidance on where to distribute test results within the company.

Ultimately, the beta test manager must understand all aspects of the beta test process. If necessary, he or she can run a beta test as well as any of the team. The beta test manager needs to be technical enough to support the company's products and operate the program infrastructure. By being able to handle these issues, the beta test manager can maintain the program when difficult situations arise.

Portia recognizes that, sometimes, being an effective manager means being able to do any job in her department. Beta testing is very close to the end of the development cycle, and thus, carefully scrutinized. The team's infrastructure problems cannot hold up a product from release. By taking on the projects, Portia is ensuring the success of her program and the project. See the Case Study on page 79.

Case Study: Write If You Get Work

Portia Adams has been beta test manager for the past two years for Nonstop Software. Nonstop makes a universal power supply (UPS) management interface for most of the major UPS hardware manufacturers. As an OEM, every version of their new application must be customized for their clients.

Each customer supplies specific requirements for their interface, and communication between each company's UPS and the software is unique. Thus, a single base application multiplies as each customer provides details to make the product function with his or her hardware.

Portia often faces scheduling nine or 10 simultaneous beta tests when the product enters its final phase. She has a team of five beta test engineers, and each takes on two different customers. The versions are somewhat staggered in delivery as each company is tying the software to their latest product release. Nonetheless, the projects fall within weeks of one another.

This morning, Portia received news carrying a mixed blessing. Paul Sloan, one of her beta test engineers, has received a promotion and is being asked to move over to his new department immediately. While Portia is pleased for him, she now has a vacancy, and testing is expected to start in the next week. Even if she could find a qualified replacement candidate, there is no way to get a new person up to speed on the product.

Portia first examines the workload for her department. While each of her engineers is loaded, the variability in the development schedule might allow her to delegate Paul's work out to the other engineers. Unfortunately, there is little room in each engineer's schedule for these additional projects, and Portia worries that the extra load will compromise the quality of the test.

Contacting the project manager for Paul's assigned tests, she informs him of the situation. She starts to evaluate the potential of bringing in a QA engineer to assist. QA is also buried in version testing. It quickly becomes evident that this option is not possible.

Getting the product to market in a timely manner is the most significant concern for the company to succeed. If Nonstop does not meet the demand of its customers, it risks losing these contracts. Portia became manager through promotion and is very familiar with running a beta test. Although it has been a while, she assumes the responsibility of getting Paul's projects beta tested. She begins to send mail to all the test participants, notifying them of Paul's promotion and that she will be handling the project.

Qualifications

In discussing the qualifications of a beta test manager, consider that this position requires a lot of different experience. The beta test manager should have balance in technical competence, customer service skills, and management experience. Ideally, an effective manager has a varied background and a history of focus on the customer.

Selecting a person with excellent competence in the product or technology a company produces is essential. From the seasoned technical support person to an industry expert, a beta test manager must be fully versed in the technology he or she will support. While this does not need to be code-level knowledge, understanding the impact of changes on the code is important.

The person running a beta test program must also be an excellent time manager. Beta testing does not flow on a regular path. The sporadic and constantly shifting nature of the product development process makes running a beta program very unpredictable. Being flexible and scheduling projects effectively are key qualifications for a good beta test manager.

Finally, the primary activity of beta testing involves interfacing with the customer. Thus, a beta test manager will have excellent customer service skills with an emphasis on communication. Being communicative is a key part of the beta test process, and a manager with this emphasis will operate a successful program.

Beta Test Engineer

The beta test engineer operates as a highly technical project manager. Not only is there an emphasis on debugging issues, an engineer must be focused on operating the test, coordinating projects, and ensuring the best test results. The engineer's primary objective is performing a successful beta test project.

Responsibilities

The beta test engineer's first responsibility is the selection of technically competent beta test sites. Detailed in Chapter 12, "Effective Site Selection," this critical and difficult process takes a lot of training to perfect. However, it is arguably one of the most important roles of the beta test engineer.

Once the test participants are selected, the beta test engineer takes the time to develop a rapport with them that is both professional but slightly personal. Gathering test data, providing support, and working through releases, the engineer is expected to be the primary contact to the beta test participants. By building a good relationship with these customers, he or she will be able to gather more feedback and better results.

Customer service skills are a quality not normally tied to an engineer. However, it is an essential quality of a beta test engineer. The communication between the engineer and the test participants during a beta test is the foundation for the test results. Establishing clear paths for communication and offering timely responses to beta test participants' issues are a key responsibility of the beta test engineer.

The beta test engineer also ensures contract compliance of all beta test sites. This includes making certain that the test participants respond to requests for information, submit issues, and generally participate in the test. On the frontline, the beta test engineer is the only person who can identify whether a beta test participant is fulfilling his or her obligation.

Prior to entering test, the beta test engineer works with test products to become familiar with their technologies, features, functions, and so forth. Over time, the engineer is expected to become the expert on the product and is able to educate and inform the rest of the beta test team.

As an expert on the product, the beta test engineer must continually evaluate technical data from testing and verify the existence of problems. This evaluation is central to building confidence in the efficiency of the beta test program. The development team must realize that when the beta test engineer reports an issue, it is real and needs to be addressed.

Part of the issue verification process involves configuring equipment for use in duplication of issues. The beta test engineer should have a comprehensive understanding of all the supporting technologies associated with the company's products. This involves assisting in the maintenance of the equipment in a test lab and establishing proper test parameters for use of that equipment.

Acting as a liaison between the sites and the company during the beta test, the engineer maintains and updates the test database. Adding information and updates to the project database, the beta test engineer scrutinizes data from the test results reported by each beta test site. From that data, he or she distributes the information to the development team.

Communication between the beta test manager and the beta test engineer needs to be continuous. The beta test engineer should provide reasonable details about project workload, issues discovered during tests, participant performance, and the general beta test issues. In addition, the engineer should be communicating equipment and related budgetary needs to the manager.

Attending project meetings and being properly prepared to address beta test-related issues in those meetings is a responsibility that is shared by the beta test manager and the engineer. In some cases, both might want to attend the meeting. However, the beta test engineer is the closest to the project and should be the primary contact on any project.

Aside from the duties of running the beta tests, the beta test engineer should become an expert on the product line through the review of technical data. In addition, this data should be generated into technical reports that can be used by the beta test program for training purposes.

The fact is that the beta test engineer spends a lot of time with a product from conception through development and into test. He or she will develop intimate knowledge about the inner workings of the software and will be able to provide assistance to more than just the beta test participants.

Qualifications

Primarily, the beta test engineer must have an excellent foundation in the technology that is being tested. He or she must understand everything from the code to the packaging. This knowledge can be acquired through education or experience. However, the beta test engineer should have some experience dealing with the technology on many levels. This will assist when debugging the varied issues that arise during test.

Beta testing interfaces with real customers, and thus, beta test participants have an expectation of the level of service they should receive. To deliver this, an engineer with experience in customer service is always helpful. However, one who has excellent communication skills might be able to address this need.

Aside from technical excellence, the engineer must also be effective in time management. Just as the manager must coordinate an entire team, the beta test engineer must coordinate multiple projects. This is especially important when projects overlap and the engineer has to correspond with different people about various projects simultaneously and not confuse them.

Last, the engineer should have foundations in project management. This skill set is more of a compliment than a necessity. However, organizing and ensuring the success of projects is a large portion of the beta test engineer's position, and that skill set can provide the necessary tools to meet these challenges.

Beta Test Coordinator

The beta test coordinator is the core of the beta test team. Handling the mundane items such as shipping, software duplication, product distribution, parts ordering, or other simple but time-consuming tasks, the coordinator allows other team members to focus on the important issues during test. The test coordinator does the "maintenance" that keeps the beta test engine running.

Responsibilities

The most time-consuming task involved with the beta test process is the shipping of product to and from beta test participants. The beta test coordinator assists the beta test engineer in the gathering of the materials for test, packages them appropriately for distribution, and then ships to the site. If the site has an issue or is not in compliance, the coordinator must arrange to get the product from the customer.

Preparing a product for distribution to the test participants involves a lot more than just boxing and shipping. Often, multiple small tasks must be completed to get the product into the hands of the beta test participants. From copying manuals and software to setting up access to the test infrastructure, the beta test coordinator takes the responsibility to get this completed.

With all this product distribution, the coordinator must also monitor the cost to ensure that the department is using the most cost-effective methods possible. In addition, there are numerous laws and regulations involved with some products and their distribution. Enter international concerns into this fold, and you open a whole other set of issues. The coordinator needs to be fully versed in these areas and be able to address issues quickly.

Another important responsibility is the monitoring of testing progress and contract compliance of all beta test participants. When a test site agrees to participate, they obligate themselves to provide feedback. The coordinator works with the engineer to make certain that this happens. From sending friendly reminders to the certified legal letters demanding the return of the beta product, the coordinator keeps the test participants active.

The beta test coordinator also manages the countless administrative aspects of a beta test program. Procurement of everything the department needs and the financial duties associated, the coordinator acts as a department administrator to ensure that the needs of the team are met.

Another administrative duty of the coordinator is the establishment and maintenance of a filing system for beta test documents, legal paperwork, and other important items. Beta testing involves a lot of legal paperwork. From non-disclosure agreements (NDAs) to software licenses, these items must be properly tracked for the protection of the company and the department.

Beta test programs often act as a large repository for legacy software. As versions and documents change, an effective program keeps track of this data. Often, other departments within a company want to borrow the material. The coordinator manages the software, keeps track of the versions, and manages these company resources.

Once test participants complete a project, they receive a reward for their effort. This reward is part of a beta test incentive program. The coordinator is responsible for collecting information about the performance of each tester and then distributing a corresponding award.

Just as the beta test engineer establishes a technical role with the test participants, the coordinator establishes and maintains a supportive role. The beta test coordinator makes certain the testers have everything they need to perform the test. Contacting each participant throughout the test, the coordinator acts as a secondary liaison for the test. By providing this extra assistance, the test participants have tremendous support for their effort.

Qualifications

Education or experience is certainly an important qualification for any position. However, the most important for the beta test coordinator is follow through. The coordinator must be someone who can be handed a job and guarantee its completion. Without this type of consistency, the team cannot rely on the coordinator.

Additionally, persistence is a key factor in being a successful coordinator. Test participants are often difficult to contact, unresponsive, or slow to communicate. A successful coordinator is able to balance the rigors of mundane daily tasks with the unexpected nature of a development schedule. The coordinator mixes skills of a department administrator and project manager.

As with every position in a beta test team, the coordinator should have customer service focus. Experience working with the public is helpful, but as mentioned, someone who has excellent communication skills can address this issue.

Beta Test Lab Manager

It might seem ambiguous to have a lab for a beta test program—the whole premise of beta testing surrounds getting a product out of a lab. The fact is that the lab is one of the most valuable tools a beta test program can have. The field produces many issues, and the beta test lab ensures that those issues receive proper attention.

A lab provides a place to duplicate issues. It is a venue for product training, education, and evaluation. A lab affords a test program a place to keep legacy hardware and software for the purpose of test preparation. Last, a lab is an excellent resource for supporting beta test participants. The lab manager acts as an efficiency expert to ensure that the lab is a small but efficient entity.

Responsibilities

The lab manager works with the beta test team to build and maintain efficient test workstations for reproduction of test issues. Understanding what projects will be coming into test and properly preparing the equipment to meet the needs of that test underline this effort. It is essential that the lab manager continuously evaluate these systems to ensure they are meeting the requirements of the test engineers.

In conjunction with this effort, the lab manager should also work with the test product to become familiar with its technologies, features, functions, and so forth. The lab manager should be as well versed in the product as the engineer is, and should be prepared to educate and inform the other team members of this information.

Another key responsibility is the procurement, update, calibration, certification, and retirement of test software and equipment within the lab. Every item in the lab should be carefully monitored to ensure that it meets the needs of the test engineers. Lab inventory should be tracked in a database, and budgetary decisions should be based on the data maintained in that database. The lab manager should act as an inventory control manager. With the vast array of items in the lab, the manager should establish a repository for hardware and software that can be properly used for testing.

Coinciding with the equipment allocation, the lab manager also monitors the testing progress of all projects that are in the lab and manages lab resources to ensure that all projects have space for operation and promote efficiency. The manager determines which software and hardware is allocated to which test engineer, and makes certain that the resources are properly shared.

Helping to build the systems to duplicate issues is only one facet of the lab design. In some cases, the lab manager might design specific software tests to duplicate issues. These are not automated tests, but rather methods for verifying the issues reported by testers. These methods can incorporate automation, but should not replicate the quality assurance process.

The lab manager should assist in the tracking of test versions submitted to beta test. In addition, he or she should evaluate the technical data from testing and verify that the problems reported have been fixed on the follow-up versions of the software. This verification ensures that beta test participants do not receive bad software candidates.

Depending on the size of the program, it might be necessary to have a lab technician to assist with the operation and maintenance of the lab. The lab manager must focus on speed and efficiency. If test system setups are being delayed or issues are not getting the time they deserve, a lab technician can be valuable.

Qualifications

The lab manager needs to be exceptionally technical and have a comprehensive understanding of a variety of hardware and software. This person should have varied experience in the field and in a lab environment. The lab manager should be especially fluent in computer architecture, network design, and software operation.

Some programming skills are necessary to be an effective lab manager. Depending on the software being developed, code skills can be valuable. At a minimum, a good lab manager will be able to read the software's code and be familiar with the commands and structure of the language.

Often, a lab can become very busy when multiple projects enter simultaneously. The lab manager will be someone who is especially attentive to details and has exceptional organizational skills. Accentuating these skills will be a fairness and understanding of a company's processes. This will enable the manager to allocate lab time effectively and ensure that everyone's needs are met.

Systems Manager

Beta testing is only effective when it has powerful communication tools to assist in the process. From Internet and intranet servers to telephony systems, a beta program needs to have the latest technologies available 24 hours a day, seven days a week to gather the most information from the test participants. The person responsible for running and maintaining this infrastructure is the systems manager.

Responsibilities

The systems manager is focused on developing and continuously improving the infrastructure and tools the beta test program uses to conduct beta tests. This person will supervise and manage the servers, telephone systems, network, databases, and all infrastructure equipment. In addition, he or she should manage a budget to maintain this equipment.

Working directly with different people within the company's Information Technology (IT) department, the systems manager will ensure that the beta test equipment complies with the company policies. In addition, he or she will work to make certain that company resources are available for the beta test program. The systems manager should maintain a good relationship with the IT department.

The systems manager is also focused on the integrity and security of the beta test data. Everything from implementing secure systems to controlling access to those systems is the manager's responsibility. The systems manager ensures that password changes, backups, and system maintenance occur on a regular basis.

When new tests arrive, the systems manager sets up the infrastructure to support the project. From dedicated Web sites to network access for test participants, the manager makes certain that all communication resources are ready for the test. In contrast, as projects complete the beta test program, the systems manager takes responsibility for archiving the data while keeping it accessible.

The systems manager is not only a network manager; he or she must also be able to write the Web programming for the systems. Depending on the size of the program, this task could be handled by a separate Web developer. However, it is ultimately the goal to have the systems manager write all of the underlying data.

Responsible for all of the data on the beta test network, the systems manager also runs the database and supports its underlying programming. Versed in the database languages, the manager makes certain the beta test engineers can get the test data they need. This is also a very complex task and might require a separate database administrator.

The beta test program relies heavily on the systems manager to keep everything it uses running. It is a complex, mission-critical position that is necessary in any medium- to large-sized beta test program. Like the foundation of a home, this person is rarely noticed, but everything will collapse without the support.

Qualifications

The systems manager needs to be exceptionally technical in computer architecture, network architecture, Web programming, telephony, and any communication technologies. The systems manager must also be able to troubleshoot various networking problems on a variety of different networks.

Education or experience is very valuable for this position. In some cases, certification in the related networking might be helpful. Able to capably follow and understand directions, the systems manager must be able to closely adhere to corporate policies and ensure compliance of the entire infrastructure. Overall, the systems manager will need to interface with many different IT people, and should be able to communicate competently.

Database development is also a key part of this position. The systems manager must have extensive experience with databases and should be able to program within the database's architecture. Everything from report generation to query building, the systems manager should be experienced in this critical area.

This is a large job and, depending on the size of the program, might require multiple people to perform all of the associated tasks. The systems manager should be able to effectively delegate work and should have good communication and management skills. Complimenting this will be effective time management and organizational proficiency.

Hierarchy

A good beta test program functions as a team and runs effectively when each member handles his or her role appropriately. However, all good organizations have a structure

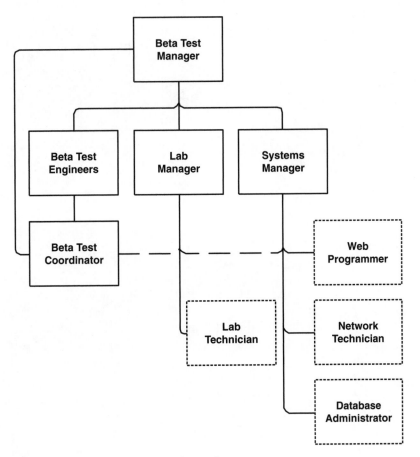

Figure 8.1 Beta test program hierarchy.

or hierarchy to ensure that a "chain of command" exists. Figure 8.1 shows a typical orientation for a team in a medium- to large-sized business.

In Figure 8.1, the positions with the dotted lines are optional. Depending on the size of the organization and the amount of work, these positions might or might not be necessary. However, they are subsets of the primary position to which they are attached, and thus, that person's responsibility.

Also note that the beta test coordinator has a dotted-line report to both the lab and systems manager. This is because he or she is responsible for administrative duties associated with the operation of the department. At times, these people will need to enlist the assistance of the coordinator to order equipment, duplicate software, or assist with general program tasks.

While Figure 8.1 shows the model for an effective organization, the design of any team should work for the manager running it. Therefore, as with the remainder of this section, use what works. Beta testing, in process or in practice, is about constant improvement.

The Process

This chapter is inordinately long for a number of reasons. First, it seemed inappropriate to break up a single, continuous process. Second, in a straightforward approach to any topic, it is best to ensure that you provide an overview and then elaborate on specific topics later. Last, as refined as this is, it could become confusing if the process was broken up to accommodate chapters.

This chapter explores beta testing one step at a time. It begins with the notification of a test and finishes with the archiving of the project data. Progressing through each of the steps, diagrams of many processes are provided. These are presented as guidance rather than as rules. The fact is that flexibility remains the key to successfully implementing this process.

Each company is different, and each company's process is unique. The material included here has been through years of refinement and testing. However, it is written without the knowing the reader's organization or product. Therefore, once you have read this chapter, take the material and adapt it to work with your system.

In addition, the perspective presented here is from a company that has nothing in place to perform beta testing and is building a program. With an existing beta program in place, you might want to compare your system to the material in this book. Walking through each step, the best practices for each part of the process are presented.

 **See Figure 9.1.**

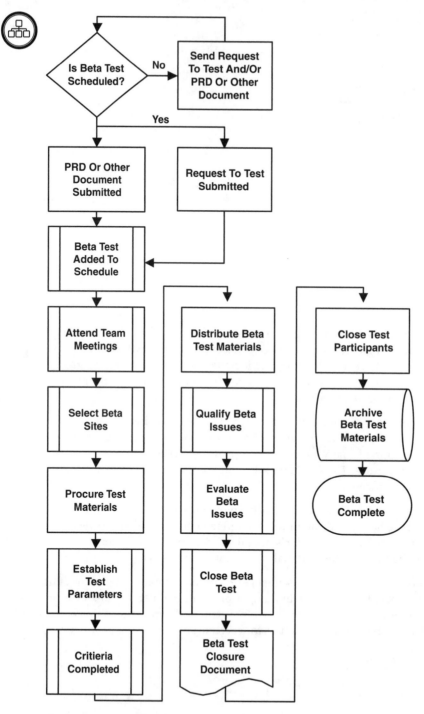

Figure 9.1 Complete beta test process.

Figure 9.1 presents the complete beta test process. It does not delve into the specifics, but provides a nice overview of how the process works. In this flow you can view the various procedures and documents that make up a beta test. Later in this chapter are more flowcharts that provide details about some of these procedures.

Reading the Road map

Beta testing is normally the last check prior to release. However, the process for beta begins nearly at the moment a product is conceived. As a product evolves, it becomes apparent that testing will become necessary, and with that, the beta test needs to be scheduled. Usually, development teams work off a schedule called a "road map."

The road map is a timetable showing the logical development path for products. From conception to "end of life," the road map attempts to draw a visual picture of the development cycle and build forecasts as to which resources will be needed to ensure successful execution. The road map is very valuable to beta test.

A beta test manager must take time to review the road map and see what schedule is anticipated and what resources might be necessary to support these new projects. However, road maps are often changed, and while reviewing the road map is valuable, it is not necessary to assume each project will be on the beta test schedule.

Road maps provide a glimpse into the future. It is key to take the time to build familiarity with the technologies and changes that the road map anticipates. However, until the development team actually begins doing real work on the project, the beta test program does not need to be concerned.

Requirements Documents

Once management has decided on a road map, people immediately set to work on designing a product. To maintain a focus on making these concepts a reality, a document is assembled to gather all the relevant information about the project. The "requirements document" acts a rationale, feature description, target market evaluation, and specification for the product.

The best way for a beta test manager to get a comprehensive understanding of a product is to get a version of the document and review it in detail. "Version" is central to understand, as these documents are rarely static. Features are often dropped or added as the product moves closer to release. However, they are still the best way to understand what the product is supposed to do.

If a requirements document is not part of your company process, a functional specification or other design document will assist in assessing the product's features. These documents typically are exceptionally technical and do lack much of the marketing material. However, they do give a detailed analysis of a product and can be useful.

The Queue

Projects come and go with sporadic and varied results. Some might go through the test process with little or no incident, while others are constantly going in and out of test. In addition, different projects have different priorities. Thus, it is critical that the beta test schedule is properly maintained.

 See Figure 9.2.

With an understanding of the product and its design, it is time to determine a rough schedule of the projected arrival time. If a team has a requirements document in a relatively static state and the development team has begun to do some work, it is time to put the project in the "queue" (Figure 9.2).

The queue is the schedule of tests that are either entering test in the near future or are actually in test. Effectively a timeline of pending and active projects, the queue represents projects that need attention. When a beta test team publishes a weekly queue report, it becomes a very effective way to forecast and manage projects for a number of reasons.

 Only put a project in the queue that involves some type of work. Putting projects in the queue that are too far out makes it look like you are trying to pad your schedule.

First, when placing projects in a queue, you have visible reminder of projects that will be coming. It allows you to anticipate the work that will be coming and establish resources for these projects. Reviewing the weekly report is a constant reminder of the project.

Second, a project in the queue immediately becomes visible to the entire development team. Program managers who review a beta test team's weekly queue report will make certain their projects are on the list. It also tells these people the amount of work in the queue.

Last, the queue is a simple and effective way to establish priority and note project slips. Once a project enters the queue, the beta test manager is stating that time is being dedicated to the project. The natural progression of projects in and out of test allows emphasis to be shifted from one project to another. This project shift sets a subtle priority within the team.

One must recognize that a beta test team does not establish priority; it simply acts on directives from other teams. It is a service organization and should take priority guidance from those who establish it within the company. The queue simply assists in creating priority where none exists.

Project slips are also important to watch and track through the queue. The sad reality of product development is that projects often do not meet their forecasted schedule. Whether the issues are from extraneous sources or from within, they impact the beta test queue. Tracking slips and their cause can help improve processes and better anticipate risk.

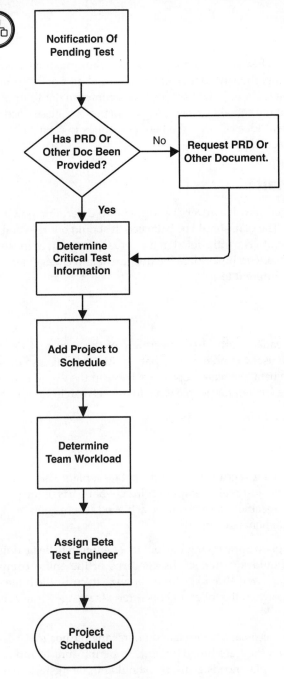

Figure 9.2   Adding projects to the queue.

The Plan

Now that the project is on the schedule, it is time to gather the information to write a test plan. The test plan is a comprehensive document designed to give an overview of the beta test to the development team. In one aspect, it is a commitment to do a beta test, yet it tells very little about the actual test itself. A good plan is a concise document that gives everyone an excellent idea of what the beta test hopes to achieve without going too in-depth about the actual process.

Elements of a Beta Test Plan

All good plans provide an overview. However, it is difficult to determine how much detail to include or to remove. The plan should be balanced. It should offer several specific details about the project, but very little detail in the actual execution of the test. A well-run beta program will be able to boilerplate the document and change necessary portions to accommodate the different tests.

Summary

The summary provides the reader with a basic overview of the plan and provides enough information to allow a user to understand what product is being tested, when it will be tested, and what the beta test team hopes to achieve in the test. It is usually only a paragraph or two and is written for people who do not need an in-depth understanding of the beta test.

Goals

The goals of the beta test are the most critical part of the beta test plan. This is where a person will specify what data the test will attempt to collect, what parts of the product need to be assessed, and what specific tasks need to be achieved. These goals are gathered after reviewing the requirements document.

Goals need to be specific enough to appear tangible, but loose enough to be flexible for implementation. The goals should also reflect the concerns of the entire company rather than any individual group, and should be broad enough to cover the interest of multiple groups within a company. In the following case study (see page 95), we see an example of some good goals.

Bill provides the team with the necessary material and offers tangible goals that can be realistically achieved. However, they are broad enough to permit him to input and remove specific tests. A beta test plan needs goals, but should not tie the test manager to anything too precise. In its ambiguity, the plan leaves the test manager the flexibility to get the best data.

Case Study: Going for the Gold

Bill Malden is beta test manager for Siegel Industries, which manufactures huge environmental control systems for large buildings. They are an industry leader in providing software that manages the power and output of everything in skyscrapers to warehouses. They have developed a high-speed proprietary protocol to speak to air-conditioning units, lights, and other industrial devices.

This protocol is so effective that Siegel has decided to move from the industrial market into the home arena. It has been working effectively over much of the test wiring they use in the lab as well as at the CEO's home. The company feels it has a good shot at making it in this different market and has added the project to their road map.

In the past, Bill had an established relationship with select buildings around the country that were using their software. With this change, he is expected to go out and locate test participants who have an interest in home automation. Everyone on the project team understands that this challenge is new, and the project manager is asking Bill to deliver a test plan early to the development team so they can provide input.

Gathering data from the Product Requirements Document, Bill begins to assemble the material he needs to author a comprehensive plan that will cover the necessary scope of this project. Although it is more than eight months before he will begin testing, the development team expects him to provide a fairly accurate plan.

Bill has written many test plans in his time and decides that with some modifications to his regular plan, he should address the concerns of the team. At the next meeting he delivers a completed plan with the following goals:

- Test and evaluate the home automation software.
- Compare the product to its competitors.
- Establish test participants who are described in the "Participant Profile" of the Product Requirements Document.
- Verify compatibility with different aspects of the product's operation in multiple home environments.
- Verify the operation and usability of the home automation interface.
- Verify the operation and usability of the software with varied devices.
- Test and evaluate the physical features of the product.
- Test for operation on the supported operating systems.
- Test the technical accuracy and usability of the documentation.

The team feels that this sufficiently covers the needs of test. Bill explains that as the product becomes closer to release, he will be able to refine these goals and understand what will be the biggest concerns for the beta test.

Specifications

The specifications are nothing more than specific items requested by someone within the company. In the previous case study, Bill might have received instructions to include some type of test during the beta test. Using the specifications section of the plan, he could note the exact request and make certain that it is performed.

Including specifications in the plan leaves no room for miscommunication. If a particular person or department has expectations of the beta test, this section allows for those expectations to be specified. With this clarity, the beta test manager understands what needs to be done, and the requesting party sees their concerns being addressed.

Budget and Materials

The plan is a forecast of the beta test itself. Providing details about the anticipated expenses to perform the test and the required materials only makes sense. It provides tremendous benefits for a number of reasons.

First, when it comes time to perform the test, hardware and software become scarce. Everyone has his or her own interest at heart, and there might be temptation to start to take materials from beta. Being last in the process, the anticipation might be that the material might be replaced or changed prior to the start of test. By specifying the items necessary to begin test in the plan, a test manager is making certain that the program's needs are recognized early and are properly budgeted.

Financially speaking, the plan should not go into depth about cost, but rather list common associated costs and what should be budgeted. If the software requires some specific equipment to test, that should be included. However, incidental items such as disks or packaging to ship the product can be left out. In general, the test manager should be generous in his or her estimations and deliver more realistic numbers as the test gets underway.

Site Quantity

The number of sites is often difficult to calculate. Everything from the complexity of the product to the number of people managing the test needs to be considered. There are too many factors that will impact this decision to determine a reliable number. Because of this, a range should be specified. By doing this, the manager provides a little flexibility in the decision.

 We discuss the best way to estimate the number of sites for a test in more detail in Chapter 12, "Effective Site Selection." However, a manager should consult the development team and assess their needs. Providing a number that hits within 10 percent below or above the requested number is sufficient.

Reporting Information

This portion of the document explains to the reader how the results from the test will be reported. Basically, the object here is to give the team some visibility into how they will get the test data. Whether the manager provides real-time feedback over the Web or will simply report progress in the weekly team meeting, the method is not as important as much as the path.

By giving this information, the beta test manager alleviates any confusion on how the data will get into the team's hands. The document should detail the method in a number of ways and provide the beta test manager's contact information if there are any issues during test.

This might be a simple and seemingly unnecessary effort. However, often when test starts, things are so busy that it makes sense to clarify this information up front and eliminate any confusion. Furthermore, it reminds the development team that they will be getting data during the beta test and that they will be expected to respond.

Participant Profile Design

The design of the participants is yet another section of the plan that needs some specific attention but a generalized approach. Gathering data from the participant profile section of the requirements document, the profile should reflect the intended audience for the product. However, it should also include specifics that focus on the desired demographic for the product.

It makes sense to approach the development team prior to writing this section of the plan to be certain that everyone's concerns are addressed. The test participants are the focus of a beta test, and if the wrong sample of the population is gathered, it can damage the credibility of the test. In addition, there is a possibility that the test data will be invalidated by the lack of qualified test participants.

 Once you have that input, leave the criteria flexible enough to ensure that it is specific but not restrictive. Chapter 12 goes into extensive depth on the process of test participant selection. After reviewing that chapter, you should be able to strike the balance between specifics for the plan and the actual selection standard.

Communication

The communication that happens between the test participants and the beta test team is key to the success of the project. This section of the plan stipulates the rules governing communication and provides channels for the team to get information to and from the test participants.

Development teams are encouraged to communicate with testers. However, it can become problematic if the correspondence is not properly documented or if the test team is unaware of the communication. In these cases, the tester is not working with the test team but with an extraneous person who is impacting the tester's output.

By enforcing strict communication paths between the test participants and the development team, all of the correspondence can be documented and the test participant will remain focused on performing the beta test. In addition, the development team will understand the importance of the tester's feedback.

The plan should detail the methods of communication available to the sites and a process for the development team to get information to and from the beta test participants. There is no need to go into detail, but rather general guidelines and locations for the test data. Whether that is a Web site, weekly mailing, or telephone number, it is starting place.

Schedule

As early as a beta test plan is written, it is unlikely that any schedule published will reflect what will really happen. Projects are constantly shifting and formal schedules are normally not formed until just before products begin serious development. However, not having some type of schedule in the document is an impact to its credibility. How can a plan be executed without dates? Therefore, a generalized timeline including the distribution, test performance, and closure dates should be included.

Inevitably, the project timelines will change, and it makes sense to include a notation on the plan of that fact. It should also direct the development team member to a location to obtain an accurate schedule. This can be in the form of a Web site or a telephone number for the beta test manager. Either way, it ensures that the document does not need to be updated and that a path exists for the most recent information.

Closure

Closure specifies what will happen at the end of the test. Each company and beta test program handles closure differently, and detailing those procedures is valuable. Whether it is a distribution of incentives and gathering of test material or an archiving of data, the plan needs to show the anticipated process.

When tests end, it causes issues when there is no process in place. Later in this chapter, closure is explained in detail and suggestions are offered. Whatever processes a beta test team uses, it should be documented in the plan.

Addendum

Finally, a section of the plan should leave room for changes. The whole purpose of leaving this document flexible and open is to make changes unnecessary. However, there are times when the changes are so significant that the plan becomes nearly obsolete. Providing room for an addendum allows the document to be altered without be rewritten.

This section of the plan can be small. It can simply state that the document is subject to change and that any significant changes will be attached to the original plan. If there are tremendous changes, balance the value of an addendum to rewriting the plan. As mentioned earlier, a good program perfects its plan as the process becomes more refined. Once a boilerplate has been built, it might be easier to just generate a new test plan.

Meeting Attendance

It might seem rather mundane to include something like meeting attendance in a book about beta testing. However, it is quite the contrary. The work associated with beta testing fluctuates often and can impact a person's schedule. In addition, development times on software can vary from several weeks to several years. Beta testing falls near the end of the process and it makes no sense to attend meetings when a beta presence is irrelevant.

Proper management of time is critical to multitask. Attendance at team meetings is an essential part of the beta test process. However, it can be difficult to determine when to attend and when not. Figure 9.3 helps explain the decision-making process on whether to attend team meetings.

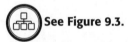 **See Figure 9.3.**

Meeting attendance requirements should be established with the person who is running a meeting prior to deciding whether to attend. By working closely with the team

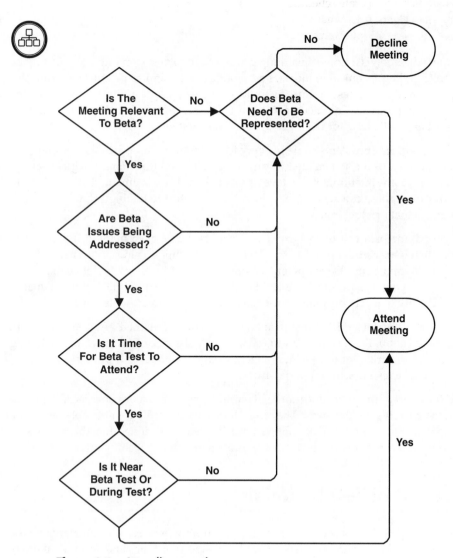

Figure 9.3   Attending meetings.

leader, the beta test manager can establish an effective balance that permits participation with relevance to the process.

Product Education

The beta test team needs to have as much expertise on the product as anyone on the development team. It is not enough to know how to use the product. The beta test team needs to understand every nuance and detail of the product before entering test. By engaging in product education, a test team is effectively prepared (Figure 9.4).

 **See Figure 9.4.**

Product education is a time-consuming process. It involves spending hours using the product, reading technical manuals, and working with similar products. During this preparation, the beta test engineer should take every opportunity to document the information gathered. This documentation will assist in training the remaining beta test staff and will allow for reference during the actual test phase.

During a beta test, problems come in every form. From the simple to the complex, the beta test team must be able to identify any issue that could threaten a product's release and bring it to the attention of the development team. The documented materials from the education phase can act as a compliment in the effort to distinguish between support and actual product issues.

In the end, the beta test team's expertise benefits the team in many different ways. First, when issues are reported to the development team, it is important to be able to speak with credibility. Development engineers need to understand that the issues coming from the beta program are valid and need to be dealt with. Nothing damages the credibility of a beta program more than frivolous or unverifiable issues.

Second, a well-educated test team operates in a self-contained environment. With proper education, there is no need to rely on the assistance of other teams, including support, engineering, or marketing. In fact, when the beta team is properly prepared, they become a resource for those departments.

Last, the effort of product education will naturally assist on later versions of the product and on derivative products. The education is an investment in the beta test team. The information gathered will continue to have relevance long after the beta test is complete. Few products are developed without some legacy technology.

Procurement of Test Materials

The gathering of the test materials is a time-consuming process. Very often, not all the pieces that make up the product are ready at the same time, and to make matters

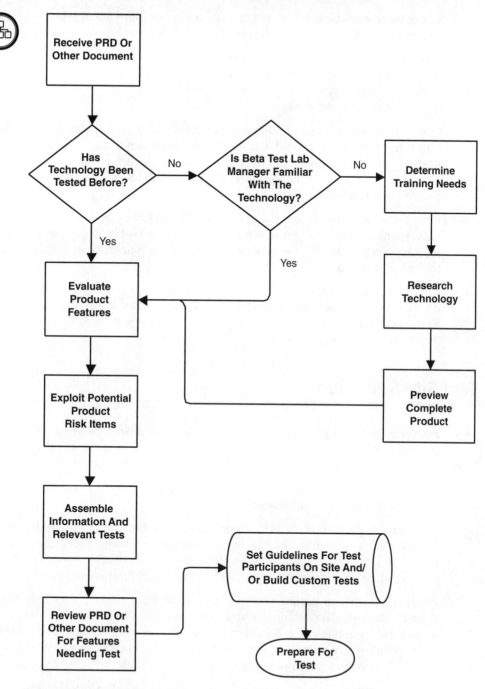

Figure 9.4 Product education.

worse, the responsibility for each of these pieces varies. Normally, this task is left to the beta test coordinator. However, in small programs, this can be a tremendous burden.

Start early with the effort to gather the materials. Begin the process by letting those who have the deliverables know that you will need the material soon and that they should be prepared to deliver. In addition, continue to follow up with these people until the material is delivered.

Once the material has been collected, set up a system to catalogue and track it. Use a simple numbering system, and tie a description or version to that number. The fact is, there might be more coming in the future and it is important to note revisions and quantity immediately. As the test materials become distributed, being able to track the location will be critical.

Prior to distribution into beta test, the materials should also be closely watched. People wanting the latest and greatest material frequently visit beta test. Clearly mark all property, and if some of the beta test resources are shared, make certain they are tracked in some manner.

In addition, beta test material is often very close to release, and while it is not a retail package, it carries the same perceived value. Because this value is very high, it should be treated as such. For example, if the retail price of the software application is $200, then treat it as if this is its value.

Test Site Selection

 Elaborated on in Chapter 12, this is one of the single most critical aspects of the beta test process. A successful beta test depends on good site selection combined with proper test management. Both components must be there for a test to gather effective results.

The process of site selection is complex. Using the flow chart in Figure 9.5, a basic overview of the process can be established.

Test participant selection needs to happen as soon as there is a reasonable expectation that the product will enter test. Factoring in items such as outstanding issues, number of revisions, and marketing schedules, the beta test team should determine when the product will enter the test. Once that has been established, site selection should begin.

Whether it is from an existing pool of testers or soliciting of new participants, the sites should have up-to-date information about their configuration. Based on the information provided in the requirements document, the selection process is difficult and prolonged. Often, people will not have the correct configuration, be unresponsive, or will be unwilling to test. Therefore, it is important to budget sufficient time for the selection process.

The selection duration varies depending on the specifics of the test. If obscure configurations or difficult-to-obtain equipment are required by the test, selection could take several weeks. In contrast, if the criterion is very simple and common, the selection process might only take a few hours. In addition, the number, geographic distribution, and the expectations of the test can all contribute to the length of the selection period.

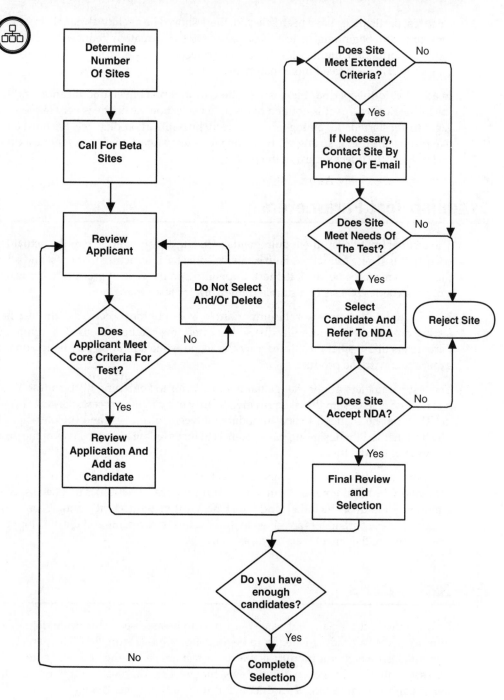

Figure 9.5 Selecting beta test participants.

Once test participants have been selected, there should be a relatively small amount of time until the beginning of test. Test participant information changes, and often a tester's information might be lost in between selection and notification. Thus, this window should never exceed more than two months.

In addition to this period, there is also the critical time between notification and test start. Once a participant is notified of his or her selection, he or she is very excited and eager to get started. Beginning test as close to the notification time gets the most effective results. If a user is strung along waiting for a test to start, the level of interest drops and reduces the effectiveness of the participants.

Establish Test Parameters

The test parameters are the requirements a beta test team will give to the actual test participants. These guidelines help establish some basic structure to the test and allow the sites to meet the needs of the test. Depending on the type of product, these can be a complex series of tests or a simple framework for test progression.

When specifying parameters, it is important to work out the objectives of the test. Beta testing does focus on getting feedback, but often this can be too broad an approach. Parameters allow a beta test to narrow the scope while still allowing the freedom to experiment with the product.

The test parameters might change many times prior to beginning the beta test. While it is necessary to design these requirements fairly early in the process, they are not static. They can be changed to accommodate the needs of the test and the participants. The best method for designing parameters is to focus on the key objectives of the product and build from there.

Test parameters should be a balanced reflection of the test participant profile and the contents of the requirements document. In addition, any other issues that need specific attention should be included and must be written with clarity and focus. Once designed, these parameters are given to the beta test participants and the development team to ensure they meet their needs as well.

Pre-Test Criteria

Before a product officially enters test, it needs to be assessed. This evaluation determines whether a product is ready to begin beta testing (Figure 9.6). The parameters that establish whether a product is ready for test are called the "pre-test criteria." A series of feature and functionality reviews, the pre-test criteria attempt to prevent test participants from receiving a product that is not ready for beta testing.

When the product is in its early stages of development and the beta test team is working on getting educated about the product, there needs to be consideration about what the product does and how it works. As the features are evaluated, a checklist of the key items is built. Once the product is submitted for entry into beta testing, a comparison against the checklist is performed. If any of the features are not working, distribution into test needs to be evaluated.

 **See Figure 9.6.**

Evaluation

The key word noted here is *evaluated*. Evaluation involves many factors. How much time is allocated to test? How serious are the issues? Will the customer experience with the product be negative based on the product's current state? Will the product perform effectively with the issues? Will the beta test be effective without these features or this functionality? Taking these issues into consideration, whether or not the test should proceed is established.

The criteria are not a pass/fail measurement, but rather a guideline to protect the customer. For example, if several small features are not working on a product, but anticipation is that it will be rolled into the product during the test, it might be ready. In contrast, if one vital component of the product is not working and there is no expectation of when it will be fixed, test should be held. Balance of the interests of the company and the customer are key in this decision.

A beta test manager usually does not get much argument from a development team when credible issues are presented and the beta test team demonstrates the impact that the issues will have on the beta test. However, this is a sensitive issue and opinion has no place. Only supported facts presented with the potential impact will be sufficient to prevent test from beginning.

Build Expectations

The pre-test criteria are the most effective gate for ensuring a quality beta test. However, the development team needs to know that its product will be evaluated prior to its distribution into test. The test manager should communicate to the developers that the product will go through an evaluation phase. Presenting the criteria to the team prior to the assessment gains a lot.

First, the development team must have a clear understanding of what will happen if the product is not ready for test. If the beta insists a product is unprepared for release and the development team believes it is ready, there will be a big conflict. Giving clear and specific expectations prior to receiving the product will make help avoid conflicts.

 Chapter 11, "When to Start Testing," goes into greater detail about when or when *not* to start test. Part of the pre-test criteria involves the concept of viability. These decisions should not be arbitrary, but rather based on a series of well-founded tests and assessments. By creating realistic expectations with the development team, the transition into beta test should go smoothly.

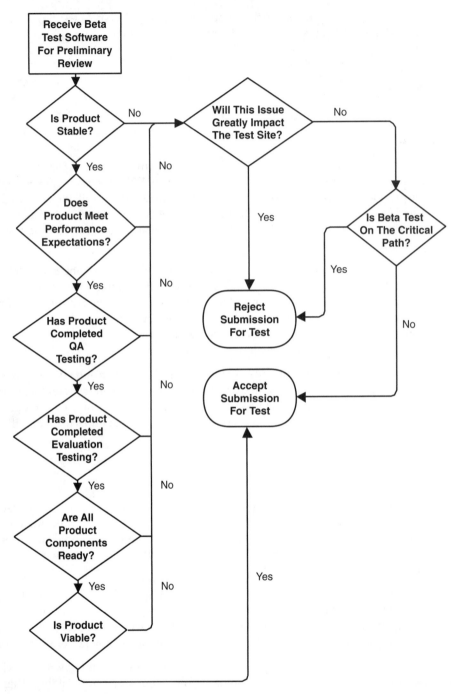

Figure 9.6   Pre-test product evaluation.

Legal Agreements

When a beta test begins, there is a lot of excitement and interest in the product. The test participants are eagerly anticipating the arrival of the product. However, prior to beginning test, various legal steps must be taken. The following are some of the key documents necessary to ensure that a company has properly prepared for the test.

Non-Disclosure Agreement

Beta test products are normally not too secret. With beta test arriving late in the development process, marketing has usually already announced the product. In addition, some samples might already be distributed. However, this is no reason to avoid the traditional non-disclosure agreement (NDA) when signing up test participants.

The fact is, the product might not be secret, but the test results are. During the beta test process, the best and worst aspects of a product are explored, and it is possible that word of any failures could damage the product before it enters the marketplace. An NDA is not a guarantee of secrecy, but rather a method to enforce it.

When test participants sign this agreement, they are agreeing to keep quiet about their test experience. Everything from the product to the paper the manual is printed on is protected by the NDA. Therefore, if a test site decides that he or she needs to tell the press about his or experience, the company has a method to keep the site quiet.

The NDA is a signed formal agreement in which the company agrees to give a test participant confidential information about the product and the test, and the site agrees not to share this information with anyone else for a specified period of time. This agreement is key in any beta test and should be in place before the test product is revealed to the participant.

Software License Agreement

Beta test software can be copied and illegally distributed just as easily as regular software can. In some cases, it might even be easier, as protection and registration features might not be in place for the test. Thus, a software license agreement should be set up prior to beginning test.

A software license agreement is a legal contract between the company or software publisher and the user of that application. In this case, the users are the beta test sites. The site agrees that for the privilege of seeing the test software first, it promises to comply with all rules stated in the agreement.

This document, when paired with the NDA, might overlap slightly, but it is better to have both in place as a precaution. However, if a test team wants to reduce the number of agreements a test participant must sign, a lawyer might be able to combine these two agreements into a single operable document.

Test Contract

Although not required, it might make sense to have the company lawyer draw up a test contract for the participants. In this agreement, the rules of test are specified. In addition, repercussions for not participating in the test are also listed. The contract allows the beta test team to obligate test sites to participate.

In addition to this basic function, it can also include items such as testing duration, ownership of the product after the test is complete, or warranty and servicing requirements. When properly designed, it is yet another tool to keep the participant focused on providing feedback.

Distribution of Test Materials

Once all the material has been gathered for the test and the test is scheduled to begin, the product must be distributed to the test participants. Simply placing the material in a box and shipping it is not sufficient. The distribution process requires professionalism, care, and attention to detail.

Welcome Letter

This small formality really starts a test off properly. When a test participant receives a welcome letter on the company stationery, it effectively sends the participant the message that the test has begun and that the company means business. The customer's perspective is immediately shifted to the goals of the test.

The letter should be comprised of three parts. The first is the actual welcome. This text should enforce that the testers have been selected to participate from many other people and that this is a unique opportunity. It should also delicately enforce the testers' importance in the process and that they will be watched.

 Small details really make the difference. Custom folders, binders, and stationery really increase the professionalism of a project and make the site take the test seriously.

The second portion is a simple explanation of the product. This should be a short paragraph or two explaining the finer points of the product, and needs to enforce a refined goal of the test. This is also a good point to remind the test participants that they are under a non-disclosure and need to keep all the information they gather in test very secret.

The final section expresses thanks for their participation in the beta test. This thank you should enforce the importance of their role and that the product's future depends on their valuable feedback. The welcome letter is a document that officially anoints a test participant and when properly written, it will allow the tester to feel a part of something significant.

Parameters Document

Test participants need to be given clear guidelines about their responsibility to test. The parameters document establishes the rules of a beta test and makes certain there are clear directions for the testers. The parameters document ensures that the test participants know what is expected of them.

First, it enforces the legal documents that the test participants signed. Whatever documents they agreed to, the parameters document reminds the sites that they did sign it and have to adhere to the stipulations specified.

Next, this document was initially designed when the test plan was conceived. Taking the content from the plan, this new document delivers the message to the beta test participants. The parameters specify any specific tasks needed to be performed during test. It should also provide a basic timeline of the test events and any relevant information that will assist with performing the test, such as contact information or Web site locations.

Last, it also helps guide the participant as to the type of feedback you are looking for during the test. While it might not be specific, it does give general guidance. It might even reinforce that guidance by providing details about the incentives. In all, this document is mainly to keep the test site informed of your expectations.

Test Package

The package for a beta test comprises the elements that make up the actual product. This means that everything that will ship with the real product should be distributed as part of the beta test package. Manuals, third-party software, supplemental applications, and the software application itself should all be included in the materials sent to a beta test participant.

Of course, distributing the test software is rather obvious. However, it is the form factor that is of concern. Even with the latest technology allowing downloads, it is still important to send an original master copy of the software. There are a number of important reasons for doing this.

First, most people download software on a regular basis, and while it is convenient, it is intangible. When the actual software comes in the mail, it gives it value. People attach this value to things they can touch. A download reduces the perceived worth of the product, and thus could potentially reduce the amount of feedback on the test.

Second, there will inevitably be changes. Almost every software package will require revisions during the test and subsequently require a download. By sending the master, the potential file size of the revisions will be reduced.

Finally, the shipped material serves as a backup in case an application becomes corrupted during the beta process. This is a test, and often things do not go as planned. By having a master from which the test participant can return to a controlled state, you eliminate the risk of the test participant experiencing downtime.

Accessories

Providing everything the tester needs to perform the test is crucial to ensuring a successful test. Beta test participants should have not have any excuses about their performance. If the software requires a specific application or accessory to function, it either needs to be specified as a prerequisite or shipped to the tester as part of the package.

An accessory is something that is necessary for the product to function, but would not normally be packaged. In the following case study (see page 111), we see what can happen when an accessory is excluded from a package.

Had the company provided everything needed to complete the beta test, this issue would not have happened. Thinking through the steps to properly use the product is an effective way to gather what might be necessary. Whether it is software or hardware, making certain that the proper accessories are provided or are prerequisites for the test must be a top priority in getting the test materials prepared.

Managing Testers

Tester management is about ensuring you get the most feedback from your test participants. Chapter 14, "Getting Results," focuses on many different techniques that will assist in getting results. The main emphasis in this section is to understand the role it plays in the process. Management of test participants relies on many important tasks to be performed.

Communication

Active and consistent communication with the test sites makes the difference between success and failure of a beta test. Through communication, test participants must feel the test is important, active, and that their contribution has value. Without communication, test sites become distant and unconcerned. Eventually, the site will give up and efforts to get feedback become useless.

A beta test relies on the team communicating on multiple levels on multiple occasions. This means that communication starts with something as simple as a telephone call to the complexities of an online bulletin board. There are two forms of communication available: interactive and noninteractive.

Interactive

Interactive communication techniques involve communicating with test participants in real time. This method of communication has the advantage of being personable and immediate. It also provides excellent gratification for the test participant. Moreover, interactive communication is very fast and provides instant results.

Case Study: A Wireless Product

Nautical Concepts is a Connecticut-based software developer creating navigation software. Their industry-leading application operates on a laptop using the latest in mapping, cellular, and GPS technology. It provides real-time weather and navigational data while in coastal waters, and navigational data at sea.

At a recent trade show, Ben Loma, CEO of Nautical, met with the CEO of Indigo Yachts. During their meeting, Ben discovered that Indigo had built a USB interface into the dashboard of their latest yachts, which connect into an on-board GPS. Their intention is to support applications like the one Nautical develops.

In addition, Indigo says that they will be happy to add the Nautical software to their accessory catalogue if they can demonstrate that it works. Indigo will be publishing their next catalogue in about five weeks, and Nautical needs to get confirmed data before that time if they want to be included.

Ben returns from the show and is hot to test the application. However, they can't go out and purchase several yachts to see if it works. Dylan Carling, beta test manager, is asked to find owners of the correct Indigo models and distribute software to test the application.

She makes contact with Indigo and they provide her with a list of potential customers and an internal engineer who works with the dashboard. Ben is checking daily and Dylan is getting a tad frazzled having the CEO watching so closely. However, she understands the potential impact this has and works hard to get the software out to testers.

The process of finding willing users is slow and Dylan feels the pressure. The Indigo models that are supported have only been available for a short time. After three weeks of work, she finally gets enough test participants for the beta and distributes the software. She notifies Ben that the software is in the hands of her users and the data should be coming in shortly.

However, in her haste to get the software to the customer, Dylan neglected to send a USB cable to each of the testers. Nautical is not a hardware developer and she never considered the cable as part of the package. In addition, previous users were expected to have their own GPS and cell cables.

To make matters worse, the cable needs to be longer than average to accommodate the distance between the laptop and the yacht's interface. The testers are unwilling to buy the cable to use the software. Dylan now must quickly purchase USB cables and distribute them to the test participants.

The cables are acquired, but a serious amount of time is lost in the process. In addition, the software does not work with the built-in GPS, and the time to assess the issue is so short that it doesn't look as if Nautical will make this important window of opportunity.

However, interactive communication has many downsides. It is exceptionally time consuming and labor intensive. In addition, its instantaneous nature does not allow for preparation and can actually require follow-up time. Finally, it lacks uniformity and makes consistent communication with test participants challenging.

Telephone Calls

Naturally, a telephone call seems to be a logical method of communication to use during a beta test. Telephones are ubiquitous and simple to use. In addition, they are global, providing a method of communication that works whenever and wherever. However, telephone calls are actually the worst method for communication on a beta test for a number of reasons.

First, telephone calls consume the attention and time of a beta team. Every person expected to answer calls has to take a moment from his or her normal work to handle a call. This can be very counter-productive when a test is in full swing and there are many issues to handle.

Second, telephone calls offer no real documentation or record of test activity. It forces a test team to have to log and transcribe the correspondence to ensure it gets registered as part of the test feedback. This adds one more time-consuming task and brings no real benefit.

Last, the telephone is addictive to beta test participants. Because of the immediacy of the results provided by a telephone call, test participants will start to call before trying to solve issues on their own. In addition, they will not use the other forms of communication, thus creating more work when it really isn't necessary.

The telephone is not an enemy but a dangerous device that needs to be managed closely. It is not out of the question to discourage test participants from using the telephone during the test. In fact, providing every other form of communication can successfully redirect test sites away from the telephone.

While the telephone can be a beta test's worst enemy, it does have some benefits. It certainly has a place, and customers should be given an opportunity to use the telephone in certain instances. First, telephone calls are personal and are useful at the beginning of a test. The test sites will sense the importance of their role in the test when a call comes in from the test team.

Next, the telephone remains the quickest form of communication available. If an issue requires an instant answer, there is no substitute for a telephone call. This is especially useful when a single issue is holding up a project and knowing whether it has been corrected will determine whether the product ships.

Last, the telephone is an excellent tool for clarification and enhancement of communication. If a test site reports something and has not effectively documented the issue, a telephone call is the fastest way to get the accurate information. The fact is, not every test site will have good writing skills, and the telephone might be the only method to clarify the site's submissions.

Chat Software

Chat software offers the real-time and interactive communication of a telephone call with the benefit of text documentation. Chatting has many benefits over a telephone, but is still limited in many ways.

On the positive side, chat software does allow a beta test team to communicate with test participants when they need to talk without picking up a telephone. It is not quite as time consuming as a telephone, as it does leave room for multitasking. In addition, chatting provides a method of documentation.

In contrast, chatting does take attention away from normal work and thus can slow productivity. In addition, chatting lacks the formality of a bug submission process, and often information delivered through this form of communication is incomplete. Also, not everyone is an efficient typist, and for some, chatting can be painfully slow and frustrating.

Chatting should be offered as a form of interactive communication, but should be focused as a secondary method for communication. Directing users to the noninteractive communication methods will allow increased efficiency and more documented information.

Real-Time Web Boards

The real-time Web board is similar to a chat room, except that the information is posted to a forum and can be read after the session is complete. This form of communication is very useful for history, but a lot of derivative data exists. The style of communication on a Web board is conversational rather than informational; thus, there is a lot of posted data that has no meaning for the person reviewing the text.

Noninteractive

Noninteractive communication is the best method to communicate with beta test participants. This form allows time to formulate correct answers to questions, professional response to issues, and consistency in every response. A team looking to provide the best service to the beta test participants will emphasize this form of communication to the test sites and will enforce the test team to respond using these channels.

Email

In the past 10 years, email has become almost as ubiquitous as the telephone. Test participants are used to getting abundant amounts of email, and often it is the preferred method of communication among computer users. Aside from the fact that it is text based and documents feedback, there are many benefits to using email and only a few small inconveniences.

First, email is almost as instantaneous as a telephone call because it travels to the recipient in seconds. The speed of email allows test participants and a test team to get information to one another with little or no hindrance. Its speed is certainly its strongest asset because it improves communication among all members of a beta test.

Second, email is global. Tests can have participants located all over the planet. Email breaks communication barriers by allowing people to communicate via text, effectively eliminating the issues that sound can have, including telephony problems, accents, and language barriers.

There are some minor issues with global testing. First, test participants should have a relatively good understanding of the test team's native language. Second, keyboards differ from language to language, and sometimes text does not come across properly. However, requiring these two as prerequisites for participating in the test will reduce the amount of miscommunication.

Third, email has the capability to carry attachments. While this is not an ideal method for file distribution, it is fast. If a software application in test has a small update, there isn't a faster way to distribute that update. Email ensures that each person gets the file and that the same message about that file is conveyed. However, large files are problematic and can cause more distribution issues than using a Web-based method.

Finally, email is standardized yet flexible. While many technologies continue to be changed and innovated, email remains static and simple. It is straightforward enough that anyone can use it effectively, and it has enough flexibility that it can answer many of the communication needs of a test.

Mailing Lists

A powerful tool for communication, mailing lists are force-fed email. They make the participant see the correspondence among all the participants in a list of email addresses. If one user posts a message to the list, all members are copied on the posting. This is a good and bad scenario for the test participants.

On the positive side, participants are forced to communicate as they see all the correspondence in their mailbox. On the negative side, a mailing list can generate a huge quantity of email and this can turn a test participant away from the project. The overwhelming nature of a mailing list makes it a useful but risky tool.

Mailing lists can be moderated. This means that every mail message must be approved before it is posted to the list. This can be a time-consuming proposition if this is the primary form of communication for a beta test. However, it prevents unwanted email and allows a selective amount of mail to go the test participants.

The most effective method for using mailing lists is as a broadcast communication tool that allows users to hear the latest news about the project. It provides immediate results, allows mass distribution, and encourages communication. However, the list must be used in conjunction with other communication tools to ensure that test sites have some method with which to converse.

Usenet

Usenet is a public discussion system with global distribution and a large technical base of users. It consists of "newsgroups" with names that are sorted by subject. "Articles" are "posted" to these newsgroups by people on computers using software designed to interface with the Usenet. Once the article is posted, any reader of the newsgroup can view it. Some newsgroups are "moderated," and require that the posted message be sent to a moderator for approval before it shows up in the newsgroup.

Usenet is an excellent place for discussion, but is not very effective for beta testing. First, the public nature of this service is directly contrary to the private nature of a beta test. Second, Usenet is extremely large, with nearly 60,000 different discussion groups. It might be difficult to find a group that could be used for a beta test. Last, Usenet is not necessarily safe. Viruses, illegal software, and other dealings are regularly distributed through Usenet and can cause issues for people trying to do business.

It is possible to set up Usenet privately or to host a local Usenet group that will allow use of the same interface, but it has several complications, including privacy, file posting, and the previously noted issues with viruses. Local groups can be useful, but mailing lists are more effective for this purpose.

Fax

Faxes are almost useless when it comes to communication. Although possible, it is difficult to grab electronic text documentation from a fax. In addition, faxing is slow, cumbersome, and often poor quality. Its black-and-white simplicity limits its scope, and in the end causes more frustration than it is worth.

Fax is usually used with the legal documentation. Companies use faxes as a means of authentication of signatures on the various agreements used during test. However, there are now better electronic forms that provide similar authentication to achieve the same result.

The fax is not entirely without use. Often, someone wanting to show something in hard copy has no other simple method of sending a copy. Faxing remains a relatively low-cost, simple solution to send a document. However, it is certainly not the best form for receiving and sending information.

"Snail" Mail

The traditional postal system, fondly nicknamed "snail mail" for its slow performance compared to email, remains advantageous for one reason: it is professional. Nothing adds more of a professional touch than real mail delivered personally to a test participant. Although it is slow, snail mail offers a special personal touch for the test site. From sending the official welcome to the thank-you letter at the close, there is no real substitute for a signed letter in the mailbox.

In contrast, there is no worse method for gathering beta test data. The primary reason for this is the slow nature of the mail system (hence "snail"). This speed makes it completely ineffective. Using paper surveys is antiquated and ineffective for many reasons. From the penmanship of the tester to watching a mailbox for a response, traditional mail is worthless for the purposes of gathering test data.

Timing

Test management starts with proper timing. Everything from file distribution to the duration of the test must be managed with a balanced and measured approach. Test participants need to receive updates, files, and communication on a consistent basis to see that the test is moving forward.

Sending test sites too much work up front buries them and can cause frustration with the test. Material needs to be balanced over the test period to ensure that the sites have an adequate but not overwhelming amount of work. This is also applicable in every other aspect of the test. Too many email messages, documents, files, and test components will cause the tester to back away or possibly even quit.

In the following case study, we see how proper timing can help balance a test and ensure the best test results.

Case Study: Too Much Time on Their Hands

Loren Carlos is the beta test engineer for new archiving software. Majestic Software has produced an archive application that allows users to encrypt a compressed file and send a key to another person who might then open it. The program has been a challenging beta, as the test sites continually find issues with the product and have been testing for more than a month.

The development team has been following the beta progress intensely and has been diligently working on the software to correct the issues the test participants discover. The sites have been testing the same application for the past few weeks and are starting to get frustrated that a new version has not been distributed.

Loren attends each team meeting and begs for a new version. The development team keeps promising a new version, but every time they are ready to deliver, another issue is discovered in the beta test and they want to implement it before distribution.

Finally, the frustration of not having a new version and the continued discovery of new issues takes its toll on the beta test sites. They start to complain in the user forum that this product is too problematic to continue testing, and many discuss quitting the test. Loren assures them that a new version is only days away, but that only causes more problems because testers tell him they won't test until a newer and more stable version is available.

Loren is placed in a precarious situation. Comments such as this normally would cause him to remove the complaining participants from the test. However, he agrees with the test participants and feels that forcing them to continue testing will only aggravate the sites further.

Loren approaches the development team and asks for a new version of the software. He explains that any version, even one that is incomplete, will allow the test sites to see some progress and understand that their concerns are being addressed.

The development team, although hesitant, agrees to deliver a new version of the application later in the day. Loren thanks the test sites for their effort and notifies them that a new copy of the software will be arriving by the end of the day. Once delivered, the sites tackle the software with renewed enthusiasm.

In this case, the test sites had spent too much time on the original version of the software. Had the sites been delivered regular updates in a timely manner, they would recognize that their issues were being addressed. In addition, Loren would no longer need to deal with issues that are corrected in each version.

Scaled delivery of updates balances the beta test participants' time and effort. It allows them to see progress and ensures that the effort put forth is focused on the discovery of new issues. In addition, proper timing extends the interest level of the test sites and keeps the sites' attention.

Professionalism

The quality of feedback from a beta test directly correlates to the level of professionalism exhibited in the handling of the test sites. Beta test participants take a test seriously when they are treated seriously. This is not to say that some level of personal contact is unacceptable, but rather, keeping a professional appearance keeps the test participant involved at a higher level.

Professionalism promotes a beta test in many ways. Primarily, it instills a sense of purpose in the test participants. When test sites see a certain level of professionalism, they understand that they are part of a professional team and that their role on the project matters.

Professionalism reflects positively on both the test team and the company. A beta test that is run with a professional air indicates that the program is effective and an important part of the development process. When a site sees professional behavior from a test team, it assumes that the entire company is also professional.

Finally, professionalism also brings out the best in a beta test team. The members of a beta test team who realize the importance of professionalism in the test follow processes more closely and work to be efficient. It is a symbiotic relationship in that the professionalism feeds the process, and following a process exudes professional behavior.

Acting on Test Results

Like the echo of a deep canyon, response to testers must be continuous and repetitive to make certain the participants understand the importance of their feedback. Whenever an issue is reported, the first thing a beta test team should do is respond and then continue to respond to the tester until the issue is resolved or the communication clearly shows an attempt to assist with the issue.

Set up communication standards for your department. Create an established amount of response time for each type of beta communication. For example, on initial test issue submissions have a 24-hour turnaround time.

The information reported by the test participants comes in a variety of forms. Whether it is a complex technical issue or a simple suggestion, each piece of feedback is valuable and requires a response. It can be helpful to build up a library of "boilerplate" responses that appropriately respond to the varying submissions, sending them off as the material gets reported. However, automation is not an option.

Beta test participants do not like automated responses to their issues. They have taken the time to send in some feedback and they expect an answer. It is good to indicate that their feedback is received, but it is even more important to convey that the feedback is being reviewed. Eventually, the test team needs to send some type of response to the issue.

If an issue is not real or has little merit, the message can be a considerate "thank you and we will consider your issue." If the test site sends in a complex technical summary of a problem, the appropriate response could be several pages explaining how the company intends to deal with it. A measured response to each issue will get the best results, but any response is better than no response.

Test sites need to understand that their contribution to the test is recognized and that the company values the participation. This is one aspect of getting the best results and it is elaborated on in Chapter 14.

See Figure 9.7.

Figure 9.7 simply demonstrates that all communication, no matter what the nature of it might be, must be responded to in some manner. Even if the response is negative, the customer still expects some form of response. This flow chart shows that the cycle of communication always ends up with the test participant receiving some type of response.

Qualification of Test Issues

Every issue reported by the test participants in beta test has some relevance and importance. However, the level of importance and relevance varies from issue to issue. Qualifying the issues as they arrive will assist in the categorization and distribution of test information. More importantly, it will provide a method to manage the large amount of data that comes in during a beta test.

As issues arrive, they must be assessed. This assessment can be a simple acknowledgment or an in-depth investigation. It is not the methodology, but rather the practice of qualification that is important. Each company will have a different method for addressing issues. However, this is a process that needs to be established prior to beginning the test.

Figure 9.8 provides one example of an effective method of issue qualification.

**See Figure 9.8.**

In this example, a simple attempt is made to duplicate the issue. Through this process, the site receives some resolution to their issue and the development team also receives assistance with the issue duplication process. Depending on the technical competence of the beta test team, the issue duplication might not be an option.

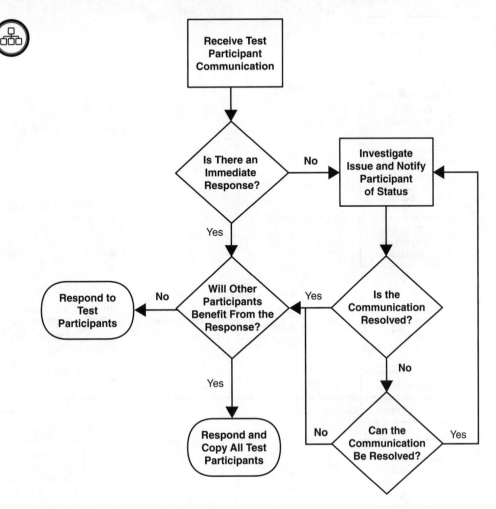

Figure 9.7 Communication response.

Qualification Criteria

There are four things to consider when qualifying data; the source, the number of reports, the nature of the test results, and the impact on the product are each factors for qualification. The source of the data is basically a focus on the test participant. Is the person a highly technical user or a novice? What quality of data has been reported until this point? Is the user comprehending the product properly and understands the issue he or she is reporting? By qualifying the source, the test team can understand how to handle the data being reported.

Next, quantity of reports needs to be assessed. If there are 20 test participants and 10 report an issue, that effectively means that 50 percent of your customers will see this

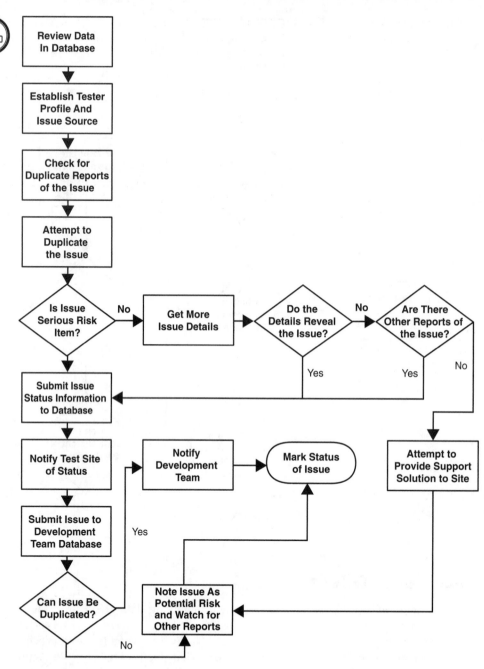

Figure 9.8 Qualifying issues.

problem. Of course, statistical data is relative to the size of the test and the number of reported issues. However, a good team will look at the number of reports relative to the size of the test, and qualify the impact of the issue if the product shipped with it.

The nature of the test results is essentially the type of issue that is being reported. What portion of the product is being impacted? How does the issue relate to the rest of the product? Can the issue be separated from the product in its entirety? Everything from documentation issues to code-level failures should be qualified. Next, establish a viable path for response and responsibility.

Last, the impact on the product is certainly the most important criterion for qualification. Determining whether a product can ship with the reported data is something to be considered every time an issue is reviewed. If there is even a hint that the reported issue might impact the release of a product, it should be brought to the attention of the development team immediately. Considering the impact of every issue ensures that no serious issues sneak through the beta process.

Benefits of Qualification

As data arrives, the qualification process does three things. Primarily, it eliminates redundant information going to the development team. This is critical, as the reputation and validation of a beta program resides on the data it delivers. If the test continuously produces superfluous or repetitive data, the test loses its impact.

Next, qualification measures the quality of data delivered by the beta test participants. Thus, a test site that provides highly accurate data with very detailed information might be someone to include on future tests as well as future versions of the software. In addition, as more and more issues are reported, you will be able to determine the technical competency of the test site.

Finally, this process establishes a methodology for handling issues. As each data point is qualified, a path for dealing with these points becomes clear. If it is a bug, it needs to be distributed to the proper engineer. If the issue is something that could have been cleared up with documentation, the problem should be routed to the technical writer. If the user has made a mistake in the installation of the product, there might be something to document for customer support. As issues are qualified, the best way to address these issues becomes apparent, and that path adds efficiency to the beta test process.

Over time, these data qualification points become very evident. The more issues a beta test team works with, the more opportunity the team has to learn how to properly qualify issues and get them to the right people.

Evaluation of Test Data

Different from qualification, evaluation actually involves investigating the reasons for an issue occurring. This means taking and looking into the report and establishing valid reasons for the issue to appear. While this does border on qualification, evaluation takes a deeper approach and requires a beta test team with resources for evaluating issues.

Evaluation involves having a deep understanding of the product being tested, and having the resources and time to make certain that the issues being reported are accurate. Resources include people, hardware, software, and related tools to verify the accuracy of the report. Qualification looks *at* the problem, and evaluation looks *into* the problem.

The distinction between evaluation and qualification is very important for a number of reasons. First, without making the distinction clear to the development team, there might be some communication issues. When a beta test team reports a qualified issue, it is stating they have looked at it and believe it needs attention. When a beta test team reports that an issue has been evaluated, it is stating that it has actually verified the existence or nonexistence of the problem.

Next, evaluation is a large commitment while qualification can operate with limited resources. As issues can be qualified with only superficial investigation while evaluation establishes a complex process of research. A team that evaluates issues normally has a lab, and the team members are recognized as experts on the software.

Last, evaluation establishes a pattern of *action*, while qualification only establishes a pattern of *distribution*. When a data point is evaluated, it can be reported as a bug, it can be given status; even a method to address the issue can be possibly determined. Qualification only says what the issue is and where it needs to go. A development team must be aware of the commitment the beta test team is taking on prior to the test starting.

Issues versus Bugs

When test participants report data, it is an issue. When the issue is established as a problem, it is escalated to a bug. The fact is, the word *bug* carries a stigma and can create a perception that is not necessarily beneficial to the beta test or the problem. When the development team hears the word *bug*, they assume *problem*. However, not all issues are problems, but rather perspectives on a problem.

An "issue" means that the test participant experienced something that he or she perceived as abnormal or unexpected. This expectation is the reason a company performs a beta test. Every issue has value, and every issue should be qualified and evaluated. If the issue appears to be something that could impact the product's quality, it might become a bug.

Issues that are not typically bugs are items such as feature requests, user interface questions, or design questions (e.g., colors, button placement, etc.). These are submissions that are based more on taste or opinion than on some occurrence or problem. However, multiple submissions of this type could escalate into a bug. If every test participant in a beta program complains that the color of the software is ugly, that is certainly something to consider as a bug.

Once an issue becomes a bug, it is much more serious. It is a negative reflection on the product and could potentially impact the consumer if the product is shipped. Bugs need to be addressed in some manner, but it is not the responsibility of the beta test team to take on this burden. There is a critical caveat to being in a beta test:

 Beta teams are employed to discover issues, not address them.

It is easy to become consumed with finding answers to issues as test participants crave solutions. However, taking the time to resolve test participants' problems deviates from the course of a beta test and can consume a lot of time. Always remember that the purpose of the test is to reveal product limitations, not to resolve them. Leave the resolution decisions to the development team.

Process for Evaluation

There is no real way to provide a specific example of a process for evaluation because it depends on the product being tested. If you are testing a word processing application, the path to issue duplication will be different than if a spreadsheet issue is being duplicated. However, there are some common methods of duplicating issues that can be explored.

Verify Your Data

The customer will report the problem and it will need to be verified. The first step is to make sure that the report has all the information necessary to duplicate the issue. It is not simply seeing that the issue is properly described, but also that any associated materials and processes necessary to duplicate the issue are provided.

If the test participant does not have complete data, it is best to contact him or her and get as much detail as possible about the issue. If possible, walk through the steps of duplication with the customer and see if the same issue appears. It could be a single instance occurrence, or the test participant might have misidentified the issue as a problem with the beta product when in actuality it is something else having a problem.

Last, if the issue does repeat itself for the customer, be certain to gather as much information about the customer's test environment to make certain that the issue can be duplicated by the test team. Often, issues can be elusive and inconclusive. With as much information as possible, an issue can often be determined quickly and efficiently.

Look for Repetition

If an issue is appearing to more than one beta test participant, it will make the path to duplication much simpler. There will be many more data points generated to help find the issue and confirm its validity. Look at all the issues that are being reported and try to determine a common path to the problem.

The path to a problem can be discovered in many ways. It might be helpful to look at the profiles of each tester to determine a common element among all the test participants. Another possibility is to look at the operation being performed when the issue exhibited itself. Last, the path might be as simple as a common mistake made by the test participants. The sooner a test engineer can establish a path, the sooner the issue will be duplicated and reported to the development team.

Follow Through

Once an issue has been reported, it might take several attempts to duplicate it. The variability of computer hardware, installed applications, operating system versions, and other factors will make it a challenge to replicate some issues. Once a test engineer begins working on the issue, he or she should continue to follow through until the issue is duplicated, resolved, or closed.

Issues that are duplicated are reported to the development team as bugs. Those that are resolved should be communicated to the test site. Whether the resolution be a fix in the software or that the issue was simply a user error, the site needs to know that the issue has been dealt with. In these cases, follow through is simple.

However, when the problem cannot be duplicated or the team has decided not to address the concern of the tester, following up with the participant becomes much more difficult. Depending on the seriousness of the issue and the importance to the test participant, this situation can become troublesome. The best method of approach is to explain the situation to the site and reaffirm the importance of the site's contribution. When issues remain unresolved in the eyes of test participants, it conveys a message that the company does not care about them or their concerns.

 Always be honest with beta test participants. Provide as much detail about the company's position on their issue. In the end, the site will usually understand.

The Balancing Act

Being in beta test is a constant balancing act in that the needs of the test participants must be considered against the needs of the company. While the company does pay the beta test employee, the role of that employee is to ensure the quality of the product. Often, companies might make decisions that seem contrary to the benefit of the test site and effectively the customer. A conflict might arise and the beta test team will sit in the middle of this conflict.

This uncomfortable situation is unpleasant and common. More often than not, many issues discovered during a beta test will have to go unresolved in order to meet a schedule. Therefore, the test team will need to selectively pick which issues to advocate resolution and which issues to relegate to a later version or to go unresolved.

Taking a position on issues is always a dangerous thing, and in most cases should not be the role of the beta test team. Always use objectivity when reviewing issues. Speaking to the facts will carry much more weight with a development team than expressing an opinion. However, if a serious issue appears to be neglected, it might make sense to express a concern and explain the foundations for this concern.

What to Report

Understanding that not every issue will be handled, it is the responsibility of the beta test team to act as filter for the development team. Alas, the great question that comes is, "what should be reported and what should be neglected?" The strange fact is the answer is "everything and nothing."

A properly run beta test generates a lot of data. Good testers send in bugs, quotes, comments, feature requests, ideas, and other items. All of this data is excellent and useful. However, a team on its way to releasing a product might be overwhelmed by the amount of data coming from a beta test. Rather than taking a selective approach to providing data, establish a method for all the data to be viewable, but place emphasis on the issues that need attention.

Create a four-tier system that allows the development team to choose how in-depth it would like to go into the beta results. From a superficial glance to an exhaustive research on the issues, providing all of the results reported from the test ensures that no issue goes unheard.

Tier One

This data is the critical information that cannot be overlooked. It is the material that could severely impact a product's release or could be damaging to the company. This material must be reviewed and put in front of the development team. Issues of this importance are focused on in the form of a special report or in immediate communication to the development team (e.g., telephone call, email, etc.). Only a small percentage of the test results will fall into this tier.

Tier Two

Tier-two data are issues that have some level of importance and need to be viewed. These issues should be noted to the development team as part of a review process. However, if there is no process to review beta test data, then the information needs to be made available in some form that is accessible to the development team. Whether it is online or in a weekly report, this data needs to be seen and that message must be passed onto the developers. Tier-two data represents the bulk of the beta test results.

Tier Three

This level of data is the material that is either repetitive or of debatable importance. These are often exaggerated suggestions, extraordinary circumstances, or strange claims. In this area, you might group all of it into a single report or provide some type of classification system for identifying this kind of issue. They might have merit, but are not necessarily worth dedicating a lot of time to deliver. The tier-three issue is something best delivered online or in a report and represents only a small amount of data.

Tier Four

The last tier issues are items that have little or no significance or have been confirmed to not be issues with the product. One might wonder what the value of sharing this information with the development team might be. However, all data from a beta test has some value. Naturally, serious issues gather the most attention, but many of these lowest-tier concerns are often interesting and should be reviewed when the pressure to release the product has passed. It might make sense to wait until the project is complete to deliver these items.

Distribution of Test Data

 The data that comes from a beta test is valuable to many people. Thus, it is important that there is some method for distributing the data to the different teams. In Chapter 10, "Improve Your Program," an analysis of how to innovate this process is discussed. In this section, we will discuss the flow of test data and where it needs to go.

Technical Data

When information comes in of a technical nature, the qualification process should dictate where the information should be distributed. It is important to establish a clear path of ownership for products. In the following case study, results from the beta test are distributed to one department, but there are many owners.

As we see, Mike runs the beta test purely through qualification. He is not doing any serious debugging. His emphasis is purely on getting the issues to the right people. However, he does make certain that the reported issues do exist prior to bringing in the responsible party. His focus is on getting the issue to the right person. See the case study on page 127.

In the case where the issue was unclear, Mike knew that handing it to the wrong person would be a problem. He brought in the producer and leader of the team, Karen. She made the decision on how to proceed and Mike made note of her response. His effort made certain that the right people looked at the right part of the product.

Marketing Data

Opinions, ideas, and quotable comments are all material that can be pulled from beta test results. These items offer excellent insight into the customer's opinion of a product, and getting it to the marketing team is critical. If something comes in that could

Case Study: Stealing Thunder

Blasted Softworks is an action game developer focused on the first-person shooter market. Their latest product, *Thunderlords*, is a network game based on the ancient Norse folklore. Each character in the game has the ability to shoot lightning from its fingertips in battles to determine who will be the master lord.

A collection of polygons and textures, the characters represent a new innovation in three-dimensional rendering. Each Thunderlord is drawn in tremendous detail and has special traits that need to be tested. The game is beginning beta testing to ensure the traits work properly and interface correctly with the other characters.

During preliminary tests, Mike O'Neil, beta test manager, has set up several computers in the Blasted labs and has invited local gamers to test the new game over their lab network. Immediately, some of the testers begin to see issues.

The first problem is that a character becomes translucent when it fires its weapons. This strange phenomenon occurs on every lord and could have multiple owners. Mike realizes that the main person responsible for this issue is the model designer and he passes it on to her.

Next, the game loses color during several of the explosions. Mike does some analysis and determines that the team that writes the 3D engine should address this issue. He gathers several screen shots and passes them along to the engine team immediately.

The beta sites are enjoying themselves but they have several comments about the difficulty. Some complain that the competition is too difficult and that some characters have too much power. Others are frustrated that the game is too easy and that there is no challenge. Mike knows that this has a lot to do with the properties of each character. He passes the individual test comments on to the game designers.

In another instance, players complain that network lag seems to impact the performance of their characters. Mike monitors the network traffic during the game and sees no problem with the load. With this in mind, he asks the test participants to see if they can duplicate the lag as he monitors the traffic. After hours of playing, the network barely registers the traffic. Using this data, Mike concludes that the issue must be somewhere besides the network and brings in Karen Tether, the game producer to see the issue.

Karen is at a loss on where this issue might reside and decides it needs to be debugged by the QA team before she will dedicate any of her engineering resources to fixing it. Mike notes her comments in his database and informs the beta testers that the issue is being looked into.

After several weeks of testing, this first phase of beta testing is complete. The game development team has gathered a significant amount of data and begins to establish guidelines for the next revision of the game. Mike closes the test and thanks the participants for their contribution.

potentially help market a product or an item that might be an improvement to the design, marketing needs to see it.

Items of this nature come in the same method that the technical data comes in, and often when dealing with issues, there might be a tendency to put these items on the back burner. However, these comments are just as important to a product's future as a bug is. It might not have the same sense of urgency, but material of this type helps build better products.

Timeliness of Distribution

Getting the test data to the team in a timely manner is imperative. Depending on the severity of the issues being reported, issue distribution can become a literal balancing act. Which issues go to the front of the line and which issues need to be put back until there is time to address them becomes one of the biggest challenges of running a beta test.

During the qualification of every issue, an engineer learns that some issues are more important than others. Items of a critical nature naturally gather the most attention and get distributed to the development team immediately. However, there are those issues that are important and need consideration but are not the top priority.

Based on the specific qualification of every issue, a standard timeline should also be established that corresponds to its severity. As noted earlier, issues with moderate severity might go out in a daily report. Items with minor severity might go out once a week, and issues with no severity might be distributed on a biweekly basis. While this decision is arbitrary, common sense dictates getting the data in a timely manner so that it can be addressed.

Following Up

When issues are handed off to different members of a development team, they cannot be left to be resolved. The simple fact is that the only person who can be relied on to respond to the beta test site is the beta test engineer responsible for the project. Therefore, it is crucial that the test engineer follows up on each issue that he or she hands off.

Beta test sites expect a response to each issue they submit. If an issue is handed off and fixed, there must be a clear path of ownership of that issue. The site reported it, the test engineer qualified it, and the development engineer fixed it. The only problem with this is that the first two people are communicating together on a regular basis; the third is not in the communication loop.

It is the responsibility of the test engineer to keep on top of every issue that is passed on and to follow up with the test participants and let them know the status of their issues. In some cases, the development engineer might not be able to be in contact with the beta test engineer. In those cases, there are alternatives to getting a response.

One option is the release notes that are delivered with the product. Those notes often indicate when changes are implemented and what has been fixed in the latest version. If that is not an option, check and see if access to the company's bug-tracking database is available. Some beta teams actually use this system for tracking bugs, while others use their own system and the software team maintains their own. Notes on the fixes should be included in that database. Last, if nothing else is available, verify that the issue has been fixed through an issue duplication process.

No matter how it happens, following up on issues that leave the realm of the beta test team remains an valuable task of test data management. The distribution of data is rarely one-sided. Inevitably, when an issue is brought to the attention of the development team, some course of action will be planned. It is the role of the beta test engineer to ensure that course is followed.

Management of Test Materials

Beta test materials are often hot properties. With beta following so close to release, the beta test material is often the closest thing available to a real product. Thus, beta teams are often solicited for the latest software. While this is certainly a privilege of being in the beta test process, it is also a large burden. The pressure to get the materials to a variety of people unrelated to the beta test is tremendous. However, it is a mistake to allow a beta program to act like a software distribution house.

Beta test materials are test resources and need to be managed closely for a number of reasons. Primarily, beta test resources are for the test and need to be allocated for this purpose. Sharing them with other organizations puts the test at risk. It also creates precedence; other teams will assume that they can pilfer from beta test on every project if they did it once.

Next, you cannot trust anyone with the software. Plain and simple, people do not always do what they say. Sad as it is, the fact remains that people will give software away. Most don't perceive that giving an application away is wrong. Without proper management of the test materials, the first beta test participants will be people who downloaded the application from a pirate Web site.

Next, beta materials are often in a constant state of change until the test starts. This variability means the software is not controlled and issues could exist in the application. Because of this, the software could be more dangerous in the state it is in and cause issues for those who use it.

Last, beta materials are very close to a released product that has tangible value, and lost software could mean lost revenue to a company. Keeping tight reins on the materials from test can be challenging and it does make sense to catalogue these materials in some manner. Whether you use a complex database for tracking each item or simply number and log each item on a sheet of paper, some method for keeping tabs on the material is necessary.

Beta Test Closure

Closure is the last phase of the actual beta test. It is the point in the test where the product is approaching release and things are beginning to wind down. Closure seems like an obvious step in the process and one that might be slightly inconsequential. However, closure functions as a method for getting test data, a process for measuring test performance, and a key final step in the test process.

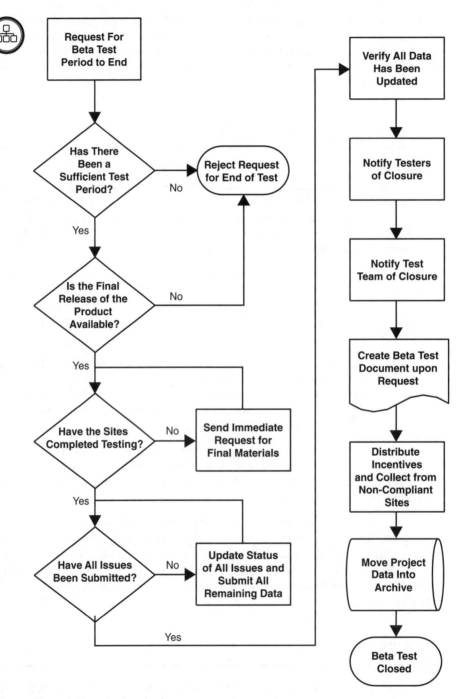

Figure 9.9 Closing the beta test.

 **See Figure 9.9.**

Figure 9.9 provides a basic overview of all aspects of project closure. You will notice that there are several gating items to get a project to closure. However, these items are not always going to be available. Use Figure 9.9 as an example of an effective process, but do not assume that each of these steps will occur.

Participant Closure

The test participants have just spent several weeks working on a product. They have dedicated time and effort. They have been responsive when needed and productive in their output. So, how do you end this period of productivity on an effective note? Closure is the process that effectively ends a test.

The test participants are notified that the test is coming to an end. A specific date is not given at this time because it might change. Sites are instructed to make certain that any remaining issues are submitted and any requirements of the test are delivered to the beta test team. In addition, the test team confirms that the sites have all the materials they need once the test is closed (e.g., manuals, master disks, etc.).

 Never **tell a beta site a specific closure date until you are actually ready to close the beta test.**

Once this is performed, the state of the product is determined. If it appears that the product is ready for release, the release candidate of the software is distributed to the test participants to ensure that everyone is on the latest version. Then, a specific date is set for official closure and all participants are informed of this date. Once this date has been established, test sites tend to drop in their level of participation. They understand that the test is almost over and their work is done.

Incentives

Incentives are one aspect of this process. The incentive is the proverbial "carrot" at the end of a test. It is the one item the keeps the tester motivated to perform even when things get challenging. There is a science to properly gauging the right amount of incentive with the test. In this section, that science will not be examined, but rather the step in the process that is required.

Testers who have successfully completed the testing within the parameters specified at the beginning of the test are entitled to the incentive. If the test participant has not quite met the parameters but did do enough to be of value, a smaller incentive might be in order. No matter what the level of performance, incentives should be distributed immediately after the closure date has passed.

Test sites are not truly closed until they receive a thank-you note and their incentive. Now, incentives are an optional item. Depending on the product, being part of the test might be sufficient incentive enough. It is really the discretion of the test manager whether he or she gives incentives.

Test Participant Ranking

Coinciding with the incentive distribution is the test participant ranking. Each site needs to be ranked based on his or her performance. There are many important reasons for ranking test sites, and in Chapter 12 there is elaborate description of the criteria needed to ensure proper ranking. Here, the only concern is that it happens.

Once the test has been completed, look at each tester. Did he or she provide all the information requested? Was the tester a value to the test? Did he or she provide valuable information? As each of these items is considered, a corresponding rank will be assigned.

Having a good ranking system will assist with future site selection and will help with the establishment of a corresponding incentive program. In addition, it will build a strong user base for impromptu tests that need good, solid people on short notice. Ranking is an important tool in the closure process.

The Closure Document

The closure document is a comprehensive overview of the beta test and its results. A critical indicator of the end of test, the closure document allows everyone to know how the test was performed, the outcome, and what should be done going forward. By generating a closure document, the development team has a way to show management that a beta test was performed. In addition, the closure document establishes the state of the product just prior to shipment.

The Ideal Document

The ideal closure document is basically a simple summary that tells the reader everything he or she would want to know about the beta test without actually reading every bit of communication from the test. In the best case, the document is relatively short and concise. It covers every aspect of the test, but only provides the crucial data.

The sad fact is that most people do not read the closure document. The test is complete and the important data has already been dealt with. If things went well, the product is shipping and everyone is working on new projects. So, why take the time to create a closure document? There are many valid and important reasons for this document.

The closure document is a record of the performance of a test. As a product matures in the market, there might be a need to perform a new test. The closure document will explore what was done in the original test and will help build a new test plan for a new version of the product.

Beta tests produce large amounts of data. The closure document allows that data to be archived and kept off-line. If someone wants to understand what happened during the beta test, all he or she will need to review is the closure document.

Ultimately, the closure document is a milestone in a project and it signifies the end of test to not only the beta test team but to the entire development team. With the delivery of this document, the beta team is telling everyone that the test is done and no more work on this project will be performed.

Without the closure document, there might be some latecomers who want something from the beta test or someone might doubt the test was performed down the line. A properly designed closure document addresses all of these issues and is an important part of the beta test process.

Project Summary

The summary for the project should only be a few paragraphs and explain the rudimentary details about the test. Number of test participants, duration of the test, a description of the product, and the high and low points of the test should be included in this summary. In addition, it makes sense to provide numbers about the quantity of feedback that was gathered during the test.

A good summary allows someone in a management capacity to take five or 10 minutes and completely understand what happened during the beta test. This can be a challenging task, as all the work that goes into a beta test is not easily summarized in a few paragraphs. However, this summary is a key aspect of the document and the reader is unlikely to read much more than this section.

Project Participant Summary

Listing the test participants in a summary table, this section basically describes the demographics of the test participants. It should include the site's name, company, position or title, geographic location, and any test specific information such as hardware or software required to use the product.

This section should not be a contact sheet and should never include contact information. If a person within the company wants to contact a test participant, make that information available outside this document. This portion of the summary is only trying to demonstrate that the test successfully addressed the demographic needs of the project.

Issue Summary

The issue summary is a difficult but necessary item to include in the closure document. The development team can often construe it negatively because they see this list of issues as the "dirty laundry" of the project. However, it is important to document any issues discovered during test that were not corrected by the time test closed.

Inevitably, there will be a need to know what issues were discovered that were not fixed. These items might be small and inconsequential, but must be documented. The sad truth is, when the real customer sees an issue in the field, someone will want to know if it was discovered during the beta test. If there is no document indicating the discovery, the assumption will be that beta test did not catch it.

Marketing Summary

The marketing summary should include some of the more positive comments that came out during test. In contrast to the issues summary, the marketing summary illustrates the positive aspects and enforces the successes of the test. It might seem biased to point out only the positive in this section, but there are valid reasons for this.

First, marketing does not use negative material to promote a product. Therefore, comments that reflect negatively on the product might demonstrate objectivity, but they do not necessarily benefit anyone in the summary.

Next, so much feedback comes in from a properly executed test that it is difficult to determine what should be shared. Taking a focus on the positive reflects nicely on the beta test program and shows the development team that there is a lot of benefit in performing this test.

Last, the positive comments will encourage readership of the closure report. The development team and other people in the company might use this report to promote the product within, recognize the development team, or even note the excellent job the beta test program did.

This summary can be a list of quotes, a written summary including some user comments, or a customer success story. Whatever format is chosen, it should always emphasize the positive aspects of the product.

Material Summary

The last item to include in the closure is a summary of the materials distributed into test. Every item that was included in the box, distributed through the Web, or shipped to the customer should be noted. It should also include version information and build dates if possible. This tells the reader the last version tested.

When documenting the materials, make certain to catch all the relevant version information. This includes build dates, build numbers, version numbers, or version dates for every component shipped to the customer. Every manual, disk, and hardware component should be documented in addition to the software application.

 Keep a log of every version of every component that is submitted during the entire duration of the test process.

This section is especially useful for issue duplication after the test has been completed. Keep in mind that just because the beta test is finished, the product is still shipping and issues might still appear. Thus, the information gathered during beta test is often looked over by customer support and other teams to see if problems reported from the field were reported during beta test. Sometimes, beta test information is used to confirm or deny new issues. Thus, keeping accurate records about what was tested is imperative.

Archiving Test Data

Just because a beta test is closed does not mean that the data is now obsolete. Quite the contrary, the data now takes on a new and useful form. As an archive, beta test data allows companies to continue to gather insight into the opinions and ideas of the customer long after the test has closed. As new products are developed, the archived beta test data becomes a valuable resource.

An archive can be made available online or in a form that is easily accessible for development teams to view. It might even make sense to break out all the product suggestions into a single report and deliver them to marketing when they begin road map discussions. If a new version of the software is expected, it is also good to provide this information to the new development team prior to beginning the next application.

It might seem logical to put the suggestion information in the closure documentation, but it really loses its impact in that form. Often, months go by before a new version of a product begins development and by that time, teams have forgotten the document and the results from beta test.

An archive is a place to reference previous tests. Thus, a beta team can learn from its previous experience and leverage that experience for new tests. An archive provides valuable history, and while it is not used a lot, it becomes significant when it is needed.

Beta Test Completion

Once the test is completed, the data is archived, and the project is closed, thus begins a cycle of new tests. A good test team takes time to assess the successes and failures of the beta test. By logging these, the team provides material for improvement and refinement. The fact is that while the information provided here exhibits the best practices possible, each company has different processes.

Take care to look over all aspects of the beta process and examine closely the relationships built during the test. Communication is certainly one of the most critical components of a beta test program and this is the place where the most failures occur. It might make sense to bring in the development team partners and ask them to evaluate the beta test program.

Listening to those internal partners can be very beneficial. First, they will have real and hopefully constructive criticisms about the program. Next, whenever someone is close to something, it is difficult to see its faults. The outside set of eyes could bring some excellent insight into the beta test organization. Last, these people are also customers, and meeting their needs is important.

It is also helpful to maintain relationships with test participants who really made the extra effort during the test. If there is an extended period of time between projects, drop the site an occasional mail message and keep him or her in the loop about upcoming tests. These people are a valuable resource, and maintaining contact will demonstrate to the test sites that you value their contribution.

CHAPTER 10

Improve Your Program

This chapter has two objectives. The first explores the ideas behind using innovation to improve the different aspects of the beta process. The second examines how innovations can impact and be implemented to employ a better overall testing program.

This chapter does not examine any actual or existing technologies or any innovations. These things change constantly. As quickly as one technology is released another fades into obsolescence. Therefore, it is the purpose of this chapter to explain how to innovate rather than the innovations themselves.

It makes good sense to look into every technological innovation and examine potential methods for improving a program. Conversely, running a beta program is time consuming. There is little room to properly evaluate new technology. However, it makes sense to do so, as improvements in technology mean improvements in the process—and improvements in a process means more time.

Why Innovate?

The expression, "If it isn't broken, don't fix it." is so wrong in so many ways. Just because a process works doesn't mean it works well. In fact, striving to get the best out of a beta program means always looking for methods to improve it. This is a big task, but an important one.

Conceptually, using technology and innovation are central in any process. However, when it comes to actually deploying a new technology, there are many obstacles. Whether it is having the expertise to do it properly or having the budget to get the appropriate equipment, implementing a new technology can be as challenging as running the beta test program.

Therefore, taking on the challenge to innovate and improve a program must coincide with the goal of getting the best test results. If these two go hand in hand, both objectives move forward. With every improvement and innovation implemented, more effective results come from test. Sometimes, the benefit is small, and sometimes it is huge. Regardless, the changes still make a better test program.

Measure Your Program

Before striving to establish a better program, it is important to understand the state the program is in. Taking measurements of the effectiveness of a beta program is a very difficult undertaking. How can you measure performance when every product is different and every test has different participants?

The fact is, determining a good program or bad program is subjective. One might consider any feedback excellent, while another considers 10 or more issues from each test site as a good test. However, the good beta program generates feedback, and this is good place to start.

First and foremost, evaluate test performance by establishing criteria for a successful test. For example, set a goal to receive five pieces of feedback and one bug from every participant. This can be arbitrary criteria, but they need to be something a touch lower than what you normally expect from test sites.

Next, evaluate your delivery of data. Do you get feedback in a timely manner to your development partners? Do you see areas for significant improvement? Again, how you measure the performance is arbitrary. Perhaps, you can take a look at development team involvement or maybe determine the number of methods of delivery.

Last, take all this information and set this as your "bar." This is the current state of the program. This is not meant to be a judgment of the program, but rather an establishment of a measurement to help build a better beta program. As you consider potential improvements, you can see if they can potentially raise the bar of test performance.

Track Your Data

When the "bar" is raised, you will want to share it with everyone. Management and your partners need to know that methods to improve the beta program are being considered. These improvements are effectively designed to help improve the beta process and, consequently, improve the product. The only way to do this is to provide comparative data.

With comparative data, a beta process can demonstrate the improvement of the program and the benefits of investing in the program. Program budgets are built on this type of data, and when the time comes to justify new hardware or software, tracked performance is an excellent way to sell the improvements.

Innovation and Testing

Innovation is defined as bringing in something new. However, our perception of innovation is something not only new but improved. Innovation is a critical component of success. Whether you are innovating a product or a process, using innovation will accomplish more.

Beta testing for all its random results is a relatively static procedure. Whether there are 500 test participants or five, the process applies. For that reason, implementing improvements is more a process of refinement than change. You don't need to do anything new, just do it better.

For example, getting the most feedback from beta test participants is certainly a central goal of an effective test system. If you can improve the output of the test participants, you effectively improve the test. Taking that into consideration, adding efficiency is one way to use innovation. Getting the data quicker and easier improves the results. In the following case study, we see how innovation improves a beta test.

Test programs are about experimentation and evaluation. As a beta test program, it makes sense to consider any potential methods for improving a process. Whether those improvements come from internal partners or an external resource, a good beta test program is willing to experiment (or "test") and is constantly looking for methods to innovate.

Often, improvements are available where they are least expected. Focused on finding the best innovations, the beta test manager should consider multiple sources and keep an open mind to all people and ideas. Many might exist within your grasp, and it is important to take time and make certain that you are using all available resources.

Borrowing from the Best

There is no need to "reinvent the wheel," as innovation and best practices exist all around us. Whenever looking at a method for innovating a test process, look at other processes and see if there is something that might be learned or leveraged. Good examples live all around us in different forms, and many can be easily transitioned into a beta program.

One of the best ways to get this information is to simply ask. Call together different groups, managers, or coworkers and ask them for help. Many times, someone has had to take on a similar task and can offer advice. People love to share their ideas and opinions. It makes them feel important. By asking for help, you not only convey a message of respect, you get a lot of good ideas.

 Sign up for other companies' beta tests and look at how they run the their program. Through your participation, you might gather some new ideas!

Case Study: Practicing What You Preach

Alina Bronnski is the beta test manager for Helix Internetworking Systems. Helix produces network security software that allows connected networks to be safe from intruders through virtual private networking (VPN) technology.

Alina has been asked to perform a beta test on Helix's VPN security system called "Latchkey." The software monitors multiple VPN networks and sends a message to a system administrator whenever an unauthorized attempt is made to enter a network. In addition, it immediately starts a trace on the intruder to help identify which VPN it is coming from. Alina has been testing earlier versions of this product and sees no problem in setting up the test.

In past tests, Alina has used a regular Web-based interface to gather test data. Test participants log in to the beta test Web server and can submit bugs through Web-based forms. While it has been relatively effective, the users must operate the Helix software on a separate network and report issues through a system connected to the Internet. In addition, all issues must be pulled off the external server and moved over to another server internally. While the system works, Alina feels it is a bit strange that she is not using her company's technology.

In order to improve the process and get the most from the test, Alina works with George Carmichael, the design engineer on the project, to deploy a new VPN specific for her beta sites. By using this innovation, Alina can achieve multiple goals. The sites will be using the Helix technology, she can share a single server that will be connected to the internal network, and, ultimately, test participants will be able to use a single network to test the software and report issues.

Alina has very little time to get this deployed and asks George to provide assistance in setting up the separate network. George sees this as a way to test the new software. He can ask Alina to have the test sites attempt to get into other networks on the Helix intranet and get real-time results. Normally, he has to review the log files produced by the software. In this case, he will actually receive the alerts.

George sees this as a benefit to his project while adding efficiency to the beta program and offers his help. Working together, George and Alina build something that both innovates the beta process and improves the site's ability to test the product.

Once you have exhausted your internal resources, it might be time to start looking outside the company. Many people put their best practices out for the world to see them. Perhaps it is ego or maybe a form of altruism; no matter what motivation exists, it makes sense to evaluate the data provided.

White Papers

White papers are short, often-technical documents that provide insight on a particular technology. While they can be one-sided and focused on promoting a particular practice or business, a white paper usually contains a lot of useful information. White papers are almost always free, and because they are concise, they allow an efficient use of time to get technical information.

When using white papers, make certain you always consider the source of the document. Often, these papers are used to sell a product or service. While they are usually technically accurate, it is best to compare other white papers on the same subject. Often, the paper might be skewed toward the focus of the authoring company. This doesn't take away from the value a white paper offers, it simply means you need to look at a lot of the information before making a judgment call.

Web Sites

Web sites can be useful tools when looking for new innovations and technology. However, there is no way to verify the technical accuracy or credibility of the authors of these pages. Therefore, when reading Web-based data, review your sources closely. In addition, look for dates on the pages if possible. What you might be reading could be outdated or even incorrect information.

The best sites to visit are usually professional organizations that focus on the technology you are examining. These sites often have discussion boards with professionals discussing the technology. It might be useful to join a chat session or bulletin board and ask a few questions. In most cases, the people involved are eager to share information.

Another method for getting Web data is to use a search engine and start a random hunt for the material you need. While the process is sometimes slow, and specific data might be difficult to find initially, it can be productive and produce decent results. As with white papers, you should always consider the source and date of the information before reviewing the data.

Books

Technical books are excellent resources for researching innovation. The person writing the work has taken the time to assemble all of the material in a single publication. The comprehensive nature of books makes them an excellent resource for investigation of technical innovations. In addition, books often list other valuable resources that might be useful in the pursuit.

There are only two real detractions from using technical books. Due to the time it takes to publish a book, some of the information might not be up to date. In addition, Web sites and white papers are free. Books are often expensive, and it might take more than one to get all the information you want. Nonetheless, a book is the best way to go for the most comprehensive and accurate material on a particular topic.

Magazines and Periodicals

Magazines, newspapers, and other publications print articles about new innovations all the time. Often, they provide the latest and most interesting information available, but lack the depth necessary to execute on the information. Magazines are an excellent starting place to get some ideas, but usually they leave a lot to still learn.

Magazines are based on consistent readership, and if you can take the time, subscribing to a magazine might be the best way to keep on top of the latest innovations. Most are written for the "now," and the articles are usually very relevant and fresh to the business of beta test. Additionally, magazines are rich with advertisements. These are useful for building budgets and for knowing what is currently on the market.

Newspapers rarely treat any topic with too much depth and are not generally useful when trying to investigate a potential innovation in technology. However, they often report the announcement of an innovation first, and thus a quick glance through a paper can be worthwhile. Budgeting time to review magazines and periodicals can be valuable when used for investigating potential technical innovations.

Evaluating Innovation

Something new isn't always something good. Before deciding to implement technological innovation into a beta process, it is necessary to give it a "beta test" of your own. Innovations represent the cutting edge of technology, and thus it makes sense to make certain the new technology will bring benefits and not headaches.

Trade Shows

Every year, different industries gather together to show off their latest and most innovative wares. The "trade show" usually brings together the vendors and the customer in one location so purchase decisions can be made for the coming year. Admission is typically free of charge unless you are interested in participating in one of the educational sessions.

By and large, much of the information presented at a trade show provides a cursory overview of the products. However, many companies bring a technical expert to discuss the finer points of a product with those who are interested. Therefore, take the time to do the research on the technology you are interested in seeing. These experts are often in demand and it will help if you are properly prepared.

Most developers attend multiple trade shows throughout the year. The cost of getting to a trade show is often expensive and attendance is normally reserved for people helping with the sale of a product. However, if your company attends one of the larger shows, there might be a chance to balance your time working the booth while seeing the show, thus adding value with your participation.

Because the beta test program sees every product just prior to release, they make excellent trade show booth workers. If you want to visit a show and work, point this out to the trade show manager. You will end up being one of those "experts."

Evaluations

Often, manufacturers will allow companies to take a test drive of software or hardware before purchasing the product. An investigative period, the evaluation will let the beta program measure the benefit these new products have to offer. However, there is risk when using an evaluation product on live systems.

Whenever evaluating software or hardware for the beta test infrastructure, it is good to throw it into a test environment and give it a try. Not every company can afford to have duplicate servers and infrastructure. Therefore, take it for a test drive on a noncritical system or move it onto a computer not seeing much use. Evaluation copies usually have expiration dates or limitations. It makes sense to pull off the evaluation software once you have had a chance to look it over.

Ask Around

As before, it always makes sense to use your company resources wisely and check to see if anyone else is considering the same products. If you are testing a new innovation, it is very possible that someone else in your company might be doing the same thing. Check with colleagues inside and outside the company if necessary, and see what type of response the software or hardware you are examining has received. There might be someone who has already gone down the same path.

Additionally, these people might have the actual equipment or software installed. This would provide an opportunity to forego the evaluation but still examine the material first hand. This benefit is huge, as it eliminates the time to install and test the software on resources you might or might not have.

Finally, there might be an opportunity to reduce the cost of the product. More often than not, companies provide financial incentives for multiple licenses, or in the case of hardware, it might be possible to offset the cost by sharing the resource.

Innovation Impact

The importance of innovation can be felt in many places within a beta test program. Whenever implementing any changes, the potential return on investment (ROI) should be studied. If the innovation is expensive or impractical, it might make sense to wait a little time before considering it. However, if the benefits are tremendous and there is money in the budget, it might be time to make the move.

Either way, the most important reason for making any of these changes is to see an improvement in the beta test process. Any innovation, no matter the cost, must be thoroughly evaluated to see if it will enhance the program.

Communication

Using innovation in the communication process is an essential part of ensuring the best results. Successful beta tests are all about good communication, and thus any method that can improve that aspect of the process is important. Communication technologies vary tremendously and it is essential to use those technologies that are best suited to the infrastructure.

Innovations that will accelerate the communication between the sites and the test team or that will bring in more data are always of value. Additional value would be gained if the technology improves communication between the sites.

When evaluating potential communication improvements, there are two mandatory criteria to take into consideration. First, there must be a way to document the correspondence. Whether it is a log or a text-based form, there must be some text trail to keep the communication.

Second, the communication must not consume any more time than any existing form of communication. Innovation infers improvement; thus, any new technology that is being considered should improve the amount of time dedicated to communicating, or there is no real reason to implement the solution.

Issue Management

Normally, companies have bug-tracking systems that must be used by all development staff. However, this system is normally internal and nobody would ever even consider giving access to people outside the company. Therefore, beta test programs must maintain their own systems for managing issues gathered from beta testing.

When evaluating potential methods of improvement to the issue management system, integration with your company's bug tracking system should be a top consideration. While a stand-alone system does effectively work, most issues will need to be moved over to the bug-tracking system.

Extensible design should also be a priority consideration. Effective issue management depends on the issues being managed. It makes no sense to invest in a system that remains static while the products are constantly changing. An issue management system needs to have a built-in flexibility to ensure it meets the needs of both today's test and tomorrow's.

Real-Time Results

Normally, beta test durations are quite short. The entire test process might be three or four weeks. In that time, a beta team is buried in evaluating data, responding to questions, and working to ensure a successful test. Therefore, any method that allows people to view test results in "real-time" is a benefit to the process.

Both the program and those involved throughout the company benefit from being able to access the data as it arrives. There are numerous technologies that allow the reporting of data in real time. However, some are more efficient than others. The most important focus of the real-time data is ensuring that those people who need access can get it quickly and easily.

Security

In most companies, beta testing is a secure process in that the participants are under nondisclosure and there is a measure of secrecy involved in the performance of the test. Because of this, beta test data needs to be kept secure. From the hacker spreading viruses to internal security risks, the world of information technology has continued to innovate to address these issues.

Protection of the beta test data is a top priority when evaluating the test infrastructure. Security should be constantly scrutinized. While your current system might seem sufficient, as soon as an innovation is deployed, new ways around it are discovered. Therefore, this is one area that requires considerable attention.

The best method for ensuring that the security is being maintained properly is to invest in hardware and software that can be updated regularly to address the latest security concerns. Through this method, security can be addressed once, and maintenance is the only issue going forward. This provides the best impact with the least effort.

Customer Response Management

As noted many times before, communication is an essential part of the test. A beta test participant is a customer and should be treated with extra care. The beta program is a direct reflection on the company itself, and it is critical that the test participants are treated with the same consideration the consumer receives. If the test sites are neglected, mistreated, or poorly responded to, users will not only produce poor test results, they will also think poorly of your company.

The beta test system must have the customer in mind when considering updates and innovations. There are many things to consider. From usability to responsiveness, the system must answer the service needs of the test participant. The focus on the improvement should be ensuring that the systems have the most responsive and customizable interface possible.

Managing the relationship with the beta test participant brings together many different technologies. Because of this, keep focus on addressing usability issues with your beta test systems. Implementing updates can be very challenging, but any improvements in this area effectively contribute to better test results.

Implementing Innovations

Once you have properly evaluated the improvements and the impact they can have on your system, it is time to implement. This challenging phase consumes the most time, causes the most stress, and is the most difficult part of the process. Therefore, being properly prepared is essential to ensure a smooth transition.

Schedule Downtime

Before making any significant changes to the beta test infrastructure, it is important to notify the beta test participants and the beta program's development partners of the change. It is not important to notify any extended management unless they are impacted by the changes. If possible, make the modifications during a time when there is the least infrastructure activity.

If the innovation will represent significant changes to the system, it is better to notify your users of these changes before they happen. People will adjust more quickly and efficiently if they are aware of how they are impacted. In addition, the notification is a helpful way to show everyone that the program is receiving upgrades.

Be certain to allocate enough time to get the process completed. If you think the changes will take two days, tell everyone three. Never try to jam this process into a shorter period than necessary. Anticipate that problems will arise during the transition and allocate time to handle those problems.

Last, if the changes seem to be consuming more time than initially thought, keep people informed. Any time you move from an old technology to a new one, there are bound to be problems. If things are not going as planned, there might be the need to return to the original configuration and re-evaluate the changes. Whatever the decision, be certain to share this with your partners and users.

Make Backups

There is a thought that everyone should lose some critical data once in their life to teach the value of backups. Nothing is more devastating than discovering that something you have spent time and effort on is gone forever. Therefore, any time there are significant changes planned for a system, make certain to have a backup strategy in place.

If you don't have a backup regiment as part of your regular activities, put down this book and take care of it immediately. If you do, perform an additional backup just prior to installation of the software or hardware. Make certain the backup is done in a method that will allow a quick recovery if things do not go as planned.

Some backup methods are designed to keep up to date with incremental changes. In this case, you will want to perform a complete backup of all systems. Depending on the complexity of the improvements, it might even make sense to do a complete re-installation. In those cases, you will want to perform two backups. One will back up the entire system, and the second will back up the data. If the installation goes as planned, simply move the data over. If it doesn't, you have the complete backup to fall back on.

Deploy

Once everything is in place, it is time to deploy the new improvements. Before starting, make certain you have every component needed to install the product. In addition, ensure that you follow the schedule you designated for the downtime. Once you begin, you should be prepared by gathering together the product manuals, customer support numbers, and any other information that might make the process flow smoothly.

As the installation proceeds, it makes sense to take detailed notes. Whether you jot them in the manual or create your own installation document, keep a record of everything that happens during the installation process. Beta testing is a time-sensitive process and if something unexpected takes the equipment down and you cannot retrieve the backup, you will want to eliminate any further complications.

Notification

Hopefully, everything goes smoothly and in a short time, the beta test systems are back up and running. When this happens, take the time to send notification to the test participants, internal development partners, and key management people. The notification should provide an overview of the changes, discuss why the changes were made, and recognize any assistance provided.

The whole idea behind sending notification centers on earning recognition for the beta program. Recognition is important because funding and other decisions are made based on a program's exposure. If people know that there is a beta program and that it is working to improve its systems, they might take notice of the work being done.

Once people learn of the improvements made to the system, they recognize a number of things. First, they see that the beta program is focused on providing the best possible service. Second, it demonstrates the technological competence of the people administrating the program. Last, the notification helps let others in the company know that you have deployed a new technology and could be used as a resource for anyone else looking to do the same thing.

The only exception to this notification would be any security changes. In this case, you will want to keep your notification list small and internal. However, it is still important to let people know that changes were made. It is especially important to notify management. Security changes demonstrate a concern for the company and your systems.

Measurements

Once the changes have been made, watch the progress and try to get some tangible measurement of their impact. Everything from user quotes to statistical data should be gathered. The fact is that this data is very useful. It can provide a justification for future updates, establish a basis for others to make the changes and confirm the decision to make the change.

Take the time to determine how much the enhancements have actually changed the test. Don't be afraid to see some dropped performance or minute improvements. Sometimes it takes time for the impact to be really felt. If the time and research to this point have shown that this will improve the beta results, the results will improve.

If the beta program has been measured for a long period of time, it is good to create comparative data and calculate actual numbers that can demonstrate the value of the changes. Presented in a percentage, these figures should be compared to the "bar" mentioned earlier in this chapter. Often, data of this type helps build a financial case for this and other improvements.

Return on Investment

The ROI is the foundation of any good business decision When deciding whether to deploy improvements in a beta program, there must be a rational path to showing that the improvements work. A balance needs to be achieved where the output of expenses is surpassed by the output of data. Whether it is more beta test feedback, better efficiency in the process, or more valuable data, the ROI effectively is established when a company has a better beta program and better product quality.

Outsourcing

Outsourcing is a viable alternative to running a beta program internally and a great way to innovate a beta test process. Beta programs are not very expensive, but often, a significant amount of resources must be dedicated to maintain the beta infrastructure. By outsourcing, a company can keep an internal beta presence but reduce overhead by using the outsourced system.

Outsource companies promote their business by doing one thing right and doing it in the best possible way. Because of this, a company can reap the benefits of their experience. With their expertise involved, an internal beta program can leverage the outsource company to get the most from the beta test with limited internal management.

If a beta program is running ineffectively, an outsource company can come in and provide immediate results. Their expert knowledge will allow them to produce a more effective test. Additionally, the outsource company takes ownership of the project. Thus, they have to ensure that the test produces results, while an internal resource might not.

As an added benefit, an outsource company usually has the latest innovations deployed on their infrastructure. Their business depends on giving their customer the best possible product. Therefore, the need to innovate and improve is handled by someone else. This enables a company to dedicate these valuable resources to other areas.

Last, outsourcing doesn't always need to replace a beta program. In many cases, it can be used to improve an existing program, provide help when a beta program is overloaded, or consult on methods to improve a company's process. Outsourcing is another excellent way to help innovate the process and get the best beta test results.

CHAPTER 11

When to Start Testing

L ike a stone rolling down a large hill, the product development process gains momentum as the product approaches release. It is a big stone, and most people do not want to get in the way of it. Beta test sits directly in the path with its placement at the end of the schedule, and beginning test is always a sensitive subject.

The question of when to start testing is often difficult to answer. Starting isn't just about beginning the beta phase; it is about sending something to the test participants any time during a test. This is not an arbitrary decision but rather one that takes a mixture of scientific data, rational discussion, and experience.

When making the decision to start testing on any version of a product, it is key to provide the development team with well-founded criteria on whether a product is ready to be distributed into test. In this section, we provide an analysis of the method of getting to this conclusion, and the method of delivering it.

In this case, the pressure to get product ready for the trade show is large. Mark takes a position that is well founded and supported by his manager. In making this unpopular decision, he is showing that his interests are focused on providing a reasonably good product so he can perform the best test possible.

A beta test team should make every effort to get the product into test without compromising the integrity of the test program. Beta sites will willingly accept a product that is in an unfinished state, but it must be usable. The difficult question of when to start testing is one that a test team will struggle with on almost every project. Yet, through communication with the development team, an understanding of the technology, and a clear set of pre-test criteria, a decision to enter test can be achieved.

Case Study: Slow Motion

PhotoTech, an annual trade show for the digital photography industry, is in six weeks. Ocular Systems has a new image management software that they are planning to demonstrate and are working diligently to get it ready for the show. In order to ensure that the product is ready for demos at the show, they plan on doing a short beta test phase.

Alpha test has been encountering a number of issues during their initial test phase and it is not looking good. Images are loading very slowly into the application, and when some are clicked, they cause the operating system to crash. In addition, the application uses a lot of system resources. The application cannot even be opened with another application running.

These issues are making the prospect of a demo at the show unlikely. Yet, management is demanding that the software be ready for the show, as this is a huge opportunity to show the product to thousands of digital photo enthusiasts. The development team is working night and day to meet this demand, but the product is still rife with issues.

After two weeks of hard work, the development team delivers what it believes is a beta test candidate to the test program manager, Mark Lincoln. The beta test participants have been selected and Mark is ready to distribute the software. However, prior to distribution, Mark takes the product to his lab and begins assessing the product to make certain it meets the pre-test criteria.

Within a few minutes, he realizes that the product is nowhere near ready for a beta site or a trade-show demo. Images load so slowly that it makes the program unusable. In addition, the program failed to install on the first two attempts. Mark does not even bother to continue testing, as the product is obviously not ready for the test participants.

Notifying the development team of his rejection, he tells them that the product will not go into beta test unless these issues are corrected. He explains that he knows that many people have been working hard to get it ready, but he knows the beta test data will only confirm what he is seeing and it is obvious that the product is not ready.

The team does react negatively. While they understand the product is slow and has some other issues, the pressure to have the software for the trade show is immense. They want the beta test sites to start testing other aspects of the product and as it improves, they will make the software available.

Mark understands their concerns but believes delivering the product in its current state would only frustrate test participants and make the test useless. In addition, he does not have the resources to provide support to 30 testers who will not be able to install or use this product.

The conflict becomes more intense when Mark's boss, Jeff Ryder, receives instructions from upper management to get the product into beta test. Jeff is supportive of Mark and his decisions, yet he feels the pressure and needs to show valid reasoning for their actions.

Both wonder if management has seen the product and understand the state it is in. To clarify the position they are taking, Mark and Jeff offer to show the issues that are holding the product back from entering beta test to the management team. Management agrees and brings in the development team to address the concerns expressed by Mark and Jeff.

In the meeting, Mark's issues are confirmed, as the product will not install during the demo. No matter what the other issues are, the team understands that beta sites cannot use a product that will not install. His other issues are noted and the development team is ordered by management to get them resolved before submitting a new candidate to beta test.

Handling Conflict

Before discussing the many issues within this chapter that deal with establishing a basis for acceptance or rejection of a product into beta test, it is important to understand how to handle delivery of the news. Providing clear reasons for either an acceptance or a rejection is the only way to ensure that the message is one of readiness and not an opinion.

Acceptance

Naturally, acceptance is the easier of the two responses to a product's readiness. When acceptance is granted for a product, it sends the message that the product is ready to start testing. Therefore, the biggest concern is being ready to test when the news of acceptance is delivered. Inevitably, the team will want to get the product into the hands of the testers as soon as possible, and thus, the beta team should be prepared to ship immediately.

Rejection

Rejection is by far the most difficult of all emotions. Rejection indicates that something is wrong and that unless the issue is corrected; the product will not commence beta testing. Once the news that the beta test program has rejected the product arrives, arguments will abound. In some cases, there will be accusations and even anger over the decision. A beta test team must be prepared to weather this situation.

Clarity

When delivering the bad news, the basis for the decision must be on hand and ready to be clarified. There must be a clear and valid reason to tell a development team that their product is not ready to ship. All of the associated data must be delivered. The rejection and acceptance criteria should also be delivered at the same time.

If the team feels the rejection criteria is unreasonable or unfounded, it is the responsibility of the beta test team to establish even more data to support the argument. Much like a court of law, the rejection is an accusation and can only be supported when evidence suggests the accusation is true.

As noted earlier, there is a lot of pressure to enter the beta test, and saying no does not help the beta test program; it only creates more exposure and more pressure to ship. Thus, it is essential that rejection be only used in cases where the product is definitely not ready for beta testing.

Flexibility

When criteria for tests are established, it is easy to become married to the idea that these rules are set in stone. When this happens, the system becomes more important than the test. Rigidity is something best suited for principles associated with running a program rather than the program itself. The fact is, there are many variables in the product development process and change is inevitable. No matter what criteria is established, there should always be some give to ensure that a product can ultimately be released.

Being flexible buys a lot with a development team. It demonstrates that the beta team is working in the interest of the product and the company. The beta test team will be viewed as working with, not against, the team. It establishes the grounds for a good relationship with the developers, and more than likely, the developers will reciprocate the flexibility when the beta test team needs it.

Try to offer potential ways around the rejection. Encourage the development team to provide additional candidates, and make an effort to show that you want to get the product into beta test. The developers will realize that the rejection is not the fault of the beta test program but rather the product itself.

Empathy

No matter how pathetic the test product looks, there needs to be a measure of empathy in the delivery of the rejection. Developing a product is no simple task, and pressure comes from all directions to ensure that schedules and budgets are met. Empathy will soften the anger that comes from the rejection, and open the door to discussion on ways to get the product accepted.

Profit versus Quality

Beta test must balance the needs of the company with the goals of the program. While it is important to be an advocate for the customer, companies must make business decisions that coincide with the best interest of the product and company. There might be times where these two goals come into direct conflict with one another.

Understanding the needs of the company in the case of each product is essential. Market window and product availability concerns must be taken into account when making the decision to hold up a product. While quality is a valid and important matter, profit for the company is of equal concern.

If a rejection could cause a potential catastrophe for the company, it might make sense to endure an exceptionally bad product. Rejection is used to get the most out of the beta test. However, if a product will miss a critical market window, it might be necessary to test with the bad product.

No Surprises

Notice of the rejection or acceptance should not come as a surprise for a product development team. Communication during the entire beta process should make the news of the status not only anticipated, but never in need of delivery. A well-run beta program has strong and open communication with the development team and notifies them of potential impacts to the schedule.

By establishing this type of rapport, a beta test program can promote the needs of the test participants early in the development process and potentially divert any customer-related issues before they occur. In addition, the communication will allow beta test input into the design and more opportunity for product education.

During the actual pre-test evaluation, consistent communication with the development team is also important. The team might have some information that will be useful to the testing and the actual beta test.

Excellence

If the beta test team is actually judging whether a product is ready for beta test, there must be a foundation of credibility on which to base this decision. From the lab to the team's reputation, every aspect of a beta test program must represent professionalism, consistency, integrity, and technical excellence.

A beta program that does not have excellent qualities ends up being circumvented or ignored. It takes time to build a reputation for excellence in performing tests. However, when it does happen, the team's decisions will not only be respected, they will be adhered to.

Establishing Viability

Once the product has been submitted to the beta test team, a series of tests will need to be performed before distribution to the test participants. Those tests are guided by several principles that underlie the motivation to perform the test. A product must be assessed and determined if it is even a viable test candidate.

Viability means that the product is capable of functioning under favorable conditions during the beta test. It establishes that the beta test participants will not be expected to test a product that isn't ready to be tested. However, what determines this? The following factors all need to be considered to determine viability.

Balance of Issues

How many issues the product has and the severity of those issues need to be considered before testing. A tenuous balance needs to be struck when deciding whether a product should even be pre-tested. Weighing between one severe issue or hundreds of small issues, it is a judgment call.

The only effective way to measure an issue is to understand the impact it will have on the customer. Prior to consideration, discuss the nature of a single issue with the responsible development engineer and get an understanding of the following:

1. How likely is it for a test participant to see the issue?

2. What is the potential impact the issue will have on the test participant's system?

3. What is the anticipated time to have the issue corrected?

With this information, an assessment of the issue's impact can be determined. If there are multiple issues, each must still be reviewed in this manner. In some cases, there will be no need to ask the development engineer for this data. The nature of the problem will make the answers to these questions evident.

Achieving balance between the number of issues and their individual severity is a difficult task and takes experience with beta testing as well as the product to properly determine. It is also a challenge to understand the competence of the test participants and how they will handle the issue.

Once each issue has been assessed, judgment of all the problems combined and their impact will determine whether the product is ready to even be considered by the beta test team. If the product has too many problems, it might be useless to even begin evaluation. The only real benefit would be the potential product education or to gather an understanding of the issues the product will encounter once it is in test.

Product Type

Viability must be assessed based on the product and its complexity. A simple driver either works or it doesn't. Thus, the measurement for viability is simple. However, a complete software application will obviously take a lot more into consideration before deciding whether it is ready for the customer.

The product's complexity is only one factor of many that will be tied to the product type. In addition, it will be necessary to see what the software touches and how great an impact it will have on the rest of the test participant's system when installed. Any software using system resources must be carefully scrutinized before distributing to the test participants.

Participant Competence

The technical level of test sites definitely impacts the decision of whether a product is ready to go into test. If the product requires experts in a particular area of technology, then distributing the product with more issues might be possible. In contrast, if the software is designed for use by a computer novice, the criteria might be stricter.

The level of the user directly correlates to the level of issues that are tolerable. In fact, a good test mixes the levels of user technical competence, and it might make sense to send the more knowledgeable test participants the product. As the software becomes more stable, distribute to the remainder of the group.

"Testability"

Asking the question "Can the software be tested?" might seem rudimentary. However, it is a common issue that is often overlooked. From unrealistic system requirements to missing components, a product that is incomplete cannot be tested.

Often, there will be arguments that the missing components are not necessary to perform the testing and that they can arrive later. The only response to this argument is "Will the product ship without it?" If the answer is no, the proper way to handle this is to remind the team that the purpose of beta testing is to assess the quality of the product in the state in which it ships. Excluding any component challenges the credibility of the test.

If the development team comes to the beta test group and wants to provide a candidate that has different system requirements from those of the anticipated release candidate, the response is the same. However, there might be room for flexibility if a particular part of the product needs focus.

Testability basically infers that the product can be tested. It is up to the judgment of the beta test team to decide whether the product meets the criteria established to perform the beta test. In addition, the relationship between the test participants and the beta test program must be considered. This can be severely damaged if a product is sent prematurely.

Schedule Concerns

When speaking of schedules, we are referencing every schedule that could be potentially impacted by the rejection of the test product. Beta test schedules are often in a constant state of transition. Projects schedules are fairly rigid and often fall behind tentative dates. Other project schedules are leveraged on both the beta and, ultimately, the project schedule.

If a product is not ready for release, the issue of schedule becomes a looming monster for a beta test program. If another beta test is sitting behind the one being slipped, there could be a resource issue. In addition, anyone leveraging the beta test team will also be impacted.

When considering a potential rejection, it might make more sense to put the project on temporary hold or to review what could be accepted. Meeting schedules is certainly secondary to ensuring a quality beta test. However, reality dictates that all of these factors be addressed before throwing out a rejection.

Pre-Test Evaluation

Before a product enters test, it needs to be assessed. This evaluation determines whether a product is ready to begin beta testing. The parameters that establish whether a product is ready for test are called the "pre-test criteria." A series of feature and functionality reviews, the pre-test criteria attempts to prevent test participants from receiving a product that is not ready for beta testing.

When the product is in its early stages of development and the beta test team is working on becoming educated about the product, there needs to be consideration about what the product does and how it works. As the features are evaluated, a checklist of the key items is built. Once the product is submitted for entry into beta testing, a comparison against the checklist is performed. If any of the features are not working, distribution into test needs to be evaluated.

Evaluation

The key word noted here is *evaluated*. Evaluation involves many factors. How much time is allocated to test? How serious are the issues? Will the customer's experience with the product be negative based on the product's current state? Will the product perform effectively with the issues? Will the beta test be effective without these features or this functionality? Taking these issues into consideration establishes whether the test should proceed.

The criteria are not a measurement but rather a guideline to protect the customer. For example, if several small features are not working on a product, but the anticipation is that it will be rolled into the product during the test, it might be ready. In contrast, if one vital component of the product is not working and there is no expectation of when it will be fixed, test should be held. Balance of the interests of the company and the customer are key in this decision.

A beta test manager usually does not get much argument from a development team when credible issues are presented and the beta test team demonstrates the impact that the issues will have on the beta test. However, this is a sensitive issue and opinion has no place. Only supported facts presented with the potential impact will be sufficient to prevent test from beginning.

Build Expectations

The pre-test criteria are the most effective gate for ensuring a quality beta test. However, the development team needs to know that its product will be evaluated prior to its distribution into test. The test manager should communicate to the developers that the product will go through an evaluation phase. Presenting the criteria to the team prior to the assessment gains a lot.

During each phase of beta testing, the method for pre-testing varies. When a product is in test, the time is exceptionally valuable. It is important to establish expectations about how to get the software from the development team.

When stating "pre-test," the reference is not prior to the beginning of the beta test but prior to beginning any testing. Pre-test can be used before sending a simple update or prior to the actual beginning of the beta test. Either way, there are different methods for testing, from prior to shipping to the test participants to during the actual test.

During Test

While a test in progress, it is essential to ensure that the evaluation phase is exceptionally efficient and expedient. Not only are the test participants usually anxiously awaiting the new software, the development team is also following closely to hear the results. Evaluation during test should focus solely on issues that are being evaluated.

Comprehensive reviews during the test are counter-productive. The energy spent on reviewing the entire application normally results in finding nothing and longer than necessary delays. The pre-test review should consist of a focus on the issues that expect to be corrected by the change in software. In addition, basic operational testing should be performed.

Revision Management

Revision management means keeping changes on the software to a minimum. While the best test is in progress, changes are normal. However, it makes no sense to send participants every minor change as it becomes available. It consumes a lot of time and it makes it challenging to track the issues coming in from test sites.

Revisions should be scheduled prior to beginning test, and the development team should work with the beta test team to effectively schedule build deliveries on the dates specified prior to beginning test. In addition, documents that note the changes in each build are useful for setting up evaluations.

With proper scheduling and anticipated builds, the pre-test phase moves much quicker and the product is effectively in test as soon as it is available. This management of time and resources improves the overall beta process and gets better results.

Beginning Beta Test

The product has passed the pre-test criteria. All information indicates that it is ready to be tested. At this point, a number of processes need to be completed to ensure that the product is prepared for release into beta test. From getting the software into a distributable form to logging the material distributed, these steps need to be complete prior to dispersal to the test participants.

Document

Before distribution, the software should be documented. In addition to the basic version and date information, it might be useful to document the sizes. This is to ensure that the actual candidate that is distributed does not differ from the one that was tested. Sometimes, test materials change between the time of evaluation and distribution; and even one change could impact the performance of the product.

In some cases, it might be necessary to perform a *checksum*. A checksum treats all the data in a software application as numeric values. The checksum is calculated by adding all the numbers together and then comes up with a hexadecimal number representing the file. If a single file is changed in the application, the checksum value will differ.

Proper documentation acts as a safeguard against distributing the wrong software or changed software. The results of pre-test criteria evaluation are invalidated if the product distributed differs from the one tested. Properly documenting the software contents ensures that this does not happen.

Distribution

Assembling the test material and getting it into a form that makes it easy to distribute is the next focus. Without violating the integrity of the software, the product's components must be evaluated and the best method for distribution should be determined. Factors such as size, design, and the form the product will take when it ships need to be considered.

If the software is small, there might be a way to archive it using a compression program and post it on the Internet. In contrast, large files might need to be shipped to the test sites. Either way, it is very important to ensure that the test materials remain untainted by the distribution process and resemble how the product will perform when it is shipped.

For example, if the test participants can download a disk image and burn it to a CD, that effectively eliminates the need to ship the CD to test participants. However, if testing the software involves evaluating the usability of the CD interface, then Web-based distribution is not an option.

Virus Check

Whether you get them or not, computer viruses do exist and can be damaging. Whenever files are passed around among multiple users, there is the chance that files can become infected. Therefore, before distributing any software to test participants, it is *always* necessary to check for viruses. Everything from the master disk to files posted on the Web or sent via email, everything must be virus free.

Sending material with a virus to beta test participants is a disastrous occurrence. Once this happens, much of the productivity that would have been spent on the actual beta test is now spent trying to remove the infection. In addition to the problems, if damage to the test participant's files occurs, the company could be held liable for that damage.

Applications for virus scanning are inexpensive and readily available. In addition, it is good to stay informed of what virus is currently causing problems and make certain that anything received from beta test participants is also scanned. It also makes sense to discourage file sharing among test participants.

Third-Party Software

Materials that are not the responsibility of the beta team to test but are included in the package should be gathered and included with the beta package. Whether or not the software is being tested as part of the package, it needs to be included. There are a number of valid reasons to ensure that this is included as part of the beta package.

Primarily, the main reason for including any third-party software is to ensure compatibility with the primary product being tested. Normally, companies evaluate any software that is bundled with their product; however, a beta test does add a "real world" element and can act as a further confirmation of that data.

It is also important to include this software, as it might be integrated into the installation routine. For example, if a software application includes an electronic manual, the reader software might be integrated into the installation. It is especially important to test this as part of the evaluation, as it can certainly impact the product.

Finally, the software being bundled might include something necessary for the application to work. An example of this would be a company that bundles a movie application to handle the video portion of the application. Without the video software, that functionality is gone. This is another case in which a third-party application needs to be distributed and tested with the application.

CHAPTER 12

Effective Site Selection

O f all the parts of a beta test, the test site is the single most important component. The test participant is the test. Their feedback is what makes a beta test. Without feedback, the beta test serves no purpose; it does nothing.

There is an intertwined balance between test participants and test results. Good test participant selection normally equates to good test results. Of course, other factors ensure a successful beta test; yet the test site is the foundation of the program.

The person who manages a beta test selection process is part psychologist, part scientist, and part tax collector. The psychologist portion focuses on understanding human nature. The scientist digs into the statistics and makes the system work. The tax collector enforces the rules and makes certain everyone is carrying his or her weight.

In this chapter, we discuss the psychological, the scientific, and the collection methods necessary to effectively select test participants. Using these techniques, you can achieve great efficiency in your site selection process and guarantee better test results.

Expectations

Before you read anymore in this chapter, there are certain expectations that need to be set. While a lot of information is provided to help with the selection process, the fact remains that you are dealing with human beings. Because of this, it is highly unlikely that you will ever achieve a perfect selection process.

There will always people who look like perfect candidates, who fit every aspect of the model, and who seem exceptionally motivated to test. Then, they do absolutely nothing on your beta test. Some go off and get busy and forget about it. Some have a terrible tragedy in their life. Some are thieves who are out to rip you off. Some die.

The random factor of test participant dropout underlies this entire chapter. In the back of your mind, you will need to remember that some test participants are not going to work. Do not expect failure. Rather, anticipate inactivity and make a plan to deal with it.

Later in this chapter, we will address dealing with inactivity and how to keep test performance at a high level. However, always remember that these methods are not full proof either, and you should set your expectations for this fact.

The practices explained here are designed to get you the most qualified, motivated, effective test sites possible. Using this chapter and the material in Chapter 14, "Getting Results," you can significantly increase the performance of your beta test.

Getting a Number

Before we begin the selection process, we need to ask a question: "How many sites?" That question is one of the most vital pieces of information to have before beginning test participant selection, and it is one of the most indefinable. Nobody on a development team can ever seem to make a decision on this and yet, there are many tangible factors to help determine this number.

During the plan-authoring phase, an estimated number was included in the document. However, that number was purely a guideline and will inevitably change. The number was included to help budget appropriately. Yet, as the test approaches, many factors change that figure.

The marketing, development, or the beta test team should decide the number of test participants. In most cases, someone will throw out some numbers for consideration and then solicit the beta program for a recommendation. The answer must consider many factors.

First, depending on how the software operates, there might be a limit to the number of copies available for the beta test. In some cases, you might be able to freely distribute the application. In others, the limits might be set by the need for registration codes. You will want to determine this number early in the process, as it impacts the other decisions more than any other does.

Next is the question of how many people the beta test program can handle. Depending on the skill and proficiency of the team, this number can vary from 10 to 10,000. Before responding, be certain you understand what resources are available and what can be done.

Third, it will be necessary to understand the type of product being tested. If it is a simple driver, the test numbers can be fairly large. If the program is very complex, the number might need to be smaller. However, this decision mainly hinges on the capabilities of the beta test program.

Additionally, the complexity of the participant profile might have an impact on the number. If the test participants are exceptionally difficult to locate, this can keep the test very small. Conversely, if the criteria are very broad, it can be challenging to narrow the candidates down to a reasonable number.

In addition, the duration of the beta test can impact the number. The longer the test, the less likely you will be able to sustain interest in the test. Therefore, you will need a very large test base to accommodate the fallout. If the test is very short, a large number of test sites will consume too much time and you will not be able to address their issues.

Finally, communicate with the team and see how many people they want to include. This will guide and refine the decision based on the information you have already gathered. If the team has unreasonable expectations, you might need to remind them of these factors and help drive them toward a reasonable number.

Of course, there are other factors you could consider. For example, you might need to perform a nontraditional beta test. There might be a need to break up a test into phases. Moreover, the test might have some different requirements. These also contribute to the number but are not very common.

Arriving at the correct number of test participants eventually requires consensus of all parties involved in the project. Once decided, the complex task of site selection begins to take form. You will want to solidify this number and inform the development team that once the selection process begins, changing the numbers can complicate the situation. Therefore, there should be no changes.

However, it is unlikely that the number will remain static. Additional software might come available, or marketing might want to expand the scope of the test. It is useful to remain flexible and do your best to nail down the numbers as early as possible and try to make the teams stick to them.

Profiling Candidates

Whom do you want to test this product? Before you can even establish any type of beta test selection process, you need to build a profile of the ideal test candidate. These are the people who will be participating in the beta test and providing feedback. You cannot simply go out and pick people at random and hope for the best.

Test participant selection requires focus and a designed plan of attack. Their role is central to the test; therefore, a concerted effort toward designing the application, reviewing the applications, and selecting the candidates is necessary. Therefore, before beginning this process, create a profile of the candidate you need.

Some time ago, you might have developed a beta test plan that established test parameters and a participant profile design. With this information, you have begun the profiling process. The profile establishes technical and demographic information that is necessary to perform the beta test. During the plan development, that information was gathered from a requirements document.

Review the beta test plan and the requirements document just prior to beginning the selection phase of testing. It is necessary to keep a clear idea of what type of test participant is needed to perform the beta test. These documents need to be fresh in your mind as you go through each step toward starting the beta test.

Often, things have changed since those documents were designed, and thus, it might make sense to coordinate with the development team to ensure that no new requirements have evolved. If the changes are small, there is no need to regenerate the beta plan. However, if they are significant, it might make sense to revisit the document and make some updates.

Bringing all of this together into a single focus helps ensure successful candidate selection. With a clear profile in mind, the beta test program can begin the process of finding the appropriate test participants.

The Application

The application is a significant component of the test selection process. Test sites need a method to tell you they have the qualifications you need for the test, and if the application isn't written correctly, it will not tell you what you need to know, or even worse, tell you the wrong information.

Time should be taken to design the application based on all the needs of the project and the development team. A marketing requirements document or functional specification is a good place to start. The application design must suit the needs of these documents. Then, move forward with feedback from individual team members.

There is a tendency to attempt to design a single application that works for all projects. While you might be able to build a foundation for the application with some of the common elements used in all tests, each application should be tailored to the project it is serving. This way, the project will have the people it needs.

Contact Information

The contact information is one of those rudimentary functions of the application that can remain constant on any application. From the mailing information to the email address, this section should be detailed enough to get a hold of people and ship to them. However, it is should not be so detailed that the applicant feels that it is an invasion of his or her privacy.

Because beta test happens during all hours of the day, it does make sense to provide a way for people to provide multiple addresses and telephone numbers. However, it should not be a requirement for people to give more than one address or telephone number for the purpose of test. Offer a primary and secondary option and allow applicants to decide how detailed they want to be.

Profile Information

The profile information is basically the data that tells you "who" these people are. Information about their occupation, their company, and their interests should be captured. This information is used to determine if the person is appropriate for the test. Each product has an audience, and the profile information ensures that the applicant is part of that audience.

This data becomes very useful in helping to understand the experience and interest level of the applicant. If someone is applying to be a beta test site for a Web-programming tool and he or she is the Webmaster at his or her company, you need to know this. On the other hand, if he or she is a CPA interested in Web programming, that is also of interest.

Keeping profile information allows you to build a demographic database of user information. With this data, a beta program can select test participants who match the profiles specified by the development team. In addition, it will assist in the qualification of issues submitted by the test site during the beta test.

The amount of data gathered should not be overwhelming to the test participants. If there are too many questions, the sites might not respond or just throw in any answer that seems appropriate. Application design should allow a user to provide enough viable information to answer the needs of the beta test. If necessary, you can always come back and ask for more.

System Information

Probably the single most important aspect of the application, the system information provides specific details about what the software will be tested on. Querying everything from intricate information about a motherboard to as broad as the operating system, this part of the application requires the most attention.

Prior to designing this portion of the application, there needs to be a complete awareness of all technical issues that might need coverage during the test. For example, if the test requires that the person have a word processing application installed, there might be a need to identify the version number or manufacturer.

A flexible application is usually the most effective for gathering. People need to have the capability to enter in a lot of different information about their system. The variety of hardware and software manufacturers and the multitude of potential configurations make it nearly impossible to design an application that covers it all.

On the same note, the level of detail necessary to properly assess the candidate software and hardware might require that the application process become a two-step approach. The first step gathers general information, and the second goes in-depth. This is not preferred because it does add more time to the selection process. However, candidates are unlikely to complete an application that is too extensive.

There are utilities that can provide detailed system information and, depending on how extensive that information is, you might be able to get candidates to provide the output of those programs. However, the more detailed information you need, the more likely people are going to be to leave an incomplete application.

Invest a lot of time thinking about what data is critical and what is not. A good application gathers as much as is needed, but doesn't inconvenience the applicant. If the application must be long, use a method that steps through the different sections, giving the candidate a break from the interrogation.

Test Specific

All of the items we have mentioned to this point sound very specific to the test. However, they are all normal criteria for a software beta test. Yet, there might be times where there is some type of data, software, or hardware that is a prerequisite for the test. In those cases, that should be a separate portion of the application.

Draw attention to this section by placing it in a prominent location on the application and make it the focus of the test. If it is extremely out of the ordinary, you might want to provide an explanation about the requirement and give instructions on what information you need.

For example, if you designed software that operates on an automobile-based GPS system, you might want to know the make and model of the car. On a typical software beta test, make and model of automobile are not normally requested, and thus, making an extra effort to separate the data from the standard application will help comfort the applicant and get the data you need.

Privacy

In order to get participants to complete a detail application, it might be necessary to ensure that the information they are providing will not be used for any purpose other than beta testing. Using it for any other purpose is misleading and can put a company at legal risk. Therefore, it might be necessary to consult the company lawyer and get some text to provide testers with the confidence that there will no disclosure.

In the text, you might want to have some expansive language that allows for the use of the data within the company. However, once all the information for the test has been gathered, it is important to remember that people have provided this information for the opportunity to beta test. Using it for another purpose is a breach of trust and will reflect poorly on the beta program and the company.

The Call

The call is a method for finding testers. It is a simple and direct approach to getting people to sign up. Written in a professional and clear manner, the call is basically an open invitation to get people to sign up for a beta test opportunity. A call has several critical components that must be included to make certain you don't receive a lot of inappropriate applications.

Timeframe

At the top of the call there needs to be a line specifying the timeframe for test application. It needs to be something that tells a potential site when the opportunity to test is available and the deadline for applications. It should not state any specifics about when test selection will be taking place.

Product Description

The first section is a paragraph describing the product being tested. This description is brief and to the point. It should not mention any specific features of the product, but it should make it sound exciting and interesting. In general, the first paragraph of a call will generate interest in the beta test but not reveal what type of product is being tested.

However, there are cases where the product can be announced. When that happens, it is good to promote the product and its features. If possible, provide an Internet link to a site describing the product. Do not use the call to describe the product. Even if the product is announced, the call should be concise.

Program Requirements

The next section explains the minimum qualifications to participate in the test. These qualifications should be detailed enough to make certain only eligible people apply for the test. If there is a specific item needed to perform the test, make sure it is included in this list.

The qualifications should be listed in order of priority from top to bottom. For example, if a software application requires a particular speed of processor to function, then that should be listed toward the top.

This section should only include requirements. If there are any optional items that might help the test but are not necessarily needed, put them at the bottom of the list and put the word *optional* after each item.

 Do your best to keep the list concise. Too many requirements will deter prospective applicants.

Directions

Once the qualifications are clear, explain to the test candidates how to apply to beta test. If you have a Web application, put the location in the call. If there is a paper or email application, provide sufficient directions on how the applicant can properly complete the document. Make sure to emphasize any particulars of the test you might really need.

Benefits of Test

In this last section, the benefits of participating in the beta test should be specified. There is no need to make any promises; just point out some of the advantages of participation. For example, the opportunity to see a new product before anyone else or the chance to earn the product is a benefit of participation.

If you are able to talk about the product's features, you might want to emphasize that aspect of the testing. Promote the new technology on its own benefits and point out that the beta test will allow a potential test participant to experience that benefit.

 Be sure to point out that being a beta test participant is on a volunteer basis only, and that there is no charge for participation.

Contact Information

In this section, provide all the necessary contact information. This should include telephone numbers, email, fax, and any other method. Although you might be uncomfortable posting this information, it is important because it lends credibility to the call and is helpful in case the site goes down.

If there is still hesitation about posting personal contact information, take measures to provide viable contact information that goes to a toll-free number, or an internal non-specific email account (e.g., beta@yourcompany.com). This will add some credibility and provide the necessary communication information for your applicants.

Posting

Once the call is prepared, it needs to be posted in various places to encourage people to apply to beta test. Post in locations where suitable candidates for your product will visit. If necessary, customize the call to match the location. The post should sound like a special invitation to participate in a unique opportunity.

Usenet

Usenet is one of the best locations to post calls. Thousands of groups organized by discussion topics, the people congregating on Usenet gather together to discuss the information about the group's subject. By posting in these groups, you are able to find people who might have specific interest in your product.

Search the varied groups and look for variations on a particular topic. For example, if you publish audio editing software, you might want to look at groups with the words *audio*, *music*, *sound*, *edit*, or any combination of those. There might be as many as 30 relevant groups that might have an interest in your beta test.

Mailing Lists

Mailing lists are a collection of subscribers to an email distribution list who share a common interest. Mailing lists are similar to Usenet in that they are usually broken out into interest groups. However, most mailing lists do not allow posting by nonmembers. In order to send email to the group, you will either need to join the list or send mail to the moderator asking for permission to post.

In most cases, joining the list to make a post is frowned upon and will produce a negative response. A mailing list is for its membership, and you will be expected to be an active participant if you want to post. If you don't want to join, contact the moderator and see if he or she will post it to the list for you.

The moderator looks at each email message and approves or rejects each based on its content. Therefore, it is important to make your call tailored to the mailing list participants and to make it sound more like a private invitation to test than an open call. Politely ask for permission to send mail to the list because you believe it will be of interest to their membership.

Web Locations

People gather on the Internet in a variety of locations to discuss varied topics. When preparing a call for distribution, search the Web and attempt to locate pages that offer discussion groups. These often take the form of bulletin boards or guest books where people post messages and respond to the messages online.

In most cases, the message boards are visible to anyone who wants to look, but participation requires a registration on the site. The registration only takes a few moments and it might be worthwhile to join, as you might want to post on these boards in the future.

Because these boards allow anyone to post and see a response, you might find someone who is critical of the call. They might view it as an inappropriate use of the board, and you will need to be prepared to provide a professional response to their criticism. Don't be defensive or angry; simply state that you apologize for their dislike of the call, but you feel that people might be interested in the opportunity.

In addition, use the company Web site to promote the beta test. If you have a dedicated Web resource where other beta information is posted, put the call online in that location. It might even be helpful to put the call on the product support section of the site. If the product is a new version of an existing software application, check to see if you can put a link to the call from the original product's Web page.

Local Publications

Sometimes, the demographics of a beta test are very specific. Because of this, you might need to seek out publications local to the area in which you need testers. Newspapers, magazines, and other local periodicals usually have a classified ad section, and it might be necessary to advertise to get the specific test participants.

Because these sites charge by the word, it might be better to write a smaller version of the call and put a Web link or telephone number for people to go to when they see the ad. You will want to provide enough data to peak their interest. In addition, you might want to spend more money on the size of the ad rather than the text, depending on the number of people you need for the test.

International Issues

If the product being tested has a need for international test candidates, there are many challenges. First, you must insist that the people testing the product speak your language. A beta test is impossible if the test participants cannot communicate effectively with the beta test team. Therefore, when posting calls, be sure to make that a requirement of the test.

Additionally, you will want to make certain that the candidates have mastered your language and have a mastery of the local language. This might seem obvious, but sometimes there are expatriates, business people, and other transplants who might not speak the local language.

Last, in the call, account for the time difference. Make the signup and test requirements broad enough that the test can accommodate people in the countries you are soliciting. Remember, some people will be asleep when you post the call and will be responding while you are in bed. Therefore, timeliness has to be stretched to accommodate their schedules.

As you post this on the Internet, remember to also post in places that might grab international visitors. Aside from Usenet and mailing lists, you might be able to post on local Web servers. You might need to enlist the aid of a translator or use a Web-based service to ensure the site has relevance to your product. Either way, it is perfectly acceptable to post in your own language.

Spam

There are times when people will see the call and perceive it as spam. Spam is a blanket distribution of commercially based mail over the Internet. Normally, the same message is sent to a large number of people who did not ask to receive it. Spam is a terrible thing that usually involves suspect products, get-rich-quick schemes, and other efforts to get money from naïve people.

Being classified as someone who distributes spam reflects very negatively on the company and the product. If you are accused of spamming, it might be necessary to defend yourself. Point out that you only posted the information to people who are interested in your product. Second, enforce that beta testing is strictly voluntary and has no direct cost associated with participation. Last, point out that the call is posted for a short time and that the total number of posts is limited.

Selecting Applications

After the call has been sent, a supply of interested candidates will begin to flow in. These people will have mixed qualifications and varying levels of interest in the project. You are almost ready to begin the selection process. However, prior to this, you must review applications.

In this section, every matter for consideration is provided. Some factors are simple and unambiguous, while others are complex and require a lot of thought. Over time, you will be able to strike a balance as to which characteristics are best suited to your test.

Numbers

The goal of the application review process is to select an appropriate number of beta test participants for a beta test. All of these subsequent steps are focused on doing this efficiently. However, to get the end result, there needs to be a sufficient number of candidates to be able to narrow it down to a list of actual potential participants.

Once the application process has closed, the arduous task of evaluating every application begins. This is a gradual process, eliminating candidates for one reason or another. All of the effort is focused on a specific number of test participants. Therefore, to begin the process, there must be a large number of applications.

At the completion of the application evaluation phase there should be close to double the candidates to the number of actual participants to be selected. For example, a 30-person test will have 60 viable applications. This field has been narrowed from hundreds, possibly thousands of applications down to this number. Each of these is completely qualified to perform the beta test and meets most if not all of the test parameters.

Application Evaluation

The scientific part of tester selection involves the analysis of information on the beta test application. This is the rudimentary approach to eliminating ineligible and unqualified test applicants before any type of detailed review of the applications. Using this process reduces the number of applications to review and ensures that every person identified is a potential test candidate.

The best approach for review of any application is not inclusion but elimination. A large amount of criteria needs to be considered, and taking an approach of elimination simplifies this process. However, it is critical that the criteria for elimination are mandatory and static. Otherwise, this process will potentially eliminate good candidates.

Set up three to five specific criteria that every candidate must have to participate in the test and begin to review the applications. As you quickly scan the applications, start sorting out those who do not meet any of those criteria.

Don't throw away the applications; they might be perfectly suitable applicants for another test. However, they no longer have any relevance to the project you are working on at this moment. If possible, notify the candidates of their rejection in a clear and professional manner. Sometimes, you might get a response and discover that things have changed since the application was submitted.

Once the field is narrowed, it is time to move into deeper investigation of the qualified applicants. The next step involves actually looking at the different qualifications on an individual basis and balancing them against the whole application.

Hardware and Software

The specified hardware and software for the project must be appropriately balanced with the remainder of the test material. For example, you shouldn't have everyone with the same operating system even though it does meet the criteria for the test. Variation is key in a good beta test, and more importantly, it is what the real world is like.

If possible, find data that shows the statistical usage data for the required elements of the test. The company's marketing department should have this information as it relates to your product. Test coverage should mirror the real-world usage models. If 40 percent of your company's customers have a printer and that is a required element of the test, then 40 percent of the beta test sites should have a printer.

The real challenge comes when weighing the test criteria among each of the sites and deciding which sites have the best profile for the test. It is especially difficult when many of the same people have similar configurations and there is little differentiation between them. However, no two people have identical systems, and there is always something to key in on and select them for the first round of review.

Demographics

Demographic data is far less complex and scientific than the hardware and software selection process. While the information is usually specified, there is a lot more room for subjectivity. Whether a person lives in a specified location is very matter of fact; however, their occupation, title, income, or interests leave a lot of room for flexibility.

Before eliminating applicants based on their demographic profile, make sure they are completely unsuitable for the test. For example, if the test calls for Information Technology managers and a person applies as an IT supervisor or a CIO, he or she might still have the qualifications needed to perform the test.

In contrast, if you need candidates who read Spanish and you have applicants who are Italian and can discern the language, they are not suitable for the test. Judging qualifications using the demographic criteria should involve common sense. However, the best judge is usually experience.

Participant Characteristics

The human being is a strange and complex animal. We are both unpredictable and predictable in the same instance. We follow patterns of behavior regularly, but then deviate for no apparent reason. In learning the process of site selection, you need to be tuned in to the human psyche and how it behaves.

Still preliminary to the actual selection period, people will make contact with you to express interest in the test. Just before moving into the selection phases, it is good to assess how people behave through the various communication channels.

Keying in on human nature and its normal patterns of predictable behavior is part of the process of participant selection. As you watch the application process, you will note common behavior patterns that indicate the type of test participant the candidate will be. By using these observations, you will have another valuable criteria for judging candidates.

 ## Case Study: Forge Ahead

Victor Lee is the beta test manager for Forge Innovations. Forge is a developer of a powerful software application for the creation and distribution of streaming audio over the Internet. Used by hundreds of Internet radio stations, Forge's technology delivers MP3 audio quality over a 56k connection.

Victor has begun soliciting for test candidates for its exciting new personal software called *Slipstream*. **This software takes Forge's streaming technology and allows people to push a broadcast to family and friends on demand. Rather than keep a stream open to the public,** *Slipstream* **offers a comfortable interface and no need for a server—simply tell the software where to direct the stream and it will send it.**

The call was posted last week and already there has been an excellent response. He has received more than 100 applications. Many people have written to express interest in participating, and one person in particular stands out among all the applicants.

Brian Mancuso is a young composer who has been looking for this type of solution. He collaborates with other musical artists to produce music over the Internet. He has been uncomfortable sharing his music with strangers for fear of having his compositions stolen. He wants to use *Slipstream* **to share audio with specific people without sending them any files.**

Brian has been sending mail daily since first discovering the post in a Usenet group. In addition, he has left Victor several voicemail messages. In each of these messages, Brian elaborates on his qualifications and sells himself as the perfect test candidate.

Victor has been very busy preparing for the test and has not had a chance to respond to Brian. However, that changes immediately when he receives a page from the company public announcement system that he has an urgent call. Picking up the telephone, Victor is startled to hear Brian's voice eagerly selling himself as a test participant.

While Victor is annoyed and a touch shaken up by Brian's enthusiasm, he knows that Brian has the potential to be an amazing test participant. His persistence, motivation, and qualifications make him an ideal candidate for the test. He tells Brian he has been accepted as a candidate, provides him with his cell phone number, and asks him politely to use that if he needs to contact him further.

Brian might have stepped a little over the line to get to Victor, but his enthusiasm and interest are something to be harnessed, not discouraged. Sometimes, candidates like this can scare a beta test manager away with their forthright nature. However, people with this type of initiative make excellent participants and will usually exceed your expectations.

Enthusiasm

When people really want to do something, their enthusiasm shows. Enthusiasm is an excellent and important quality for test participants. People who exhibit enthusiasm for the test will show this enthusiasm in every aspect of their communication. Understanding how to perceive this enthusiasm through reading test applications, email, and telephone calls are something a good beta test manager develops over time. Through constant interaction with test participants, it becomes obvious who is motivated to test and who is not.

Some signs of genuine enthusiasm are excessive communication. Interested people will send email, call, and instant message. They will do whatever it takes to get your attention and let you know they really want to test. Another sign is a detailed attention to the application. They will include information that is not asked for and will provide comments if there is an opportunity.

Enthusiasm does die and some people lose interest once the actual product arrives. Therefore, there are many other personal criteria to examine. Do not base your selection solely on someone's enthusiastic response to the test.

Responsiveness

Critical to a beta test is responsiveness. Sites need to be able answer requests for test data and perform tasks immediately. Responsive people understand the importance of the test and put the beta testing over other priorities. In addition, responsiveness demonstrates concern. Test participants who are responsive are showing they have genuine interest in the test and its results.

There are not many ways to measure responsive behavior in beta test participants prior to a beta test beginning. In fact, most test participants that become long-term beta partners have been selected for this purpose because of their responsive behavior. Nonetheless, any effort to assess a test candidate's responsiveness is of value.

Start by dropping the candidate an email or a telephone call and see how quickly he or she responds. If the site responds immediately, follow up with additional correspondence. If a pattern of communication seems to be apparent, use that as a measurement. In addition, it might be effective to add additional tasks to the application process and see how quickly the candidate completes the task.

Good candidates will respond within an acceptable amount of time. For normal tasks, 24 hours is satisfactory. However, depending on the complexity or simplicity of the task, that amount of time might need adjustment. Different people have different expectations about timeliness and responsiveness. Be clear on what is acceptable and see if the candidate responds appropriately.

Detail Oriented

Beta test participants are asked to report issues they discover during the use of a product. If the reports they provide do not offer enough detail, excessive amount time will be spent gathering the additional data. Taking time to determine how detail oriented a site is is certainly an important part of the selection process.

At first, a test team should look at the application for signs of this characteristic. Does the candidate use upper- and lowercase letters? Has the candidate completed the entire form? Has the candidate provided additional data beyond what was requested? All of these questions drive to the answer of an applicant's attention to detail.

Over time, it becomes easy to see who has taken time to complete an application and who has not. While there are varying degrees of detail that can be provided, motivated applicants will do their best to complete the application in detail. Like responsiveness, it is helpful to set expectations about how detailed you need the applicants to be. Provide guidelines at the top of the application and see if the instructions are followed.

Product Experience

Candidates who have different and varied experience with products of your type can compliment a beta test. Whether it is their work or their hobby, customers who intricately understand your product are effective test candidates and should be your first consideration when selecting for the beta test.

Professional Experience

Nothing is more valuable on a beta test than people who have spent a lot of time professionally using your company's product or similar products. Being professionals, they have been paid to use the product, and thus, will have excellent experience to test it.

In addition to having an in-depth understanding of the test product, people with professional experience usually have a vested interest in participating in the beta test. Their participation is part of their professional education. In fact, it might be even part of their job to participate in the beta test.

Providing valuable feedback, people with professional experience are normally top performers on the beta test and will become a valuable resource for your company. If you notice that they have prior experience using another company's product, this is a huge benefit. Their insight will be very useful from a competitive standpoint.

The ideal professional person is the consultant. These people make a living making recommendations about products and services. They are considered experts in the field, and people pay them top dollar for opinions and ideas. Therefore, they make eager and informed beta test participants.

Sometimes, people put "consultant" on a beta application because they have no job or are very young. Be sure to check out their Web site and the information they provide on their application.

Previous Performance

Prior performance on one of your tests is an excellent criterion to use for selection. A candidate that has been on previous beta tests for your company and has demonstrated effective beta testing skills is tried and true. That person ought to be at the top of your list for selection as a participant.

A beta program must have a system in place that identifies top performers and gives them priority selection on future tests. Part of a relationship-building system, those participants who demonstrate a willingness to work, an expertise in the product line, and a desire to be on other tests need to be focused on. These people are invaluable resources that must be tapped whenever a new test opportunity that suits their talents comes along.

Test participants do experience burnout and if some candidates have been on multiple tests in a very short period of time, it might be smart to give them a break. They might protest and express tremendous interest. However, once the test starts, they immediately become bored and before long, they are dropouts. To make matters worse, these people are former stars and you certainly don't want to push compliance issues. Thus, the product is wasted on them.

Keep in mind, if the product is very exciting, these candidates might or might not have another good test in them and it might be worth the risk of burnout. Although it is a gamble, so are any of the test candidates. It is a lot less likely that a former performer will burn out than an untested candidate will not perform at all.

Beta Testing Experience

Experience on previous beta tests outside your company is a certainly a plus for many reasons. First, sites who express interest in beta testing usually make good testers; they like beta testing and are eager to get into other opportunities. Next, they have experience testing and they usually understand the commitment. Last, they have insight into other products and might bring some of that to your test.

There are potential risks. Previous test experience does mean that they might have certain expectations about how a beta test should be run or what type of feedback needs to be provided. In addition, that previous test experience could also cause beta test burnout. Last, you might want to inquire about these other tests. If the site speaks freely about them, it brings up concerns of confidentiality.

Often, test candidates who offer up previous beta experience might provide the contact information for the beta test people at other companies. There is no reason not to give these people a call and pick up some first-hand information. Testimonials are usually good indicators that a person will be an effective test participant.

Hobbyists

The hobbyist is a different candidate. They are people who are excited about your product because they have a hobby that involves the use of your software. For example, someone whose hobby is digital video might want to test a nonlinear video-editing product to produce his or her movies. Because of this interest, they are often good testers, but have too narrow a focus on a product.

Hobbyists are only looking at your product as a tool to serve their hobby. On the good side, they usually have extensive experience using a variety of comparable products. In contrast, these people are almost always very opinionated and consider themselves experts on their hobby. Because of this, they can be argumentative and demand a lot of attention.

That opinionated nature can pay off, as they will initiate discussion on the product and get people into the product. Their experience is valuable and if they aren't too much of a headache, they can be great test participants. Understanding their idiosyncratic behavior, a hobbyist should be at the top of your list when making candidate selections.

Final Application Review

The last step in the application review process is to decide who will actually receive notification of their selection for the beta test. Selection does not mean participation, it means opportunity. This opportunity infers that they will be sent notification of their selection and that they must complete further steps to participate.

The only applications that remain are people who are qualified for the test. Because of the difficult process of getting to this number, there is a need to make certain that the applications are valid. Take a moment to review each application again and make sure everyone is qualified. With this final evaluation, the application review process is complete.

Selecting Test Participants

Now that the application base has been narrowed to a manageable number of qualified applicants, the test team must narrow the field even further. However, this process is much simpler and less labor intensive. The selection of test participants uses much of the same criteria during the application review, but now, you are interacting with the candidates.

Using email and telephone calls, the next three phases reduce the number of candidates through attrition. As participants do not respond, do not comply, and do not perform, they are removed as candidates. In the end, only those best qualified and most enthusiastic are included in the test.

Not Enough Candidates

Before we go into the selection phases, there is the occasional problem of not having enough candidates. If you are in this situation, there are number of potential reasons. Before you assume that there is no interest in your product, there are several things to test.

Have someone look over the writing in your call. Perhaps the requirements look too stringent or the test doesn't sound interesting. Verify that there isn't incorrect information in the call. Maybe the date or the number of testers was wrong. These small things can deter interest in participating in the test.

Be sure to spread your coverage of the calls to multiple locations. If that hasn't worked, expand your coverage to include other Usenet groups, Web sites, and mailing lists. In addition, verify that the post occurred. Sometimes, the posting is uploaded to your local server but it hasn't gotten out over the Internet.

Finally, look to other sources. Be creative. Perhaps the marketing organization could provide a list of customers to query, or you could post an ad in an online magazine. There are many other channels to investigate that could potentially provide additional candidates. Sooner or later, one channel will generate test candidates.

First Selection Phase

During this first phase, the sites are nearly double the final selection number. At a minimum, there should be at least 50 percent more candidates than participant positions. The paring down of the sites is significant in this first phase.

Notification at this point in the test states very clearly that the candidates are being considered for the beta test. They are not officially selected. You are providing them an opportunity to express further interest and to provide any additional information. Inform them that you will be attempting to contact them during this first phase to discuss their interest.

People who respond quickly to the notification should be given priority selection. A quick response is an indicator of responsiveness, and the sites who jump on the opportunity are normally motivated. As the responses roll in, separate them from the list. In the end, you will want shave off 10 to 20 percent of the applicants in this process, perhaps more if you have a lot of extra test candidates.

Sites fall off for various reasons. Some are no longer interested in the test. Others have had a change in focus or in their lives that no longer permits their participation in the test. Some just don't respond. Whatever the reason, do not discard their applications at this point; they might be needed later. Simply put them in a place that can be revisited later if necessary.

At this point, there will be a need to review the applicants who have responded and see who meets the requirements. As the sites respond, take another look at their applications and make note of what parameters are being covered by their selection for test. If there are sites that offer no real technical advantage to the test but did respond, put them aside for secondary consideration.

Your primary focus at this point must be on ensuring that the test parameters are met. Select test candidates who best meet the criteria first, and supplement the remaining spaces with those who complement the test best.

Second Selection Phase

The second selection phase begins when you believe you have all the candidates you need to start the test. You will still need to have an additional 10 to 30 percent selected for this phase so that you can narrow the field. This phase begins with the notification that the sites must complete a non-disclosure agreement (NDA).

Send out the message that test sites must complete the NDA by a specified date. They must have it signed and returned by a designated time or they will be dropped from consideration. If you are using regular mail, allow time for transit. If you are using a fax machine, make certain that you allow for busy signals, empty paper trays, and so forth.

This period is very short in that it begins with the notification and ends once the NDA has been received. Once again, this is a measurement of responsiveness. Those sites who respond quickly are more likely to be good test participants. As the NDAs start to come in, check off the eligible candidates and watch who has completed phase two.

Inevitably, there will be some test participants who have issues with the document. If some people have issues, do not relegate them to the back of the selection pile. This is an indicator that they pay attention to details. See what their concern is and see if it is valid. If it is, you might need to work with the legal department to get the issue resolved.

This phase should shave enough people off that you will have almost exactly the number of people necessary for the test. You might have a couple of additional people, but for the most part, the candidate selection process has refined it down to only those who are needed for the test.

If there are many additional test candidates, select a number close to what you need and notify the remaining candidates of their rejection. Do not string them along any longer, as it will only frustrate them. If they have made it this far, you might offer to put them on a later test or some other reward for their follow through.

NDA Phase

This phase beings when all the NDAs have been returned. You will need to make certain that those who responded have also completely filled out the agreement and have not made any changes to the document.

Another short phase, this time is the final moment to coordinate the test team and make the final decision about who will be on the test. Go through each application one last time and take all factors into consideration. You will want to rank the sites according to the following criteria:

1. Test parameters
2. Qualifications

3. Responsiveness

4. Communication

5. NDA completed

By this time, the list of who is in and who is out should be very clear. However, this period of time allows a moment to ensure that the right people are ready to go. Those who are not selected should be put in a place where they can be quickly accessed—you might still need their participation.

Test Participants Notified

Once the final selection is complete, the test candidates can be notified of their final acceptance into beta test. Sending them a formal email indicating as such is a good idea, as it enforces the professionalism of the team and is a rewarding experience for the candidate.

Provide the team with the details of their participation and the tentative test schedule. It is also good to reinforce the amount of effort that went into their selection. Emphasize that they have been chosen from many applicants for this exclusive opportunity and that they are important.

Breaking the Curve

There is a model for beta test performance (Figure 12.1). This type of test includes an expectation that some members of the beta test team will not participate in the test. In this beta test model, the test participants perform on a bell curve. For example, in a test with 50 people:

- Five will do nothing.
- Ten will do a little.
- Twenty will meet the expectations of the test.
- Ten will exceed the expectations by a little.
- Five will be the top performing test participants.

This model seems like decent performance on a beta test. By this standard, 90 percent of participants actually do something, and 70 percent of the participants will actually meet the expectations of the test. At first glance, this seems like a fairly good ratio of performance.

However, this data means that 30 percent, or one-third, of the participants do not meet the expectations of the test. Although provided before the test and clearly noted, one in three people will not even take the time to perform the beta testing as they agreed to do when they signed up.

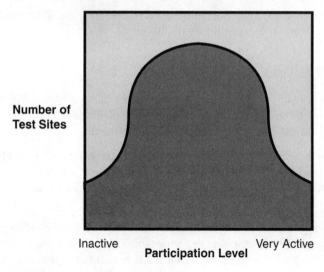

Figure 12.1   Normal test model.

Breaking the curve is about taking this model and making that 30 percent nonexistent. In the new model, the minimum performance is all test participants doing what they agreed to do and leaving no room for those nonperformers (Figure 12.2).

By working to this model, you are effectively building a test with 95-percent performance and no excuses. Although this might seem unrealistic, it is entirely possible when the sites are properly prepared for the test and managed properly during the

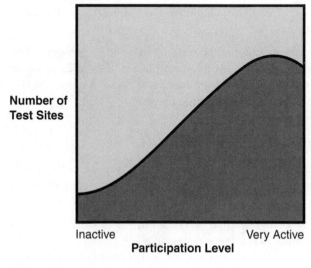

Figure 12.2   Ideal test model.

test. There still might be those who don't do the work, but they are taken off the test immediately and replaced with other, motivated testers.

Contract the Expectations

Before beginning the beta test, rather than sign up testers using a typical NDA, use a contract that obligates them to test. Using a document called a *beta test agreement*, the test participants are required to test if they sign the agreement.

In the text of the agreement, test participants are given parameters for meeting the expectations of test and are told that failure to perform the test will result in removal and replacement. In addition, they will be required to return the product and potentially pay the costs of the test.

The document is an agreement, and by their signature, they are compelled to perform the beta testing as specified by your beta test program. There is no room for deviation or noncompliance. The candidate cannot become a test participant without agreeing to these terms. If he or she feels this is an unrealistic expectation, then another candidate will be offered the test position.

Clear the Air

This might seem strict or harsh, but is it? Test participants are basically volunteers wanting to participate in the beta test. They are not obligated to sign up. Numerous other people would like to be participants in the test, and that spot can be filled relatively easy. If they want to participate in the beta test, they need to agree to these terms.

Before the test begins, this must be made perfectly clear to every test participant. Note to them that you appreciate their willingness to participate, but that you take the test very seriously and that noncompliance to the contract means ejection. Enforce to all test participants that their role in the test is critical and that nonparticipation is unacceptable.

It is helpful to point out the section of the contract that obligates them to test, and furthermore, point out the consequences of noncompliance. If candidates are uncomfortable with signing the agreement, then they are effectively saying that they have signed up to test yet they are unwilling to commit to the work.

Reasonable Expectations

Because this is a beta test and people normally have lives and jobs outside the test, there must be reasonable expectations for performance. The test must demand some time, but it should be a reasonable amount over a short period of time.

In most cases, 20 hours a week is the theoretical limit to the amount of time a site is willing to dedicate. Ten hours is a fairly reasonable amount to expect, and most people will be willing to commit to it. Twenty hours will restrict the number of participants willing to comply.

Keep in mind, 20 hours is approximately three hours per day. If a person sleeps eight hours a day, works eight hours a day, and spends an hour commuting in both directions, 17 hours are already consumed. That means a person will have seven hours to dedicate to the beta testing without room for any other activity.

It is much more realistic to ask for an hour a day during that test period with a little extra over the weekend. The participant will feel the test is fair and will more easily meet the expectations of the test and produce good data. If the work is too much, most will give up, and replacing them is time consuming.

Compliance Management

During the beta test it is exceptionally important to enforce the rules of the beta test agreement. The contract these people signed is binding and there is no room for nonparticipation. If certain sites are not living up to the expectations of the test, remove them and replace them with new candidates.

 Compliance is about immediacy. If you notice that someone is being unresponsive, jump on him or her immediately.

Compliance management involves communicating with test sites on a continual basis once the test begins. Daily email messages, an occasional telephone call, and constant interaction with the sites from the moment the product arrives in their hands is the best way to ensure that the site will meet the expectations of the beta test.

If there is any lack of communication on the part of the beta team, the site will see an opportunity to let the work fall behind. Sites must know and see that you take the test seriously and will be there. If there is any perception of unresponsiveness, participants are provided a reason for their lack of communication. All they have to do is tell you that you were unresponsive to their needs and that they tried to test.

Keeping sites in compliance is a time-consuming effort. It is better to dedicate a single person who spends his or her time calling and sending email on a daily basis to the sites to ensure that they are participating. In addition, noncompliance enforcement is a challenge.

Much like a collection agency, the person managing compliance must be persistent and ensure that the site is either prepared to participate or return the product. When a site neglects the terms of the beta test, he or she is a problem that needs to be dealt with immediately.

Identifying Problem Sites

Noncompliant test participants are a problem. They are consuming company resources and reaping the benefits of beta testing without living up to their commitment. These people are impacting the performance of the beta test and effectively hurting the product quality. Therefore, it is necessary to identify these people as early as possible and either get them to comply or get them off the test.

Problem sites are very quiet. No email, telephone calls, issue submissions, or feedback of any type is sent. Normal test participants make an effort from the moment they get the product. Some send a mail message indicating the arrival of the product; others start with issue submissions. Whatever they do, they are doing something.

The problem sites are often unresponsive. They do not respond to requests for information and they do not show any signs of participation. Some might send a single email stating that they are looking at the product but then return to nonactivity. There must be something daily from every tester in the initial stages of test, and then every other day after the product has been in test for a while.

If the sites are responsive but still do not provide any test data, they are still problem sites and should immediately return the product. Software is often a challenge to get returned. Therefore, the software developers should program some type of time bomb in the application that prevents its use after a certain period of time.

During a beta test, it would be nice if the software needed a new code on a daily basis. However, that is impractical for the purposes of testing. Therefore, the best case would be one that expires on a weekly basis only to be updated with a new version of the software or a new code.

Collection

Depending on the value of the product, there might be a need to try to collect the test material back from the problem beta test participant. When this happens, the collection process is much like a bill collector. Persistence and fear are the only methods to get people to respond.

The persistence means multiple calls a day to every number the test site has provided. In addition, follow up with email messages indicating the collection procedure. In most cases, the company should provide all costs to return the product, including packaging and shipping. This eliminates any excuse to return the product.

The fear is basically professional yet serious threats of legal and further collection action. If you have the budget, it might be necessary to turn over the product to a collection agency. Often, that will scare some sites into returning the product. However, they need to understand the seriousness of their noncompliance.

In most cases, the persistence is enough to get the product back from the sites. However, there are those who need the fear to be motivated. In addition, there will be those who do not respond at all. Only give up after every avenue is exhausted and the cost to collect is beginning to outweigh the value of the product. There is no reason to spend $500 trying to collect a $100 product.

Throughout this effort, professionalism is key. Yelling, angry voices, threats, and other forms of intimidation are unacceptable. No matter how frustrating it might be, the site is still a customer and you still represent your company. People might become angry and frustrated by your persistence. Explain that the moment the product is returned, the persistence will end.

Acceptable Excuses

Every so often, a site will come back with a reasonable excuse for noncompliance, and in those cases, it might be necessary to let the site keep the product and walk away. A death in the family, a personal trauma, later or nondelivery of the product, or some other excuse might be used.

When this happens, be gracious and offer your apologies for the persistence. Explain that the test is important to the company and that your insistence to get the product back is motivated by this factor. If the situation is uncomfortable—for example, a death or loss of employment—offer your condolences and be done with it.

The fact is, there are factors that change a person's interest in a beta test, and while the test is important, there are other things that take precedence. By being kind and considerate in these situations, you will gain favor with the customer and demonstrate the professionalism and integrity of your company.

Queue Up Candidates

Those applications that were pulled aside in the first two selection phases of test participant selection might become useful. If you need to add test participants due to noncompliance, these people still meet the profile and might be interested in the opportunity.

Drop them an email or a telephone call and see if they are interested in participating. Only do this when you are certain the other participant is going to be removed. In software tests, one or two more test sites is usually not a problem, but there are only a specified number of positions available.

Make sure that you have sufficient candidates queued up to make a choice. If they were unable participate earlier, there is a chance they won't be able to later. Therefore, having a good number of candidates available will ensure prompt replacement of noncompliant testers.

CHAPTER 13

The Test Product

The product being tested links the relationship of a beta test team between the test participants, the development team, and the company. As the test product is the focus of all the beta testing effort, an effective team must have a comprehensive understanding of every aspect of the software and how to manage it.

This chapter explores every aspect of the test product in relation to the beta test program and how to effectively test it. From its first delivery to beta test to the eventual release, a software application evolves and changes. Numerous factors must be considered to ensure the product receives the best test possible.

The Anatomy of Software

Software, when boiled down to its essential element, is nothing more than an organized collection of ones and zeros. However, the similarity ends the moment you move above this level. Each application is distinct and unique. From the programming language used to generate the code to the function it serves, software is a challenge to test.

A beta test is responsible for looking at the software from the viewpoint that while the application might be distinctive, it needs to function properly within the realities of the market. A beta test team must be prepared to examine every component of a software application so that it works the way it is designed.

The complexity of a software application is amazing. From the pointers to the graphical user interface, designing a beta test can be a complex and confusing prospect. However, most software has a basic anatomy that a beta test team can focus. Boiled down, these parts make up most applications and need to be focused on.

The Code

In all the beta tests you might perform, you might never see a line of code. However, like the DNA in our bodies, code is the building blocks of a software application and it is important to understand how it works and what it does.

Often, minor changes to the code have a major impact on an application. When testing software, a beta test team needs to understand how these changes impact the entire application. With a core understanding of the code, the development team can speak to the beta team and have confidence that both parties realize what a change in code will do to the software.

Functionality

What does the software do, and does it do it well? This question addresses the functionality of the software. When trying to test a software application, it is easy to get buried in the smallest details and lose focus. Once this happens, the software might have fewer issues but still not serve the purpose for which it was designed.

Functionality is the crucial objective of all software applications. It is the capacity of any software application to provide a useful purpose. Whether it is a minute task or a running an entire computer system, software needs to be functional. Beta test teams need to remain focused on this point.

Of course, an argument could be supported to the usefulness of some applications, and this might be realized in the beta test results. However, that is only one aspect of the test. Issues discovered during a beta test directly impact the functionality of a product. A good beta test will help determine the functionality of the software and ensure that issues do not prevent it from functioning.

The best method to look at the functionality of a software application in a beta test is to closely examine the software. Use it, learn it, and become familiar with every aspect of its operation. Then, again, ask the question, "What does the software do, and does it do it well?" By keeping the focus on this rudimentary question, the test will serve its purpose of determining market readiness.

User Interface

When considering all of the things that need to be tested appropriately, the most obvious is the application's user interface. The product needs to be tested not only for functionality but for things such as spelling accuracy, appearance, and usability. This leads to a challenge ensuring that everything in the application is being looked at.

Although often viewed as superficial, these factors often have more importance than the actual function the software performs. If the software is difficult to use or confusing to the end user, it makes no difference that it performs its function properly—it is unusable.

Testing the interface thoroughly leaves many matters open to the subjectivity of the test participants. One person might like the design of the software, while another might despise it. These issues should only be examined if there is overwhelming agreement from the test participants.

Opinions abound in a beta test and often some of them must be disregarded to ensure that only those with overwhelming support get attention. Strike a balance between the amount of time dedicated to technical problems and simple interface issues. If there are numerous reports of interface issues, it can become an issue itself.

Almost every application has some type of user interface. Whether that is a point-and-click menu or a command-line prompt, it is still a way for the user to interface with the software. Measuring the quality and effectiveness of this really comes down to measuring the functionality of the application.

However, testing interfaces involves understanding logic and usability. Rather than using subjectivity and opinion to determine whether the interface works, listen to the test participants. They are the tools used to measure the performance of an interface, and they will tell you whether it works for them.

Documentation

Documentation is the supporting piece of an application. Sometimes, it is a printed manual; other times, it is a built-in help function. Either way, this is an important part of the software because it is a resource for users to get a product functional.

The true measure of effective documentation is its usefulness, and that should be the focus of the beta test effort. Test participants should look at any related documentation and see if what is provided is helpful. Some might argue that good software doesn't need documentation. However, this is not a point to debate. If the documentation is provided, it needs to be reviewed.

Documentation that is integrated into an application should be tested as part of the application's functionality. For example, is it easy to use? Is it easy to find? Does it provide the information the test participant needs? This adds a layer of complexity to the beta test. In cases where the documentation is a printed manual, it is still necessary to examine, but obviously, the paper version is accessible if the application is not operational.

Documentation is a dichotomy. On one hand, it is a completely necessary and important part of the software application. On the other, it is a rarely used and often neglected piece of the product. Nonetheless, it still needs to be tested, and beta sites are effective at assessing its usefulness.

Preferences

Nearly every software application has the capability to be customized in some manner. From something as mundane as color to the complex configuration of a complete application, preferences are what make an application useful. Thus, a beta test should place tremendous emphasis on testing this aspect of the application.

Called *preferences*, *options*, or the *configuration*, applications have many different methods to ensure that the software meets the needs of its users. These specifications allow the application to function in a manner that is specific to its environment. Every preference added to a software application complicates the ability to test the application.

Preferences throw in variables into the beta test. The more variable ways to set the preferences, the more potential combinations there are to test. Imagine a software application with only 10 different variables with three different options each. This means there are 720 potential permutations that need testing.

On a complex product, the combinations are innumerable and it might never be possible to test every permutation during the beta test. Hopefully, the quality assurance team can attempt to cover this aspect. However, it still is a factor that needs to be addressed as part of the beta test.

Upgrades and Patches

Anyone dealing with software understands that change is inevitable. Versions, upgrades, and patches are a fact of life, and the question is never *if*, but rather *when*? With this insight, a beta test program must be prepared to address change when it happens. The test product might see many versions during the beta test, and the test sites need to understand how to handle these changes.

As a change is rolled into the test, the beta test staff should make an effort to educate the test participants as much as possible without tainting the test itself. For example, it is appropriate to tell the sites about the latest improvements in an upgrade. However, it can be detrimental to tell them about the fixes.

The test participants need to take the time to see if their issues have been corrected. If they are informed that their issue has been corrected, they will not take the time to verify that it really is fixed. However, new features excite participants and will invigorate a test when these changes are implemented. The following examines the types of changes usually distributed as part of the beta test process.

Upgrades

An upgrade is primarily an improvement in a software application and thus is usually treated to a new beta test. In most cases, the upgrade implements serious changes to the software and also includes fixes for known limitations. Upgrades can be charged for, and thus are normally very significant.

Fixes

When there are a number of issues with the software but none of them are too serious, the normal path for distribution is through a "fix." Fixes are normally distributed electronically and might or might not require a beta test. However, logic dictates that any change that impacts the core application should go through a beta test.

Often, if a beta test is performed, it will only be with people who are interested in seeing something corrected in the software. If this is the case, customer support can deliver a list of customers experiencing issues. Otherwise, it might be necessary to air the company's dirty laundry by seeking sites that have experienced the issues addressed in this fix.

Patches

Patches are immediate fixes to problems. Usually small in size but large in impact, a patch addresses a serious customer concern. More often than not, customers who need a patch are desperately waiting for its release, and they make excellent beta test participants. The patch usually only addresses a limited number of issues, but often, the software developer might want to include a number of other corrections as long as the patch is going out.

Hot Patches

Hot patches are unreleased fixes designed to test development's potential fix for an issue. When a hot patch is released, it is only to see if a concept will work. In some cases, the hot patch will be distributed to a very limited number of testers. In addition, a method to get rid of the hot patch is provided. Hot patches are certainly handled by a beta test team with sites willing to experiment with the software.

Additional Complexity

Ranging from a simple utility to a complete suite of applications, software is a complex and often challenging product to test. Much of this challenge exists in material that affects the product but is not part of the actual software. These components force modification to the testing process and often drive changes to software.

OS Compatibility

All software has to work in an operating system (OS) environment. This environment has many of its own problems and often can create complications for a product in development. Therefore, there needs to be a method to determine whether a problem is related to the OS, or if the OS is the problem itself.

In cases, where the OS is not at fault, it might take time to find the problem. Every time someone adds or removes a software application from a computer, he or she changes the OS. This means that there is really no way to get to exact matches of an operating system in a beta test. Adding to this variability are the multiple versions of operating systems available. Just like other software, the OS is constantly being revised and updated.

Because of this difficulty, a test team should keep copies of all relevant operating systems on hand and try to duplicate issues with a default installation of the OS. While it is certainly not realistic to test with an OS with nothing else installed, it does provide a starting point for debugging issues.

When the OS appears to be at fault, it might still be the burden of the software developer to create a work-around or fix. Sadly, the OS sits in control of the system, and the application, no matter how important it might be, must function within that system. It is good for a beta test to be sure to document any potential methods for getting an application working when an OS issue appears.

Other Software

One complexity that adds difficulty to testing is the introduction of literally thousands of other software applications to each beta test system. Beta test participants use their own equipment to test the product. On the positive side, this provides an excellent basis for testing an application. However, it also makes debugging problems challenging.

The multifaceted and diverse nature of each computer system offers a great test environment to ensure that a product functions properly. However, considerations must be made to guarantee that there is at least some commonality among all these computers. A beta test team should specify minimum system requirements for the software to operate.

In addition, if the test product has supporting applications necessary to function, that adds an additional level of challenge to the test. In those cases, it makes sense to provide the software application rather than have test participants use their own copy. This will eliminate the problem of version control. It will also add value to the test.

Other software is always a challenge to test for many reasons. A decision must be made whether the test team should support the extra application. The additional work involved complicates the test, but at the same time, it is better to know that the test sites are using the product properly.

In addition, the real focus of the beta test is the test product. When a secondary application is introduced into the beta test, it takes focus away from the primary product. This shift of focus is something that needs to be watched closely, and when it appears to be happening, test sites must be directed back to the primary product and reminded of what to test.

Hardware Support

If the test product is designed to support a piece of hardware, a whole new level of complexity is brought into the process. Depending on the type of hardware, many variables enter into the picture. A beta team will need to not only consider all the different variations of the hardware (e.g., form factor, manufacturer, models, etc.), it will also have to consider the versions the hardware.

Marc learns the hard way that beta testing is not as simple as it appears. In fact, the complexities of testing a product are not relevant to the size or intricacy of the product. In reality, some products, although simple in premise, make very complex beta tests. Software that interfaces with hardware is an example of this.

Case Study: Sound Off

Marc Bacon works for Sound It Out Software, a producer of educational software for K-12 students. Their innovative product allows children to read into a PC microphone and the software application will evaluate their pronunciation. Mainly designed to work with a bundled sound card and microphone, Sound It Out has produced a new version of their application that is supposed to operate with any sound card and microphone currently shipping on the market.

Marc has been enlisted to perform the beta testing on this product. His normal capacity is as a technician in the lab, but due to a recent hiring freeze, he has been moved over to the quality assurance team to help with the testing of the product. While he has participated in beta tests, he has never administrated one before, but imagines it to be fairly simple: just select some people and have the department administrator ship the product.

With little guidance, Marc starts the process of designing a test plan. He knows that this product will need to have a lot of compatibility testing, and Sound It Out only has a limited number of sound cards available to test. As a starting point, he decides to determine how many sound cards are currently on the market.

Marc is bewildered. In addition to the 20 or 30 different models of cards currently shipping, there are numerous motherboards manufactured with sound built on-board. On top of this, OEM sound cards exist that might or might not be identical to the original versions on which they are based. To complicate matters even further, there is limited information available as to what legacy equipment is on the market.

Unable to determine what his best route of action is, Marc asks Lisa Richardson, the QA manager, what she suggests. Lisa also has never performed a beta test and decides that the only way to address this issue is to narrow the field. She expects that most people will have the most popular brands, and tells Marc to see if he can find who the market leaders are and pick the top 10 cards.

Marc does this and after some research decides to find some beta test sites to see if he can match up the cards with people who are actually using the product. Using some marketing data gathered at a trade show, Marc starts to query people about participating in a beta test. To frustrate matters further, most of the people who inquired at the show about the product had very little interest in the product and more in the free t-shirts the company was giving away. Marc is starting to realize that beta testing is not as simple as he imagined.

In most companies, the quality assurance team collects the necessary hardware to perform a basic compatibility test. However, beta testing can find far more hardware used in much more realistic environments. Through the use of test participants, a test engineer can locate every potential variation need to properly test a product. However, finding those people can be a challenge. Chapter 12, "Effective Site Selection," examines the best practices for this process in detail.

To be properly prepared for a beta test that involves hardware, a beta team should get with the quality assurance team and discuss what issues they encountered in their testing. If possible, get detailed information about those products that worked without issue and those posing a risk to the test software. It might even make sense to work collaboratively with the QA team to see if the beta program can catch any of the obscure hardware in its testing.

Test products that interface with hardware need to be evaluated early and tester selection started as soon as possible to ensure that all the necessary profiles can be obtained. This means that some effort will need to be put forth early on to ensure that the marketing and engineering teams have an understanding of what type of test participant will need to be looking at the product. Many times, these decisions are made later than expected, and it might be difficult to get an answer to the question.

In all, the challenge of testing a software application relies not only on the complexity of the application itself, but all of the supplementary material associated with the product. These items need test as well, but the focus must remain on the test product. This is often difficult to differentiate to test participants and adds complexity to the beta test process.

Software Management

A software application is like a living thing; it evolves and changes constantly, and its environment impacts it heavily. It needs to be closely controlled to prevent unauthorized release, viruses, or corruption. It is a serious responsibility to ensure that software retains its integrity throughout the beta test process.

Build and Version Tracking

Software version control is probably the most critical management function. As the product is being developed, changes are being implemented consistently. Working with the development team, beta will be receiving these builds on a regular basis. As they enter the program, the version information needs to be logged.

 Whenever possible, no more than one version of the software should be in circulation.

In addition, any older version of the software needs to be removed, retracted, and possibly destroyed to ensure that only the latest is being tested. In some cases, the development team might want simultaneous evaluation of two different versions of the same application, or they might have different versions of the same application for different platforms. In these cases, management is even more critical.

If proper management of the software does not occur, there is a possibility that the wrong version could end up in the hands of the test participants. This is catastrophic, as it yields worthless test information. Because the data does not reflect the latest version of the application, issues might have been corrected, or features removed or changed significantly. Only the latest version can be considered valid testing.

Using a database or spreadsheet to log what has entered test will help keep invalid versions from getting into the test department. In addition, it allows the beta test team to track the history of an application through the test process. This information becomes useful after a test has been completed and there is interest in statistical data as to how many issues were found by the test process.

Distribution Management

A secondary yet important function of the management process is monitoring the distribution of the product. Test participants are not the only recipients of a test software application. Beta test team members, internal departments, and sometimes even real customers might be sent an application during the beta test phase.

Track the contact information of all the people who receive a copy of the software. Make certain that they are kept in the loop on all changes and, if possible, provide them with means to get that version when it is available. If possible, use expiration dates in the application so that it self-destructs after a specified amount of time.

As noted previously, at any given time there should only be one version of an application in the beta test process. If multiple versions are distributed, management of who has what software becomes a nightmare. Even worse, ensuring that everyone gets properly updated becomes a major concern.

Technical

Beta testing holds the characteristics of many different departments within a company. It gathers marketing data; it provides customer support; it reviews documentation. Most importantly, it evaluates technical information. Because of this, the beta team must make every effort to become technical experts within the company.

Being a technical organization, beta test programs need to build a reputation of being knowledgeable, efficient experts on the test product. Expertise is not limited to the actual test product, but also any associated applications and hardware. This gains a number of things.

First, as experts, the technical data submitted by the beta test team will rarely be questioned. Beta tests generate a lot of issues and the test team is expected to evaluate each one. If issues are submitted that are not technically addressed, the developers will inevitably come back and ask for more data. A technical team understands the need to provide as much detail on the issue as possible.

Next, a technical team will be able to communicate about the test product to the development team in an intelligent and efficient manner. If the developers think the beta team doesn't understand an issue, they will doubt their ability to even test the product. A beta team must be intimately familiar with every aspect of the product and be able to communicate on a technical level with a variety of people.

Technical expertise also allows a beta test team to more efficiently support the product during the beta test. It assists with differentiating user error from actual issues. In addition, the beta test participants assume that the beta test team are the experts and might bring up highly technical issues.

Finally, technical knowledge expertise allows the beta test team to have more direct involvement with the development process. With a technical team, the developers will give versions of the software to beta test for evaluation and product education. They will understand that another set of eyes is looking over the product and that issues might be brought to light.

Credibility

Credibility is not found on a résumé or in words. It is not given or bought. It is not a commodity and cannot be gained quickly. It takes a tremendous amount of time to build credibility, and only a moment to tear it all down. It is a tenuous and difficult characteristic that holds the highest praise when earned, and the greatest admonishment when lost.

People earn credibility through honest and reliable practices over time. Credibility is something fostered and developed through relationships and experience. When a beta test team truly understands a product, it earns credibility with a development team and respect for the information it delivers.

Credibility should be a focus of a beta test team in relation to the test product. This message is not only in the technical data that beta test delivers, but also in the point of quality it conveys. The beta test team is entrusted with protecting the quality of the test product, and thus must make every effort to make certain the best product gets to market.

Often, a beta test team is put up against the momentum of a product release schedule. It is important to take both the interest of the company and of the customer and show balance in the decision. A beta test program earns credibility when it establishes clear guidelines for quality and adheres to those guidelines even when there is pressure to release the product.

Secrecy

While beta testing takes place at the end of a development cycle and often the product being tested has been publicly announced, it is still important to use caution and secrecy in every aspect of the program's operation. A beta test team is being entrusted to test a company's product and must make every effort to keep the product protected.

While it is not practical or even feasible to work in complete secrecy, it remains important to remember that you never know who is listening, who might be in the room, or who might read an instant message or email. Using caution in all dealings will help prevent secrets from leaving the beta test team and test participants. Here are some important guidelines to follow:

- Never mention project names or unreleased product names in public.
- Never share any test results, even in a casual manner, to anyone but the owner of the product.
- Never mention schedules, timing, or anticipated release dates of any project.
- Never show a beta product to someone outside the beta test program before or during a beta test.
- Never note to the press, public sites, bulletin boards, or chat rooms anything about past, future, or current tests.

It is impossible to completely protect every secret in a beta test. That doesn't mean that a beta test team should not take every measure to prevent secrets from escaping. Often, a product's success or failure is dependent on its initial release into the market. A test team should look at what secure technologies and security processes are available to ensure that all precautions are implemented.

Secrecy is something that needs to be taken seriously by the beta test team and the test participants. Using caution when distributing software to test sites is a good first step. Protective measures such as passwords can be useful as well. In addition, regular reminders to test participants about secrecy are also helpful. In all, the effort to protect the product must be a foremost concern of the test team.

Include or Ignore

Once a product enters a beta test, issues come rolling in one after another. Some of these are serious concerns that impact the potential shipment of a product. Others are simply minor concerns that might need to be addressed but not immediately. There are also non-issues and opinions. The difficulty in all of this is what data to consider serious and what to relegate to the bottom of the list.

Qualifying issues is one aspect of this process. However, how does a beta test team arrive at establishing criteria for qualification? While technical expertise is valuable and will help in the validation of issues, there must be some type of reference to point to. Data is the most important ally in defending an issue and discovering problems.

Through comparative measures, a beta test team can establish measurement for issues. When assessing issues in the test product, it is good to look at similar applications or even earlier versions of the test application. This is not to suggest that those methods are the correct way to implement a feature or function; it only offers a reference point.

Baseline

When trying to determine what is an issue and what is not, it is important to accept a baseline for reference. The baseline is a starting point for the test that establishes acceptable and unacceptable criteria for the issues. In most cases, the baseline is the design standard set in previous versions of a company's software.

In some cases, the baseline might be a predefined standard created by a standards organization. Other times, it might be useful to look at the company's competitors and use that as the measurement. In any of these cases, the baseline establishes the right way and wrong way to do something.

Baselines are very useful for a number of reasons. They provide a method to determine what works and what doesn't. Baselines provide a reasonable rationale for the way things work in a test product. Last, baselines allow a company to promote best practices and ensure that they are used in the development of products.

However, it is important to achieve balance in the use of baselines and not take too rigid of an approach. The baseline is only for reference and should only be used to evaluate issues that come from test participants. If a site considers something counterintuitive or a product issue, the baseline allows the beta test engineer to see if there was a change in the design.

In this case, the baseline is initially stifling innovation to an important software application. However, later the baseline becomes a useful tool to ensure that the design of a new application follows the original's reference. The baseline is simply an informational tool used to provide reference. This information can be used to determine the validity of issues or a design.

Competitive Analysis

While the primary focus of a beta test is to gain insight into your company's product, an excellent additional benefit is the ability to get detailed information about your product's competitors. In typical beta tests, people are selected based on their experience with a particular product line or technology. With this experience, the beta test site can provide unique comparative data.

Test participants have almost always used products similar to the one being tested. In fact, many own the competitive product and can perform head-to-head comparisons. If the test product and the competitor's software can co-exist on the same machine, a lot of valuable information can be gathered.

While it should never be the focus of a beta test, competitive analysis is an excellent additional benefit. This testing generates a few issues and an abundance of opinions. Comparative data provides guidance about the test product's design. However, because a competitor might do something better in the opinion of a test site is never reason to change the product.

Case Study: Baselines Are for the Birds

Rona Mariani is a developer for Nature Link, a scientific software developer whose products are used to track migratory birds through North America. Rona just completed work on a monthly update that adds additional species of birds as well as any changes in the patterns.

Using satellite images, she inputs the last known location of literally millions of birds. Airports and airlines use the software to ensure that they do not have any issue with the wildlife. The application has been in use for nearly 20 years and is based on software developed by the University of Marquette.

One thing that drives Rona crazy is the design of the update process. Rather than provide a simple file that provides the mathematical data positioning the birds, the application must be compiled and redistributed three times a week. Although the update is simple, Rona believes it is time for a change. She has come up with a way to move the application to the Internet and to operate it through the server providing real-time data.

Unfortunately, the nation's airports and airlines have antiquated systems and are unwilling to try anything new. Every year they do a system update, and every year they evaluate the software based on the previous year's application. Any improvements to the application are designed to match the baseline application first installed nearly 20 years ago.

The company would love to pull out the old software and provide a completely new application, but the resistance is tremendous. Rona remembers when they moved from radar data to satellite and how the government fought the changes until they could be convinced that the legacy systems would not go down until the new one was operational for a year.

She proposes an idea to management: Instead of getting rid of the old software, build a new application that matches the design of the old software. However, rather than provide the data in the application, have it map to a data file that holds the information. Then, allow the application to grab that data file from anywhere the airport designates, including the Internet.

Using the baseline application as a design template, Nature Link builds an entirely new application that looks and feels the same as the original but is completely new code. At the next year's evaluation, the government is ecstatic that the software appears unchanged, but can now get real-time data from the Nature Link servers.

Defining Issues

During a beta test, numerous issues are generated. Some are viewed as catastrophic failures. Others are viewed as a cosmetic changes. Each has its own importance, and it is up to the development team to decide whether it is relegated into obscurity or if it deserves the attention of the engineers.

It is the responsibility of the beta test team to present each issue with as much objectivity as possible. Beta test engineers only define issues based on the data provided. While it is natural to want to express opinions about the issues discovered in a test product, the opinion of a beta test engineer must be replaced by the facts.

Visibility

The best method for ensuring issue visibility is to use the established issue tracking system and convey the impact the issue might have if the product is released into the market. For example, instead of demanding that an issue be reviewed, a beta test engineer should simply point out the data of the issue and explain what the sites are experiencing.

In most cases, the serious issues will always get attention because they are obviously problems that need addressing. However, the real challenge will be getting recognition for issues that are not as critical but are important to the beta test participants. Those issues need to be backed up with statistical data from the test.

A beta test is the representation of the market when the product ships. Therefore, an issue that impacts 25 out of 50 beta test participants equates to 50 percent of the market. When properly represented to the development team, correlation of beta test data to real-world statistics holds a lot of impact. Combine this with the severity and frequency of the issue and an issue will get the visibility it requires.

Severity

Severity is a form of measurement. When a test team provides a level of severity, it is reporting how great an impact an issue will have if the product is shipped. While complex to judge, severity is simple to report. For example, if an issue causes the computer to crash, lose data, corrupt or damage other products, it has high severity. If the issue can be worked around, it has moderate severity. Cosmetic changes would be viewed as low severity.

The severity of the issue is greatly increased if more test sites experience the issue. However, in contrast, an issue that might be very important might be overlooked because only a few sites experienced it. Moreover, the correlation loses its impact when the beta test has a small number of participants.

Therefore, the best way to present severity is strike a balance between the frequency and the impact the issue has on the application or system. By pairing these two factors together, the impact of the issue is easier to understand by the development team and the data has real-world relevance.

Frequency

How often the issue exhibits itself or how many beta test participants have seen the issue is a matter of frequency. High frequency infers that the issue is serious and needs attention. Low frequency questions the validity of the issue and, perhaps, its potential impact.

In cases where the beta test has only a few participants or only one site is experiencing the issue, the only recourse is to make sure that excellent technical data backs up the issue submission. It is always best to give the development team all of the data necessary to make a decision and let them decide what action to take.

Beta test teams are sometimes forced to report a particular issue because there are sites experiencing the problem and providing constant complaints. While it seems like the issue has high frequency, it is only a vocal test participant making his or her dissatisfaction with the issue known. No matter how vocal a site might be, the only measurement for frequency is the number of sites experiencing a problem.

Participant Support

During the beta test, there will be many issues reported that might or might not be problems with the product. In many cases, the issues are actually not problems, but rather a question of test participant support. The beta test team needs to do its best to address those issues immediately and make certain that other sites are informed of the potential support issue.

Just because a site reports an issue doesn't mean it is a bug. On the contrary, the beta test site is not necessarily wrong to report an issue that is in fact a support problem. Test participants often report something because it is a perceived problem. That perception alone is reason to take the time to look into the issue.

What might seem like an oversight by a test participant becomes much more serious if other sites experience the same problem. The frequency of the issue could turn the support issue into an actual bug. In addition, test sites should be encouraged to report anything that confuses them or does not work they way they perceive it should work.

As a beta test team supports the test participants, it becomes apparent which users are not savvy enough to discern a bug from a designed feature. In those cases, the user should be monitored closely and provided additional support. Help them clarify the difference between a problem and their perception.

In all cases, never speak down to the test participants and make them feel inadequate. Often, the test site that has trouble with the product is the best site, because he or she sees the product, as a majority of the population will, through novice eyes. This makes it even more important to support the test product effectively.

Finding Product Focus

When products are brought into beta test, the first and foremost goal is always to test as much of the product as possible. However, as time goes on and the different parts of the product become tested more and more thoroughly, the beta test starts to take a focus. This focus is the part of the product that really needs the most testing and becomes central to the testing.

Finding the focal point on a beta test is a natural progression of the actual test process. A solid product gets focused much more quickly than a low-quality software application does. The reason for the focus is that many derivative parts to the product become inconsequential to the test and the only thing that matters is what is being focused upon.

As the test moves forward, the beta test team should help the test participants find the proper focus and place emphasis on that aspect of the product. A good beta program is able to key in on the important part of a beta test product, and the effort of the beta test team should coincide with any engineering or marketing specifications.

It is important that the focus of the test appears to be gradual and natural. It should move the test forward without feeling contrived or managed. Test participants need to feel that they are the ones driving the product toward quality, and they can effectively do that if the beta test team is working them properly.

Losing Sight

When a test product has many issues, it is easy for sites and the beta test team to lose focus. The fact is that the more problems a product has, the easier it is for the test participants to lose sight of the overall objective of the project. When this happens, the beta test becomes useless and the product becomes difficult to test.

Losing sight on a beta project is one of the most difficult things to overcome. In these situations, pandemonium replaces order, and focus is replaced with randomness and worthless data. After the beta test sites have lost sight of the goal, they either stop reporting sufficient test information or report trivial issues.

The most common reason for losing sight is constant and unregulated updates of the software application during the test period. In these cases, the sites continuously receive updates during the test. Thus, the feedback they are reporting becomes useless as a new version replaces the old. The sites see their efforts as fruitless and they lose sight of the test.

In contrast, when no updates are provided, the effect is the same. What happens in these instances is that the test participants are given something that is needs updates but never comes. The test software must have regular and consistent updates during the beta test period to ensure that sites remain focused on the quality of the product and that they have the activity they need to keep interested in the test.

CHAPTER 14

Getting Results

W hen we perform any type of work, we have a personal reason or motivation to do so. Motivation is a something that encourages us to do it. Tapping into the motivation that drives a person is the key to getting people to participate in a beta test. If there is an understanding of what motivates test sites, there is a way to get them to do an effective job on the test.

In this chapter, we examine how to get the maximum from beta test participants by using the concepts of exclusivity, communication, and incentives. With the techniques in this chapter, a test team can use motivation to generate the most feedback from the test participants with the most efficiency.

The Exclusivity of Beta Testing

How many copies of your application do you anticipate selling? Do you think it will be 1,000, 10,000, or even 1,000,000? Regardless of this amount, how many test participants are you considering for the beta process? The fact is that it will be a small amount compared to the number of products sold. Because it is small and because it is a unique opportunity to see a new product, the prospect for someone to test your product is exclusive.

Stop Asking

It is time to stop viewing your beta program as a volunteer effort. Beta test participants are not volunteers. These people receive several forms of compensation for their active participation in the beta test. From free software to a chance to see the product before anyone else, being part of a beta test is a privilege only offered to a few people who can actually qualify to participate.

Asking people to be in a beta changes the attitude of the participant and puts a company at a disadvantage. Sites that are asked to volunteer are in control of the test. They decide whether they do anything and dictate their schedule to the test team. Turning the tables and making the test an exclusive opportunity changes the psychology and the results of the program.

The Whitewash Principle

In *The Adventures of Tom Sawyer*, Mark Twain explores a unique aspect of the human condition. When Tom is put to whitewashing the fence, his plans for a day of frolic and fun are dashed. His mind starts to analyze the situation. At first, he considers "buying" someone off to avoid doing the work himself. However, after careful examination of his pockets, this idea disappears. It is then that he has a "great, magnificent inspiration."

Ben Rogers walks by and sees Tom performing his work and decides to gloat. However, Tom seems involved and actually enjoying the whitewashing. He brushes with an artisan's flair and takes his time working to ensure every spot is covered. Tom tells Ben not only does he want to do the whitewashing, he enjoys it! He also tells Ben that he was asked to do this work by Aunt Polly because *he* is the only one she trusts with a job this important.

Before long, Tom has not only Ben whitewashing, but also all the boys in town. Twain observes,

> Tom said to himself that it was not such a hollow world, after all. He had discovered a great law of human action, without knowing it—namely, that in order to make a man or a boy covet a thing, it is only necessary to make the thing difficult to attain. If he had been a great and wise philosopher, like the writer of this book, he would now have comprehended that Work consists of whatever a body is *obliged* to do, and that Play consists of whatever a body is not obliged to do. And this would help him to understand why constructing artificial flowers or performing on a tread-mill is work, while rolling ten-pins or climbing Mont Blanc is only amusement. There are wealthy gentlemen in England who drive four-horse passenger-coaches twenty or thirty miles on a daily line, in the summer, because the privilege costs them considerable money; but if they were offered wages for the service, that would turn it into work and then they would resign.

The "Whitewash Principle" involves using human psychology to the advantage of the beta test. The fact is that beta testing really is not work but rather "play." There is no obligation to beta test, and people are using their free time to participate. Because it is play, it is necessary to keep a tone of professionalism throughout the test so that people do not digress into a play mentality.

The test site that believes he or she is on an exclusive and professional test will put forth an extra effort. Promote the fact that he or she was selected out of thousands of applicants because of some unique factor. Eliminate all essence of randomness or chance that might suggest the test participant did not come by this opportunity on his or her own merit. Let them know that they are special because of their selection.

Even if the test has 200 participants, thousands of copies of the released version of the software might be sold. Therefore, it makes sense to capitalize on this exclusivity. Feeling special, the test site will put forth an extra effort to ensure that he or she lives up to the expectations of the test. The site will regard his or her selection with pride and will feel special because he or she is among a selected few to participate in your test.

Scaled Selection

Setting up the selection of test participants (Table 14.1) in a scaled acceptance process further emphasizes the exclusivity of the test. These scales are broken into phases and should be natural and expected by testers. Here is an example of a scaled selection process using a test with a final quantity of 50 participants:

In this example, the first candidates are notified that they are only contenders for a limited number of beta test participant positions. Thus, they must pass further criteria to be part of the actual test. Selecting about 50 percent more test candidates then actually be needed, this first phase is a measure in responsiveness.

After there are sufficient candidates selected, send a message to them indicating their candidacy for test participation. Explain the commitment of testing and then give minor details about the product to entice them to participate. At this point, you will want to enforce that there are only a limited number of positions and that only the people who respond quickly are going to be considered for this opportunity.

Insist that they are being considered for this test based on the profiles they supplied through the application process. Remind these "applicants" that their qualifications for test have gotten them this far, but an honest desire to participate is more important. However, *never* tell the candidates how many positions are available, and never tell them how the selection process actually works.

Test participants who are truly motivated to participate will respond immediately to the request to participate. It will be immediately clear who is truly interested and who is not. During this phase, examine how the participant responds. Those who try to sell themselves and promote their skills should be considered first. Those who send a short but specific message of their interest should be second. Candidates who basically respond with a single word might not be worth considering. Of course, those who do not respond should be removed from candidacy.

Table 14.1   The Selection Process

SCALED SELECTION PHASE	NUMBER OF CANDIDATES
First selection phase	75 Candidates
Second selection phase	65 Candidates
NDA phase	60 Candidates
Test participants selected	50 Candidates

After this first phase is complete, the field has narrowed slightly. You will want to pull about 10 to 20 percent from consideration through this process. At this point, candidates should be notified that they made the first cut. The next task for them to perform is to complete a non-disclosure agreement (NDA) or beta test agreement.

Some sites will inevitably have an issue with the NDA or will not complete it in a timely manner. This process further exposes those candidates unsuited to perform the beta testing. If they are unable to complete the agreement in a timely manner or are unable to abide by the rules stipulated, it is a good indicator that those candidates aren't going to perform very well on the actual test.

Valuable Assets

Do not let all this talk of exclusivity go to your head. Keep in mind, good testers are very valuable and there is no place for arrogance. Do not take the "country club" attitude and bring snobbery into the test. After all, beta testing can be hard work and time consuming. Good participants need to feel their effort is appreciated.

Once the selection process is complete, the attitude of the test team needs to go from one of elitism to partnership. A candidate is now a test participant and with that comes responsibility and privilege. These people are part of the group, and the success of the beta test depends on their effort going forward.

Symbiosis

Once selected for the test, the relationship with the test participant changes. It is a relationship based on sharing, balance, and communication. It is a partnership founded on symbiosis. Symbiosis is a dependent relationship that is mutually beneficial to both parties involved. When symbiosis is practiced, everyone wins.

To achieve a level of symbiosis, a test team must focus on balancing labor with reward. There must be an effort to ensure that while feedback is asked from the test sites, there is also a level of appreciation expressed. Every communication asking for a response should thank the participants and recognize that their time is valuable.

When the symbiotic relationship is achieved, feedback is quick and accurate. Test sites feel good about the project and are willing to take the time to meet the needs of the test. Last, there is a feeling of community and partnership that is obvious among the participants and the beta test team.

Serious Business

Involvement in a beta test needs to be conveyed as something serious and important to test participants. They must believe that every effort they put forth directly impacts the outcome of the product, and that their word is what will keep a product off the shelves or allow it to go to market. The sites must believe that their contribution is essential to the success or failure of the product.

In every communication and every appearance to the test site, make them understand that this test is not being done on a whim, but rather it is a well-planned, well-executed process that requires their involvement. Their role is critical to the success of the test and there is nothing wrong with letting them know that. It only reinforces their sense of importance and makes them understand that you take them seriously.

The Power of Professionalism

A beta test conducts its operation by interfacing with the customer. Thus, it is essential for the beta test to present an image that coincides with an image messaged by the company in its marketing. This impression should be carried through every aspect of customer contact.

From answering the telephone to the daily email correspondence, a test manager or engineer interfaces with customers on many levels. In all forms of communication, it is crucial to act with professionalism. A beta test team that appears professional sends a message to the testers that they are working with an organized, efficient, and important organization.

When customers see this, they respond by also acting professional. The response is that the testers are also organized, efficient, and feel important. The actions of the beta test team set a standard the beta sites follow. Test participants often act as a mirror to the beta test organization, and when given the best, they give the best.

Customer Contact

During the beta test, there are many forms of contact. Some are obvious, while others are very subtle. A team wanting to get the most from the beta test participants will work to ensure that each of these contact points exudes professionalism. When this happens, the test sites realize that the company takes beta testing seriously, and thus, they treat it seriously.

In the following sections, some basic guidelines are provided as to what is the best approach in each circumstance. While this might seem a little meticulous, it is in these small ways that the beta test participants will see the team's true level of professionalism.

Correspondence

There are many forms of correspondence available. However, there are only a few rules that apply to all forms. Using these rules will ensure that the company portrays the best image while allowing a beta team to be comfortable with the test.

First-Name Basis

It is appropriate to use first names in communication. The computer business operates on a much more casual basis than many other industries do. Using first names also eliminates the potential embarrassment of using a proper title. Gender can be difficult to discern from email or a telephone call. In our times, most people prefer the use of their first name. In addition, it can add a comfortable and personal touch to a test.

Magic Words

Please and *thank you* are truly magic words and should be used often and generously. Whether it is in email or on a telephone call, test participants need to understand that you appreciate their effort. In this small way, they recognize that they are important to the test and that you value their feedback.

Down to Business

There is little room for humor in the business world. Jokes and the like are very subjective and could potentially offend a test participant. Friendliness is great and should be used. However, jokes need to be used rarely and carefully. For example, self-deprecating humor can often soften a difficult situation. However, a teasing jest can be taken the wrong way and turn ugly very quickly.

It is important to keep a business-like tone in most correspondence, with an occasional light remark to make people feel warm and welcome. If you are uncertain whether a remark is appropriate, don't send it—chances are it is not. Offending a test site can lead to much worse scenarios than simply poor feedback.

Letters

Using letterhead and nice stationery adds an air of professionalism that no other form of communication can convey. Thick, watermarked paper with the company logo sends a message of importance. Each letter should be personally addressed to each tester and should not convey any type of automated mark (e.g., "Dear Sir or Madam," obvious insertions, etc.).

In addition, any letters sent on this nice paperwork must be hand-signed. Unless there are 10,000 beta testers, a signature needs to be at the bottom of every letter. Each signature indicates to the test sites that you took the time to put a personal touch to their letter. An unsigned letter sends a message of laziness or lack of concern.

Packaging

Materials that are shipped to the customer should look professional and packaged adequately. Boxes should be new and clean. They should not have any markings other than those of your company or the shipping carrier. Boxes are usually available free of charge from the carriers. Never use old product boxes or some other packaging.

Items inside the box should also be packaged neatly and orderly. Avoid using old newspapers or recycled paper to package a product. With the world environmentally concerned, it might be good to use something biodegradable or environment friendly. However, be careful not to use anything too messy.

User Interface

Any Web interfaces, user documentation, or test software should also convey a feeling of professionalism. Clean, neat, and organized, these services should convey efficiency and follow the corporate messaging set by the marketing organization. If possible, a professional designer should be involved, and perhaps the company advertising department.

A representation of the company, these interfaces are the closest to touch the beta test participant. While it might require giving up a little freedom in the operation of a test program, keeping the user interfaces along the company line conveys a feeling of professionalism better than any other method does.

Communication

Throughout this book, the message of communication has been an important one. Good communication is the foundation of any beta program. In this chapter, we explore how to keep test participants active in the test using good communication skills. Sites that feel neglected become frustrated and unresponsive. Test participants tend to reciprocate the communication they receive, and it only makes sense to be responsive to their needs.

The Power of Responsiveness

An immediate and complete response to all forms of communication from every site is a strict rule that must be followed in every beta test. Test sites measure their importance based on the responsiveness of a test team. A quick response sends a message that their communication is important and that you value their effort to correspond.

In addition, when a site has an issue that needs attention, every moment that sites are not responded to is a moment they are not working on the product. A prompt response ensures little downtime and little frustration for the sites. In a beta test, timeliness is critical. Test sites are given an excuse for poor productivity when a test team is unresponsive.

Respect the Sites

Responsive behavior is also a conveyance of respect. The time and effort that a test participant puts forth is valuable. In most cases, people who participate in a beta test use their personal time to participate in the test. While the test is an exclusive opportunity, respecting this fact is important.

When you treat the beta test participants with respect, they understand your appreciation for their work and will work even harder to live up to that respect. Respect is shown in a number of different forms. First, the mentioned responsiveness is critical. Quick responses to communication make people feel important.

Next, speak to the sites with understanding and an assumption of intelligence. Don't talk "down" to them and assume they do not understand the technology that is being tested. Instead, be clear and concise with your communication. Treat the sites as though they are experts until you determine their actual level of comprehension. If they have difficulty with the material, provide more explanation but never change the tone.

In addition, recognize accomplishments and contributions. For example, when a site discovers an important issue, acknowledge this to the entire group and make a special effort to show the impact of the discovery. This shows appreciation as well as the recognition of the technical contribution of the site. If possible, try to recognize each site for some contribution he or she has made during the test.

 Be careful when recognizing individual contribution. Test participants might react negatively to it if it is excessive or focused on one person.

In addition, don't overwork the sites. Respect their time by establishing a time commitment early in the test and do not exceed that commitment. Provide all test participants with a measured amount of work that keeps them occupied but not overwhelmed. The sites are working with you on this test, not *for* you, and keeping them busy is good.

Last, provide the team with a final copy of the software for their participation. Test participants like to see the accomplishment and their contribution. When a copy of the software is delivered to the beta test sites, it signifies that they helped bring the product to fruition. It is also an excellent way to bring closure to the test.

Respecting test participants follows the old adage of "Do Unto Others as You Would Have Them Do Unto You." Beta test participants are people and have lives beyond the test. Ask the question, "Would I do this?" when setting expectations for the test. Experience will teach you that this is the best measurement for a well-balanced test.

Partnership

Beta testing is a partnership with the test participants. Aside from giving respect, it is good to treat the participants as partners in the product quality process. In a partnership, the site enters a relationship with the company that is characterized by mutual teamwork and responsibility. They understand that the work they do directly impacts the product, and thus, they have an investment in the outcome of the test.

Test participants need to know that they own some of the responsibility of producing feedback. Ownership is a key element of a partnership. Partners know that their participation, their decisions, and their overall effort contribute to the success or failure of the test process. Thus, involving the sites as partners imbues them with the responsibility of ensuring that success.

Providing the sites with free product is one simple way to make that partnership happen. However, another is to communicate to them in a manner that instills this sense of partnership. Treat the members of the beta test as members of a team. Promote their sense of community and establish rapport among the sites. Make them feel as though every effort they do individually impacts the group collectively. Encourage communication among one another and let them make their own partnerships.

Beta test participants feed off of one another. The sense of community helps them understand that they are all working to a common goal, and thus, they want to support one another. In addition, the more cohesive and complete the team functions, the easier it is to get good results from the test. The entire effort builds this sense of community. Thus, a partnership benefits the test and its members alike.

Relationship Building

When a test participant puts forth an extra effort and stands out from the rest of the group, a test team needs to focus attention on that person and ensure that he or she is separated from the mass of participants. These people are valuable and need to be capitalized on. The best way to take advantage of this is by building a business relationship with the site.

A business relationship is one that has a personal touch but maintains a level of professionalism. In these relationships, special consideration is given to the site. Whether it is an early invitation to a test, or perhaps participation in multiple tests, the site that excels should be focused on.

On the personal side of things, it might be good to have some lengthy conversations by telephone to become familiar with the person behind the test site. Learn about his or her job, where he or she lives, or what kind of things he or she likes. Build a rapport that allows the site to feel special and different than the other testers. The fact is, these people are special. Their exceptional effort separates them from the other sites and should be treated differently.

On a cautionary note, the undertone of any of these beta test relationships must always be business. Never get so personal that the site feels that he or she is excluded from the rules of the test. You might want to release that person from some of the rudimentary rules of test, but overall, all sites must retain the same profile and performance.

In addition, never let the other sites know that these people are special. Each test participant must believe that he or she is on the same level as every other test site. If a site is receiving special attention, it needs to be done outside the regular test community.

These relationships are not very common and often will dissolve over time. Even the best test participants get tired of testing. Sometimes they become bored with the same product offerings a company provides. Many times, their personal lives change and they no longer have an interest in even being on a beta test. Therefore, building these relationships becomes important because it allows a test team to get the most from the site while the level of excitement is high and the interest is there.

Designing Incentives

At the beginning of this chapter, motivation was listed as an important part of the test. Of the many factors that influence the outcome of a test, incentives can be the most useful or the most damaging. Designing a good incentive program is a very difficult process and is often the most overlooked.

Test participants love incentives and work well when they are properly administrated. However, if an incentive is too inexpensive or perceived as cheap, it can destroy a test. In contrast, an item that is too expensive might cause sites to report fake issues or mundane nonsense in an effort to win a prize. There must be a balance in the value of incentive to the value of the product. In addition, there must be balance to the amount of work in relation to the incentive.

This is a complex formula that needs to be monitored closely to measure its effectiveness. Sometimes, an incentive's value can go down or up based on its perceived value. In addition, there are the strange situations where an incentive makes no difference in the test. The sites have a different motivator or a lack of motivation that cannot be overcome.

In this section, the information provided will help a team design a good incentive program that will match the product being tested. Because each product is different, it might take some time to get the program to work effectively. Flexibility in the program and the incentives is key to getting things working properly.

Perception and Value

Providing incentives is all about perception. What has perceived value is valuable; what is perceived as worthless is useless as an incentive. As strange as it might be, people tie different values to different situations. Discovering the true measure of this is part of designing an effective incentive program.

The Carnival Principle

Standing in front of three milk bottles, a man takes a pitch and hurls his best fastball at them. For every three throws, it costs him one dollar. If he hits the bottles, he will win a teddy bear worth approximately five dollars. If he misses, he must pay again to get another try. In most cases, he will miss. However, he will continue to throw balls until he manages to win that bear, and often he will spend more than the value of the prize.

"The Carnival Principle" is a three-fold concept about providing a reward for effort. The first concept addresses the timeliness, the second measures the value, and the third addresses the delivery. In each of these concepts, one must interact with the other two to be effective. At a carnival, they are matched perfectly.

The timeliness of the reward is based on when and where the reward is given. The man throwing the ball sees the teddy bear and desires it. He wants to win. Whether that goal is based on exhibiting his pitching prowess or showing off for someone, the desire to get the reward is immediate. He will continue to pitch until he has earned it, and stop when he has won.

Therefore, in offering incentives, you must come up with something that is impulsive and interesting to your test participants. It must be shown to them and there must be clear criteria on how to earn it. Once this has been established, the delivery of the reward must be immediate when the tester has earned it.

In most situations, the test product is the best thing to use as the reward. This leads to the second concept of value. One of the reasons the beta test participants sign up to test is so they can get a free piece of software. By giving the test product as the incentive, all test participants are interested in the reward (or they wouldn't sign up for the testing) and they all perceive it to have value.

The teddy bear has value as it signifies the ability of the thrower to knock down something at the carnival. The product has value as it signifies the fulfillment of the test commitment. As long as the commitment does not exceed the perceived value of the product, this concept will work.

Last, delivery of the reward is critical. When the man pitches the ball, he knows that his reward will be immediate. If he accomplishes the goal of hitting the milk bottles, he will take the teddy bear home. However, he must accomplish this goal. In the case of a beta product, delivery is no different.

 Don't make acquiring incentives too difficult. Test participants will give up quickly if the incentive is out of their grasp.

People expect to have their reward immediately after completing the test. There cannot be any lag between completion and delivery. If there is, our gentleman will not throw the ball the next time the carnival is in town. The moment the test is complete, the site will need immediate gratification. He or she will still be excited about the product and will enthusiastically join other tests.

Perceived Value

Each of us views the world through our own perception. We have different ideas about what is valuable and what is not. In our culture, items such as diamonds have value because most people view them as valuable. However, if diamonds could be found in the dirt anywhere you looked, their value would not be as significant.

In the case of a beta test, the customer must perceive the value of the product as something worthwhile for the effort to test. However, there is one hindrance in this process: all products have a retail price. While this heavily influences the value, there are ways to increase the perception.

Items such as enhancements, fixes, additional features, and other product improvements can bring additional value to a product. In addition, the chance to see a brand new product before launch greatly enhances the value. However, getting around the retail price is always a challenge and it is best left unsaid unless your product has a very high price.

If your product has a low cost or perceived value, it might make sense to add additional incentives. You can provide something as simple as a t-shirt to some high-end hardware to add incentive to perform the test. However, the incentive we are discussing only deals with performing the test. Later in this chapter, we will discuss additional incentives.

The Work Formula

Once a value for the product is determined, the next step establishes what type of work can be expected from the beta test participants. This means, what kind of return should you see based on the perceived value of the product? In order to determine this amount, a formula has been provided to help provide a baseline.

Keep this factor in mind: this is only an example of what to consider to determine the amount of time you can expect to get from test participants for the incentive. The number established here is only a guideline and it represents the maximum amount of time. Test duration has a lot more to do with the complexity of the product than with its value. However, this number will ensure that you do not overextend the value of the product versus the time investment.

$$\frac{Product\ Price + Added\ Benefits + Market\ Value + Materials + Added\ Incentive}{Participant\ Per\ Hour\ Rate} = Hours$$

$$\frac{Participant\ Hours}{Weekly\ Hour\ Requirement} = Weeks$$

Product Price

The product price is the actual manufacturer's suggested retail price (MSRP). This is the price that people would pay if they walked into a retail store and purchased the product. Be certain that this factors every potential cost associated with use the product. If additional software is being provided to make a central application operational, include that in the value of the product.

Items such as tax or shipping do not add much to the cost, but can be used if they are realistic costs of acquiring the product. However, you should not add more to the price for any bundled packages unless you are providing more than what will be shipped with the product. For example, if third-party software is bundled as a trial version and a registration code is provided as part of the beta test, that would add to the product price.

Added Benefits

The added benefits are more difficult to put a price on than the product. These are new features, improvements over the existing product, or something special that distinguishes the product from its competitors. These benefits must be something that people are eagerly awaiting or something that greatly enhances the value of the product.

Establishing a value for these new items can be difficult, especially if they will not offered as part of an upgrade. However, if they are offered as an upgrade, use the upgrade price as an additional cost. Values in this area should range from $100 for some small benefits to $1,000 for huge enhancements. These values are correlated to a scale of 1 to 10.

Market Value

If the product is an industry leader or something very popular, additional value can be added to the product. Popularity has a lot to do with interest in a product, and thus makes the beta test opportunity more exciting and exclusive. In contrast, new products from small companies have very little market value.

Estimating market value should be based exclusively on real brand and market data if possible. If the product is number one in its segment, this adds a tremendous value. While market value is not a quality measurement, it is an indicator of the impact the beta test will have when the product is released. Thus, it does add value. Values in this area should range from a $100 for a small share to a $1,000 for market dominance. As before, these values are correlated to a scale of 1 to 10.

Materials

If the software bundles any tangible hardware, those materials add to the value of the product. Of course, the value of these materials is directly related to the cost of the item on the retail market. Even if the material is bundled with the package at a reduced cost, the test participants do not need to know this. In fact, it is always good to capitalize on these additional pieces to ensure that you get the most value from the product.

Test Participant Hourly Rate

This hourly rate is based on the level of user experience. While there are no rigid criteria for establishing a cost per hour, it is good to establish a cost that equates to real-world markets and the cost for the level of person testing. For example, a simple consumer application that requires end users would rate $10 per hour. However, a high-end software compiler requiring software engineers to test the application would rate $25 to $30 per hour.

Participant Work Weeks

Beta test participants, depending on the product, will perform anywhere from 10 to 20 hours of testing per week. This means that a site will take that time out of his or her personal schedule and dedicate it to looking at the test product. These figures are averages based on the type of product being tested and the specified commitment that of each particular test.

It will be necessary to determine the amount of test time each participant is expected to dedicate prior to the test starting. Once this figure is determined, it will be simple to determine how many weeks of work the sites will be able to commit to before they start to perceive that the ratio of work to product isn't favorable.

Added Incentives

In cases where a product has a very low price, it might be necessary to improve the test motivation by adding an additional incentive. Anything from a t-shirt, hardware, or cash can be used. However, you will want to select something that has excellent perceived value. To do this, you need to understand the test team and their interests.

Incentives are valuable tools to ensure future performance. Therefore, through a well-managed incentive program, excellent testers are given added reward. These rewards should only be distributed to exceptional testers. In addition, incentives can be offered in the form of priority selection on new tests.

Assigning a value to the incentive is simple if it is a retail item. In those cases, the item's retail price should be used. However, when using an intangible item such as a test opportunity, the value assigned needs to be factored based on the marketing value of the company. Assigning this amount should be made in contrast to the reputation and respect in the industry. For example, a small startup could establish this value around $100. A larger company like Sony could be as much as $500 depending on the product.

Case Study: Cool and Calculating

Martina Lister is a beta test engineer for Cinema Solutions, a company designing software for the newly emerging home digital video market. She has been asked to provide an estimate on how long she believes her company's new DVD menu software will need to be beta tested.

To determine this number, Martina gathers together the critical information to run a "work formula."

The product will retail at $399. While the software does innovate the DVD authoring process, it is new in this market and it does not have any share at this point. However, there are very few applications that have the flexibility for creativity that this application offers. Consequently, she throws in an extra $100 for this value. Last, they will be sending 10 DVD-R discs to allow the participants to do test burns. These cost $5 a piece for a budgeted amount of $50 per test participant.

On the "participant hourly rate," Martina knows that this product is focused for the consumer. However, she is going to need some power users to perform this test to get the best results. Based on the averages from previous tests, she determines that $15 per hour should cover this cost. Finally, she expects the sites to dedicate about 12 hours per week on the product.

$$\frac{\$399 + \$100 + \$0 + \$50}{\$15.00} = \frac{36.6 \text{ Hours}}{12} = 3 \text{ Weeks}$$

Based on the formula, Martina determines that she will get approximately three solid weeks of testing. This coincides with what the schedule can accommodate. She delivers the message that she feels three weeks of scheduled beta testing should sufficiently test the product.

Earning It

Once the duration of has been established and the test criteria announced, the test participants must earn their product. This means they must perform each task specified as part of the test. Make test participants aware of what it takes to earn the incentive, but leave a touch of subjectivity so that the sites will not do the minimum and quit.

For example, rather than state that the site must correspond with 20 email messages during the test to be eligible for the incentive, dictate that he or she must exhibit "constant and consistent feedback" during the test period. This conveys nonspecific but effective criteria for motivating testers.

Those participants who provided excellent feedback and made an effort to meet the needs of the test are eligible to keep the product. Sites who fail to meet the criteria of beta test are removed immediately and are expected to return the product. It should be rare for a beta test participant to make it to the end of test and have to return the product.

Balanced Rewards

In some cases, it makes sense to add potentially extra levels of reward for exceptional performance. If a product is low cost or if it is a very complex application, throwing extra incentives into the test will help push people a little more to get the best results. In addition, these rewards can be something small but should be scaled to measure performance beyond the minimum requirement.

By using a system of achievement levels, a test participant can set goals and work to achieve those goals during the test. The bottom tier should be someone who has made a conscious effort to perform the testing but has not expended any additional effort. The top tier should be someone who has exhibited constant and resourceful feedback. He or she represents excellence in technical prowess and responsiveness. In between, a team might build as many tiers that seem appropriate.

Once the tiers have been determined, a corresponding reward should be tied to achieving that level. That reward should increase in perceived value as the person moves up the tier. Every site must be able to achieve any of these levels. The criteria to get to these levels should be clearly documented and the reward must be clear as well.

Creating a reward system of this type is always challenging, as a balance must be made in order to properly recognize each test participant for his or her own accomplishments. However, it cannot be cost prohibitive to operate. Getting this balance requires understanding the test participants and designing the incentives that peak their interest.

Recognizing Losses

Most test participants will usually do at least the minimum to earn the product and be done with the test. Some will step up and do more and earn added incentives. Even fewer will be exceptional test participants. However, the smallest of all the groups is the nontester or the inactive test participant.

When properly administrated, the problem test site rarely can make it through the screening process. If this type of person succeeds in getting on a beta test, it is an oversight, a drastic change in his or her personality, or a fraud. Whatever reason, a good team recognizes that a tester is not performing and makes immediate adjustments.

In the following section, some characteristics of bad test participants are provided to help identify the behavior. When a person experiences any of these issues, it is best to simply ask for the product back and walk away. Depending on the situation, it might even be appropriate to flag the site's name as a potential problem and take measures to make sure the site never gets on another beta test.

Tester Burnout

Once testers have exceeded the work-to-value ration, they start to experience burnout. Symptoms of a tester burnout include lack of interest, lack of communication, frustration, anger toward the company, or idleness. In all cases, a decision should be made to get sites motivated again or to close the test.

Burnout is a bad problem, as once it occurs it takes some serious effort to get the test back on track. A burnout might speak negatively about the test process, program, or product, yet provide no real feedback of any worth. In addition, the burnout could try to cause problems among the members of the beta test by trying to sway the other sites to his or her way of thinking.

Nonparticipation

Known as the "black hole," some test participants receive the product and then are never heard from again. The reasons for this could be a wholesale theft, death, loss of job, or personal life changes. Whatever the description, the fact remains that a product is sitting in someone's hand and is not being tested.

When a situation such as this occurs, there are many potential actions to resolve the issue. However, the best method is to take preventative measures prior to getting the product into the hands of the beta test participants. If a constant flow of communication and interaction is engaged with every site, they will understand early on that you intend to work with them during the entire test.

Of course, there is no method to prevent the person who is attempting to defraud a company out of a product. In those cases, it is best to send a certified letter from the company lawyer or legal department that clearly states the consequences for the lack of response. In those cases, there is no point in trying to salvage the beta relationship; simply focus on getting the product back from the site.

If the test participant does return the product, simply tell him or her thank you and take measures to ensure that this person does not get selected for another test. If the person does not respond or responds negatively to the request, inform him or her that you will need to bring the lawyers into the process.

Hopefully, this situation should be very rare. Sadly, managing the effort to get the product back is very time consuming and counterproductive to the test process. However, allowing a single product to go untested is an even greater issue and must be addressed.

Wrong Motivator

Throughout this chapter, motivation has been a key theme. It is what drives a participant to provide excellent feedback. However, a test can be turned into something worthless when the wrong motivator is used to inspire the sites.

In these instances, the sites might or might not indicate a lack of interest to participate, but it will be evident in the quality of their work. Unmotivated testers respond slowly, provide poor feedback, and do only the minimum. Unlike other losses, the test appears to be moving forward but at a really poor pace.

If the beta test engineer sees this behavior, it might be helpful to ask questions of the sites and determine what is the problem. If they are unresponsive, it might make sense to close down the test and start an entirely new program. A bad motivator is very hard to overcome. Additional incentives or rewards only seem contrived to the test participants.

Competition Kills

Effective beta test management is about encouragement and incentive; it is never about competition behavior. A sure way to remove the incentive in a test is to make the beta test participants compete against one another for the incentives in the test. It effectively takes all the motivation to perform the work and ends up leaving only a few participants actually doing the testing.

Rather than focus on his or her own performance, the site will worry about how he or she compares to the other test sites. If any indication is given to the site that he or she is not leading in the test, the motivation to test the product is gone. The site loses the will to participate as the incentive goes out of reach.

Competition can inspire effective testing. However, it should be used to inspire the participants to compete against themselves. The mentioned scaled incentive program is designed to provide this type of competition.

Test Problems

If constant operational issues hinder the beta test program, it makes testing the product a secondary focus. In no instance should the running of the beta program interfere with the test process. If this happens, it will impact the test results and leave sites feeling frustrated and angry. In those instances when the test equipment or infrastructure is not functioning, it might make sense to either stop the test or choose an alternative method for testing until the issues can be corrected.

CHAPTER 15

The "Bug"

A "bug" by any other name...is still a bug...

In the development of software, there is one word that causes frustration, anxiety, and angst more than any other. The word *bug* holds many connotations. The definition dif fers between people and processes. Universally, it is considered a problem, but exactly what type of problem is where the confusion begins.

A quality engineer might view something as a bug, while a developer might not. If something is labeled a bug, arguments about terminology, semantics, and ideology abound. This only frustrates the problem and takes away from addressing the actual issue.

Defining a "Bug"

The differing views of how to define the word *bug* come from a lack of a real definition. The word *bug* is a colloquialism, a product of the computer age. And while bugs run rampant through software and hardware (or maybe they don't), identifying what they are is very difficult.

Beta testing is no different. The distinction between what is a bug and what it is not varies from program to program, and from place to place. When beta test managers are asked to produce a list of bugs, the question of what should be included in that list becomes a problem. In addition, as soon as the list is produced, there is already argument as to why it was included.

In order to clarify this issue and to ensure that this chapter does not delve into a religious discussion of what is and is not a bug, a definition is being provided. This definition is focused on the material produced in a beta test and is exclusive to that process.

A "bug" is defined as anything that could potentially have a negative impact on the customer's experience with the product.

It might seem broad to include "anything" as part of the definition. However, a beta test examines the entire product. It covers everything from the documentation to the application itself. Because of this broad treatment, the beta test must be prepared to identify problems that are outside the scope of a basic test process.

The customer experience is something that differentiates the beta test process from other test programs. The role of a beta test is to assess the quality and functionality of a product through "real world" testing. If a test participant has a negative experience with the product, a customer is having a bad experience with the product.

Who is correct in this situation? The developer makes a valid argument. However, with whom are they arguing? Mick is a beta test participant, and thus a customer. The

---

 ## Case Study: Buried Treasures

Mick Gomberg is feeling a bit frustrated. He has discovered what he considers a very serious issue with Ardent Innovations' latest application, *Pushpin*. This unique program allows users to stick notes into virtually any application. As a beta test participant, Mick has reported what he thinks is a bug. However, the response from the Ardent engineers is that this is not a bug, but rather a misuse of the program.

The design of the application allows its users to put the *Pushpin* notes on Web pages, documents, spreadsheets—anything. The application traces the location of the notes and ensures that the next time you open the application or file, the note appears. Mick was able to cause the application to fail whenever he used a CD-ROM based game.

Basically, he wants to stick the notes in different parts of the computer game, and when players gets to that point in the game they will see a note providing a clue. The application is supposed to write a simple 1-byte code into the file so that it can locate the note when the person gets to the place in the application where the note is supposed to be.

The problem exists because the application attempts to write to the CD-ROM instead of the hard drive. Thus, the application fails. Mick agrees that the application shouldn't work with writing to the CD. However, it is the system locking up that he considers a bug.

The development team argues that they cannot see a system lock. While it does take the application a long time to respond as it attempts to write to the disk multiple times, their view is that it should never happen since the program can obviously not write to a CD-ROM. In the view of the Ardent engineers, this is not a bug.

---

engineers are arguing with the people who purchase their product—thus, the expression "the customer is always right" takes on a whole new meaning.

Understanding the expectations of the customer is a critical issue in a beta test. The entire process of beta testing is designed to gather "real world" feedback from the customer. Thus, ignoring something as simple as an opinion can be catastrophic. Beta test participants are a small sample of the product's market, and the development team must be sensitive to the "bugs" of these "customers."

The Misunderstood Bugs

A beta bug is not like other bugs. Those problems discovered in a beta test differ greatly from those found in other development processes. Because of this, the beta bug often has difficulty being properly understood. Issues discovered in beta test can be hard to pin down and are sometimes misunderstood.

 Issues discovered through beta testing take many forms. Some are technical and specific, while others are vague and expressive.

Because of the complicated nature of the beta test issues, there is a tendency to ignore the problems. Traditional product issues list specific occurrences with the software and provide straightforward, scientific approaches to the topic. In contrast, an issue discovered during a beta test might report a symptom or a behavior the software is exhibiting. It might even include some emotional comments.

Beta test issues are often tainted with opinions and ideas about the problem. Where a lab reports specifics about an issue, a beta test might leave out some small yet critical detail. Beta test issues often require deeper investigation to get to the issue. So, if this process is so complicated, why bother? Because underneath the surface of these complicated issues lay real bugs.

Beta test issues are not purely speculative or opinionated. In fact, the vast majority of issues found in beta are valid bugs that would be found in many different tests. Yet, there is a large group of issues that cannot be found through any other test method. Beta test participants provide a unique and valuable test perspective on the product.

Through the insight of beta test participants, a company is able to determine how a product will perform in the real world. Through the beta process, products are better prepared for release into the market. Although the issues are often challenging, the fact remains that beta testing discovers real bugs.

Issues versus "Bugs"

Before a bug is a *bug*, it is an *issue*. The issue is not always a problem, but rather a complication or an incident. It is something strange and it needs to be defined and its source determined. By using the term *issue*, the beta test program can help keep a clear distinction between what are really bugs.

Deciding what is a bug and what it is not is a big part of the beta process. Test participants report any anomaly they see. From simple support problems to difficulties with other software, there are many potential culprits for an issue. Until the issue is clearly defined and every aspect of it is understood, it cannot wear the moniker of "bug."

Bug is a powerful word. It infers many different things, but most importantly, it conveys a failure in the development effort. Because of the power of this word, a beta team must make every effort to use it cautiously and guarantee that it only refers to real, documented problems with the product.

Crying Wolf

Nothing damages the credibility of a beta program more than "crying wolf." In the story of "The Little Boy Who Cried Wolf," a young boy is entrusted to watch the town's flock of sheep. At first, he cries wolf to see if people will actually respond to his cries. The townspeople respond to his calls angry about the false alarm.

The boy, finding humor in the situation, calls another time. Again, the people are angered by his false cries. They return home, frustrated and suspicious. When a wolf actually does come stalking, the boy's cries go unanswered. Nobody believes his call.

A beta program uses the word *bug* carefully. It is not something that can be cried whenever an issue appears. Each situation should be properly appraised and investigated. If the issue appears to be valid, it is still not the time to call the problem a bug. Only when the issue is determined to be the fault of the tested software should it wear that name.

Designating Bugs

As noted, when discussing issues, use of the term *bug* is carefully distinguished from issues. However, when an issue moves to bug status, it needs to carry a designation. This description qualifies the bug. A frame of reference for the bug, the designation allows a focused discussion on the impact of the bug.

Designation usually exists within a bug-tracking system. However, it is something that needs to be used in verbal communication. For example, if a test site is having difficulty with the installation of the product, it should be called an "installation bug." This might seem rudimentary. However, speaking with a designation allows the owners of the different parts of the product to listen and key in on issues that are relevant to them.

This very simple task provides clarity when communicating about bugs. Simply stating that the product has a bug invariably brings up the question "What kind of bug?" In contrast, when communicating issues to the development team, using a designation allows them to understand the part of the product impacted.

Designations vary from product to product and are completely flexible. They can reflect an individual company's corporate structure or can be generalized. Either way, it is simply a communication tool to help people understand the nature of the bug.

Technical Bugs

Bugs that come in from beta test are predominantly technical. When an issue is presented to the development team from a beta test team, it is always qualified. Qualification applies a designation and determines the accuracy of the information. In the case of a qualification, there is a possibility that the issue might not be a bug.

Depending on the skills, manpower, and experience of the beta test personnel, the issue might also receive an evaluation for technical accuracy. The evaluation goes in depth into the issue and there is an attempt to duplicate the problem. In this case, only relevant and potential "bugs" are reported.

In cases where the beta test team is small or unskilled, it might fall on the development team to evaluate the technical data. When this is the case, the decision of whether an issue is actually a bug becomes more complicated. In these instances, the issues must be evaluated like any other technical data, but additional factors must be considered.

Participant Competence

Beta test participants are often selected based on their level of experience with the product. Some are selected because they are very knowledgeable about the product line, while others are chosen because they are complete novices. This factor weighs heavily when considering issues.

Before making a decision about a newly discovered issue, the person evaluating the data from beta sites must consider the user's level of competence with the product. The level of competence is not to determine the validity of the issue, but rather to establish the frame of reference involved with the report.

For example, a highly technical test participant might report a detailed problem report including extensive details about what might have caused the issue. Novice users might report the same problem using details about what they were doing when the issue occurred.

In both cases, there is a valid problem but the information about the issue offered has a different perspective. While the novice might not have the technical insight into the issue, the problem is reported just the same. Never equate technical competence with issue validity. The technical user certainly provides more detail and understands technical communication, but that has no bearing on whether an issue reported is real.

"Real" Materials

When looking at issues that come from a beta test, there are often times where the test team must evaluate the hardware and software of the beta site to determine the source of a problem. Beta test participants' material is as varied and complex as the people themselves. This equipment is not used in a lab. Therefore, shareware, screen savers, spyware, and other anomalous and custom software are installed.

The fact that these materials are varied in configuration and use makes them valuable to a beta test. When an issue arises, don't throw it out because the test participant is using something atypical. More than likely, what might seem atypical to a company is much more common in the real world. Moreover, unless there is supportive data to the contrary, those issues must have the same consideration that other, more common issues get.

Intangible Bugs

Issues cannot be measured solely on the technical merit or accuracy. There are many intangible factors involved in the decision. Beta test sites often report issues based on subjective experience. Individually, these are opinions. However, when many of the same issues are brought together collectively, they become bugs.

Intangible bugs often come in the form of customer feedback. Because of this form, it is something peculiar when being addressed as a bug. It is not what typically makes up a bug, but actually the opposite. Customer feedback is nonspecific, opinionated, and varied. Thus, the tendency is to ignore this important submission. Because of its descriptive rather than specific qualities, it looks like an opinion rather than a bug.

Customer feedback is actually a bug of the most terrible kind. It is a bug that is hard to get hold of, yet very real. When customers send in feedback that is negative, they are basically expressing frustration with the product. This frustration has a root cause. Often, there are multiple issues and performance problems.

Identifying and understanding these problems is often more crucial to the success of a product than the specific bugs a design team is used to dealing with. Intangible bugs can be difficult to approach and correct. Strong opinions from both sides of the bug often result in arguments on how they should be addressed.

Taking the intangible bug seriously, a development team should anticipate that any way the problem is resolved, someone might walk away disappointed. Because these bugs are tied to opinions, the correct way to solve them is not always the "right" way.

Usability

Usability is designing a product that has the simplest and most intuitive method to use the software. While it is not an exact science, usability is a critical component of product design. When a beta test participant experiences confusion or frustration trying to use the product, it is often attributed to usability.

The key to usability is the intuitive nature of the software. Most issues originating from this aspect come from multiple beta sites making the same "mistake." If these users click a wrong box or fail to follow the instructions, these are usability issues. These issues become bugs when many testers exhibit the same behavior.

When an application is built, it usually follows conventions used by other software. The design of the graphical user interface (GUI), the flow of the application, and the overall operation of the software have been leveraged off of previously developed applications. In addition, some design factors are dictated by operating system constraints. Usability issues must be reviewed with this understanding.

Standardized design conventions cause users to become habitual in their use. If a button is in a certain location in every application of the same type, the test participants might consider it a usability issue. However, the ability to innovate and design needs to be balanced with this feedback. Software engineers, designers, and experts must put their opinions aside when listening to beta test participant feedback about usability.

Expectation feeds the intuitiveness of an application. Changing the design of an application will invariably cause some confusion and create bugs. However, a good design can overcome these problems. Thus, there are two ways to look at usability. The first assesses the adherence of software application to a design standard. The second evaluates the intuitive nature of a design.

Either way, these factors must be considered when looking at beta test participant feedback. Balancing the opinions of beta sites with the intentions of the designers, an assessment of the usability of a product can be realized. This realization is a wonderful benefit to the product and to future development efforts.

Look and Feel

A company invests huge amounts of time and money to create a "look and feel" in its marketing and products. From the logos and packaging to billboards and trade shows, a company works diligently to create an image that represents the ideals of the company. At the closest level to the customer itself is the software it sells.

Everyone has a different idea about what looks good and what doesn't. Just walk into your local shopping mall and see the vast array of clothing options and you will understand immediately. Because of this, look and feel issues are often ignored. The beta test participant's feedback is written off as an attitude and nothing is ever done about it.

However, beta test sites are the best place to see if the corporate messaging is coming through properly. In beta tests, the sites look at the product as though it were shipping. They have the unique experience of seeing the product as if they bought it off the shelf. Thus, a marketing team can get an untainted view of the software.

The look and feel can still produce bugs, but more often than not, those issues are something that will need some long-term evaluation. The messaging of most companies is not simply changed; it is part of the strategy of a company. The only time look and feel issues need closer consideration is when they actually impact the usability of a product.

User Experience

The experience a user has with a product is one of the key outputs of a beta test. As they use the product, the test participants provide a record of their individual experiences in the form of feedback. This insight is punctuated with the regular reporting of bugs. These issues are often larger in scope and generalized. Although general in nature, there needs to be a certain level of attention paid to these comments.

Test participants will convey their user experience through comments about the product as a whole. In some cases, the commentary might not even be submitted as a bug, but rather expressed through team communication. On a message board or through email, the sites will articulate their level of satisfaction with the product.

If the implication is negative, the site needs to be contacted immediately. In some cases, the reason for the discontent is obvious. Perhaps the product has had too many issues, or maybe the product doesn't meet their expectations. Whatever the reason, this poor user perspective is effectively a bug that needs attention.

While one user having a bad experience is not the mark of a bad product and might not justify a bug, there is something there that needs to be carefully examined. The best method for addressing this type of issue is to simply ask the test participant why he or she had a poor user experience. If the beta test team can determine a source, it might be something simple to address.

However, multiple test participants complaining about their user experience is something to take very seriously. On a normal beta test, the number of angry or frustrated beta sites correlates to the percentage of angry customers once the product ships. If the beta test has 50 sites and 15 are disappointed, that equates to more than 30 percent of your customers being disappointed by your product.

Expectations

Prior to receiving the product, the test participant has developed his or her own sense of how the product should work. These expectations are formed through use of a company's previous products, the marketing of the product, and many other influential factors. Because of this, each test participant has his or her own expectation about the product and how it will perform.

The expectation bug is a strange one in that the test participant reports that the product doesn't perform well, yet no level of performance has ever been stipulated. Expectations can be unreasonable and might need close scrutiny before considering a bug. However, the deeper question for this issue is how the site built these expectations.

Much like the other intangible bugs, communicating with the site may eliminate the bug. Multiple reports also have the same impact on these types of bugs. Unlike the other intangible issues, the expectation bug usually has a very specific set of criteria that the beta test site has in mind that the product is not meeting.

The detailed nature of the expectation bug makes it a more volatile problem. If other sites consider the same criteria but have not been looking at the issue, there is a chance it could slip through the test process unnoticed. To prevent this from happening, have the beta program open discussion with the test sites and determine the level of expectation and whether your product is meeting it.

Quantity

Looking at beta test feedback, recognizing that quantity equates to quality is important. The quantity of beta test issues is a simple, self-verification process in a beta test program. Since the test participants have diverse backgrounds and qualifications, they will report varied and differing information about the product. However, when all of the sites report the same issue, a bug has been discovered.

Properly executed beta tests generate abundant information. Sometimes, repetitive data seems to overwhelm the small individual and unique reports. However, if there are multiple reports of the same issue, the problem is obviously a bug and needs the attention of the development team.

Quantity is an important part of assessing the validity of a bug. Quantity takes on two forms during a beta test. The first addresses when the quantity of variable reports is high. This is typical of a beta test. Because sites are expected to report anything anomalous, they have a tendency to report even the most insignificant issue. Categorizing and combining the issues into a manageable form, the beta test team should be able to identify these issues and group them together.

The second form of quantity is when a single apparent issue is discovered and each test participant reports it. While the data is repetitive, it eliminates the need for issue verification. The test participants are verifying the issue themselves by duplicating the bug reports.

In most cases, beta issues require investigation when they arrive. Your typical beta test participants are not engineers, and they rarely take the time to go into intricate detail about an issue. However, when identical reports from different people with varying degrees of intricacy appear, a bug is easy is to discern.

Handling Criticism

Unlike bugs that come from a normal test process, beta issues often express opinions and evoke emotion. It isn't easy to hear that your product "stinks," and it is even harder to hear it when it comes from the mouth of a customer. However, this is the nature of some of the feedback that comes from a beta test.

When a developer sees the blunt and uncensored comments of a beta test, the tendency is to ignore the feedback. Pejorative language might not be what would normally constitute a technical issue. However, beta sites are real people and they express their opinions without regard to anyone's feelings. They don't know that developers are reading.

This criticism must not be taken personally, nor should it be ignored. Comments of this type have a basis in fact. Perhaps the test site has had a miserable experience using the product, or maybe the site is loyal to another product. There are numerous potential reasons for negative comments and it is important to investigate why the comment was made and if there is a possible way to address it.

Beta test teams are responsible for conveying the information gathered during the beta test. It cannot be changed or tainted to make it more subtle or friendly. If that were to happen, it would change the results of the beta test and invalidate the test itself. Negative comments are not noise, but feedback that should be listened to carefully.

Twisting Words

Beta testing produces a lot of feedback. Some of it is complimentary and some of it is not. The danger of this is that someone with selfish intentions can twist the data to make it sound any way he or she wants it to. This reality is something that needs to be understood before reviewing anything that comes from the "beta sites."

If someone feels a product is not ready for release, he or she can simply take a look at all the negative comments that come in from a beta test and simply report them out of context. Therefore, anyone reviewing beta test feedback coming from a source other than the beta test program should verify the validity of the comments with the beta test manager.

Any material not delivered directly from the beta test program should be considered carefully. Beta test data needs to come from the source and not through some derivative method. When data comes from outside the beta program, there is a risk that it might be tainted or confused and as in the preceding case study, out of context.

Beta test data is much easier to understand and appreciate when it is provided in the context of the test results. Any bugs or issues from a beta test can only be supported by the actual feedback from the beta test site. When the feedback is paired with the bug, it paints a clear picture of the problem.

Closing Bugs

Tying up loose ends, every bug must have some type of closure. Closure doesn't necessarily mean fixing the issue; it simply states that some action will be taken. Closure is as much a psychological issue as it is a process issue. Giving closure to the test participants benefits the company as much as the beta program.

Development teams should always offer some type of closure for every bug discovered during the beta test. Closure tells the beta team and a test participant that the issue they submitted is recognized as a potential problem and that it warrants attention. Whatever the decision, the participant deserves some type of response.

Fix

Ideally, every verified bug is fixed prior to the shipment of the product. In reality, only serious issues tend to get any attention. Thus, when the development team decides to fix a bug, communication of this action enforces the seriousness of the issue and it sends a message to team members that the issue was a valid bug and that it has been corrected.

Case Study: True or False?

Sitting in the weekly engineering project review, Louis Pershing listens attentively as the customer service manager, Sharon Martin, angrily debates that Call Maker Software's latest offering does not have good enough documentation to ship. She cites a quote from the beta test that states, "This software is too complex to use without sufficient documentation." She follows up with, "Market Maker 2.0 hasn't got a manual that's worth using."

Louis is startled to hear this, as he is the director of quality, and Pat McLeish, beta test manager, never commented on the manuals as being an issue with Market Maker. In their weekly meeting, Louis and Pat went over all the critical issues from the project and nothing came up about the documentation.

After the meeting, Louis calls Pat into his office and asks about the documentation for the project. Pat is startled by Sharon's comments. In his opinion, she is taking a small bit of information and twisting it into something that it isn't. Pulling up the test information on the beta test Web site, Pat points out to Louis that the quotes are twisted in two different manners. The first quote is not referencing Market Maker, but is actually in reference to a third-party application bundled with their software. The vendor corrected the issue with delivery of a manual.

The second comment was an issue with the test site. Through some strange behavior, her version of the document reader was only showing the first two chapters. A new version of the application was installed on the participant's system and she was up and running. Pat also points out that in both cases, there was no real issue with the documentation but with associated materials. He also points out that if Sharon had taken the time, she could have read all of this on the beta test site.

Louis calls Sharon and explains that the message she conveyed in this morning's meeting is not accurate and, in fact, the beta sites have not had any problems with the documentation. She responds that the quotes she took were directly out of the beta test database. Louis tells her that is perfectly true, but what she has taken is out of context.

Sharon is angry and frustrated and believes that she was "mislead." Louis also points out that if she had taken the time, she would have seen that the issues were not related to the beta test by simply reading the detailed beta reports online.

Fixing a bug takes valuable time and can slip a release schedule. However, the importance of product quality and the beta test participants' effort is effectively communicated when they see a bug they discovered being corrected.

Work-Around

If there is not a viable way to fix an issue before the product must ship, it might be better to offer a work-around for the beta test participants. The work-around basically establishes an alternative method for addressing the bug. This method of resolution can often satisfy the needs of the test participants while providing time to properly correct the issue.

Postpone

Postponing bug resolution is not an ideal solution to the problem, but in some cases is necessary. When the decision to postpone addressing a bug is made, there should be some general justification. Whether the problem needs more consideration or the impact needs assessing, the development team needs to communicate the reason for this action.

Postponement infers that the bug will be corrected in a later version and beta test participants will watch closely to see that that happens. If it doesn't, there is a chance of harming the reputation with the test sites.

Investigation

Investigation is a very reasonable response to bugs discovered in beta test. Often, issues might require more time to discover their true source. Because of this, test sites understand the limitations of time in a beta test and expect that all issues will not be resolved before the end of test. Investigation infers no timeframe for correction and leaves a company open to make a decision later.

When providing the result of investigation, it might be useful to ask the test participants to send the development team as much detail about their problem as possible. This last form of interaction shows the sites that the company has genuine interest in correcting the problem.

Consideration

Consider is similar to *investigate* in that the bug's resolution is being postponed for further review. However, consideration is used when the issue is obviously a bug but isn't serious enough to justify attention. When offering consideration to sites, it is important not to sound pompous or arrogant. Convey that the issue is something important but the company must consider all its options before proceeding.

Ignore

The last and least popular response to bugs discovered in beta tests is the choice to ignore an issue. While test sites appreciate the honesty, when they are informed that an issue will not be addressed because it doesn't have enough importance, it is usually a let down. It acts as disincentive to the bug submission process.

The best method for delivery of this information to beta test sites is at the end of the test, and it should be phrased in a manner that shows the bug has been reviewed but there is no viable way to correct it at this time. Test participants won't like it, but will at least know it was considered.

PART THREE

Making the Results Work

Summary

This third part is designed to help a company extract the most value from the results of a beta test. Its intention is to teach the value of the results and how they can be used in many different capacities beyond discovering product issues. You will want to read this section if any of the following applies to you:

- You are currently reviewing beta test data and need to understand how to deliver the results.
- You are a marketing person interested in how to use beta test results.
- You are a public relations person interested in how to use beta test results.
- You are an engineer looking for methods to use beta test data for product improvement.
- You run the beta test program and are looking for other methods to use the beta test data.
- You are a quality manager wanting to see how beta testing can help your quality system.
- You are a decision-maker looking to get more from your beta test program.
- You are trying to understand the results being reported by a beta test program.
- You want to determine if your beta test program is providing good data.
- You are responsible for acting on the results of a beta test and you want to understand how to get the most from the test.

This part of the book explains what type of data is generated by a beta test and how to use this data effectively. Part One, "Understanding Beta," provides a general overview of the program while exploring its benefits to an organization, and Part Two, "Building a Beta Test Program," goes into extensive detail about the operation of a beta test.

CHAPTER 16

Responding to the Customer

B eta test sites are people who assist in the quality testing of a product. They take a chance and look at a product before it is ready for the world. They put their systems and software at risk and give their time to help improve product quality. While they do benefit from their participation in the program, they still have expectations from your company. It is, therefore, critical that a company is responsive to their needs.

Not simply satisfied by a free product, the beta test participant has a need to be listened to, to be thanked, and to be appreciated. Beyond the communication of a beta test, a company should show action with the data the test sites have provided. From actual response to each issue to general announcements on the product, recognizing the contribution of beta test participants has tremendous benefits to both the product and the test.

Test participants should be viewed as a valuable company resource, not a commodity. They provide tremendous worth for the product and need to be responded to in a manner that not only respects their contribution, but also shows appreciation and encourages their continued effort.

Additionally, the development team needs to be clear on a point. While the beta program is there to enable the test to happen, the actual testing itself is an interactive process, which involves the sites, the beta staff, and the entire development team. Good beta tests engage the test participants on multiple levels with multiple people and encourage communication among every party.

Test Participants Are Customers

During this entire book, we discuss the "sites" or "test participants." Yet, we sometimes forget that before their selection into the beta test program, they were customers.

And, after the test is complete, these people will still be customers. This fact is something to always remember when dealing with beta test sites. They are real customers and deserve the same regard and respect a regular customer would receive.

Sometimes, when beta tests are being performed, it is easy to forget that test participants are actually customers. From the submission of bugs to the intimate discussions of your product, they start to feel like employees. However, even with their assistance and effort, they remain consumers of your product.

Beta test participants are focused on helping a company achieve quality. However, they remain people who either own your product or have experience with it. Because of this, their perspective is not only incredibly valuable, but important to the success of your product.

When dealing with test participants, is important to ensure that the relationship remains productive and effective. Poor communication with sites can hinder the beta process and impact the results of the beta test. Balancing a measured professional rapport with the test sites helps produce the best test results and allows the sites to feel like they are of value to the company.

Reflection on Your Company

Once the test is completed, test participants will go out and communicate a message about the quality of the product and their opinion of your company. While they might be prevented from revealing anything secretive about the product because of a non-disclosure agreement (NDA), they are entitled to express their opinions and they will certainly share them.

In the eyes of the beta test participant, a company's actions during a beta test directly correlate to its behavior after a product ships. Beta sites will judge the product's quality, design, and performance for the beta test. However, they will judge the company's quality, service, and reliability for themselves.

Unresponsive behavior shows that a company is unconcerned about its customers. In our example, Veronica feels neglected because she thinks her important issue is being ignored. While she might be participating in a beta test, she is a customer first, and the unresponsiveness of Embassy has turned her off to the product. Everyone involved in the product development process must treat a beta test participant in the same manner that you would treat a customer.

The beta program and the people who interact with beta test participants are a reflection of the company in a small scale. In all dealings, people interfacing with the beta test should make an effort to keep a professional and communicative manner.

Qualifying Issues

As issues are qualified through the beta test process, the development team needs to take the initiative to help the beta team respond properly on each issue. Every issue

Case Study: Undocumented

Veronica Grady has been participating in a beta test for Embassy Development. Embassy has just completed development on a new software application called *Document Director*. This software is a global document management system that allows large companies to use common documents corporate wide.

Veronica is the document control manager for Charlton Regents, a global luxury suite hotel with over 200 five-star hotels based in 50 countries. She decided to participate in the beta test because Charlton Regents has over 80 different standard documents in nine different languages. She has been looking for a simple document management solution to reduce the amount of document distribution and to enforce standardization. While she is a test participant, she is also using this test period to evaluate the software and see if it will answer her needs.

During the test, she finds the software to be a good product. Generally speaking, she likes the interface and feels it could be useful to her company. Her testing shows that the software works fine with the standard letter size used in the United States, but has several issues with the A4 paper size used internationally.

Veronica sees paragraphs being cut off and graphics being corrupted when going to the A4 format. In addition, the software states clearly that it has A4 support, but when using the program, it is obviously having problems. She reported the issues at the beginning of the beta test and has been waiting for some resolution from the people at Embassy.

After three weeks of beta testing, she has had no response to her issue. She did receive email notification that the problem was being investigated, but there has not been any other communication since that time. Because of this lack of responsiveness, Veronica decides that this must be a reflection of the attitude of the company, and thus, she will need to investigate another product for her need.

At Embassy, her issue is being given the most attention possible. The engineers have been working extra hours and the marketing team has been doing internal testing to help. Unfortunately, none of this effort has been communicated to the beta test team or to Veronica. Both are under the impression that the issue is either being ignored or has no priority. Because of this lack of communication, Embassy has lost a customer and hurt its reputation.

submission is a portion of time given by the site to your product. Thus, a small portion of time is given back with a response to the issue.

Normally, the beta test team provides a response to the site during the process of issue qualification. However, in some cases, the development team might be forced to address issues that the beta team cannot. This situation arises where the only response is based on the decision of the development team.

When product decisions arise that are outside the realm of a beta test program, someone needs to take ownership and ensure that some satisfactory response is delivered to the beta test participants. The customers expect some type of reply to their issues. In these cases, the beta test team can convey the message, or the development team can deliver it.

Custom Tests

In addition to handling specific issues from test, there might be instances when the development team wants to interact with the customer through a custom test. This format has the beta team design specific questions to gather more information about an issue, pinpoint a concept, or determine direction in a project.

The custom test is used to refine the data the development team needs to make a decision Therefore, it might be necessary to perform numerous tests to help get to the conclusion. These tests need to be used carefully, as they can divert the test participant's attention from beta testing.

While the beta program might administrate this process, the information is almost always dictated by the engineers or marketing people. When the results are returned, there might be a need to specifically contact the beta test site to gather more information. In those cases, it makes sense to have the person needing the information go directly to the site.

Managing Failure

Every so often a product fails; it dies; it corrupts; it becomes useless. In those instances, it might be necessary for the development team to step up and assist the beta team or the customer to get the product functioning again. More often than not, the beta test team can handle the situation and is prepared for a potential failure. However, strange situations arise that require special attention.

When this happens, the development team must understand the urgency and respond quickly. If a new build is needed or if the customer needs something specific to get running, there must be a rapid response. Every moment a beta test site is down is unproductive time. The success or failure of the test depends on the cooperation of everyone involved in the process.

Listening to the Site

Listening is not simply reading the feedback from a beta test. Listening is an interactive process in which the speaker and the audience are engaged. In this case, the beta test sites are the speakers and the development team is the audience. Taking an interactive role in test results shows the beta test sites that the people building the product are listening.

There is huge value for the engineers to communicate directly with the beta test participants on issues of any nature. This communication tells sites that the engineering team is listening to their comments. When test participants believe they are being listened to, they become more active and work harder to ensure that the needs of the test are met. They are willing to spend extra time on the product and work to be responsive to the development team.

Active listening makes the test site feel like he or she is part of the development effort on the product. The site will take ownership of his or her issues and care about the results of test. Promoting interaction between the test participants and the development team helps encourage the activity of the test and subsequently improves the overall quality of the product.

Sites notice recognition of their issues by the development team and become much more engaging when it happens In some cases, there might be some development team members who feel uncomfortable communicating with test participants. If this is the case, the communication can be passed through one of the beta test team members with the name or position of the development team member referred to in the correspondence.

Issue Resolution

Issues that come from beta test are tied to a person. Some customer used the product, discovered the issue, and now is suffering with it. When the problem is solved, it is important to take time to let the beta test team know that the issue has been corrected and when it will be resolved.

Resolution is an important part of the beta process for a number of reasons. First, test sites like to know that not only did they discover a problem, the development team recognized it as a problem and corrected the issue. By keeping sites informed of resolutions to their issues, they feel like a part of the process, and this will help the beta test team perform their job.

Next, resolution reduces noise. Sites are often unaware of each other's issues and many times will report the same bug over and over again. In many ways, this is valuable, as it confirms the existence of a problem. However, it also adds to the amount of useless data being added to the test data. Letting sites know that an issue has some type of resolution will stop redundant reporting.

Last, resolution promotes the reporting of other issues. As test issues close, beta sites have more time to look into other problems. With open issues, they are burdened by the effort it takes to deal with the problem. As issues are resolved, the site can move forward.

Resolution differs from closure in that it does mean "fix." A resolution is one form of closure in that the problem is being resolved. If there is no resolution to an issue, it still should be conveyed to the beta test participants. If the action is anything other than resolution, it might be better to give the unpleasant task of delivering that news to the beta test team.

Revisions

Normally, not every issue can be corrected in a single test period. Beta testing comes very late in the development cycle, and normally the code has "frozen." Because of this, a path for correcting issues is established. This path is usually through revisions to the software.

Whether it be an update, patch, or fix, the revision is an important part of the beta process. It helps the beta test participant gain closure to issues he or she is dealing with. This means that any unresolved issues at the time the test ends should be put on a path for revision. However, more important is providing test participants with a method to upgrade.

Revisions remain a real factor of software development, and a beta test participant must be able to take advantage of this factor. Keeping them involved in the development process after the product has released will allow the company to maintain a base of test participants to test the revisions, and allow the sites to get the upgrades they need to maintain the product.

Visiting Sites

From time to time when issues appear, there is a no way of duplicating them in a lab. The situation is so distinctive and unique that only a visit to the beta test site will determine the actual cause of the problem. When these circumstances arise, there are a number of steps taken to make sure the trip is necessary.

First, the issue should be serious enough to justify a visit. Simple GUI or minor errors are hardly worth taking time from a beta test site to see if an issue is real. When a bug exhibits itself and it can potentially stop the shipment of the product, then a visit should be considered.

Next, make every effort to ensure that the customer's issue is real and is related to the product. While this might seem obvious, often the seriousness of the issue has a tendency to overshadow rudimentary procedures. If a participant experiences a crash every time he or she uses your software, the blame appears clear. However, no issue should be considered clear until the actual source of the problem has been discovered.

If the issue still has not been resolved, it might be possible to ask the customer to send his or her hardware in for evaluation. However, people's computers, for the office or home, are personal and might contain private material. If the customer is willing, there is still a potential risk that the hardware could become damaged during transit. It is not the best solution to use, but should be considered prior to a customer visit.

Beta test participants typically welcome a visit by the engineering staff of a company. First, it conveys a genuine interest by the development team to fix the issue. Next, the site feels a sense of flattery and importance that he or she found an issue that warrants a visit. Last, the visit demonstrates the commitment of the company to produce a quality product.

Building Relationships

Every so often, there are test participants that do more than they are expected to do. They exceed expectations and put forth such a great effort that the development team recognizes their names. These people are usually experts in the software and make a significant contribution to the product, discovering multiple issues and making timely and valuable suggestions.

When a tester performs in this manner, it is beneficial to develop an association with this customer. Often, that relationship, although managed by the beta test team, grows to include direct participation with the developers. Engaging a beta test participant to be more involved with the development process usually ends up with that site building a long-term affiliation with the company and test program.

 Sometimes, a simple telephone call to say "thank you" can establish a relationship better than any incentive can.

Additional Incentives

In cases where test participants exceeded the expectations of not only the beta test program, but also the entire development team, it might be necessary to provide some additional incentive. This should be an initiative taken by the development team and not the beta program, and should be presented as such to the beta test participant.

These incentives are a tremendous reward for the test site. It is a special recognition to the participant from the development team beyond the normal incentives. This indicates how important his or her contribution was to the product. The extra incentive is an excellent way to get the test participant to want to keep working on the product after the beta program is completed. It is especially useful when attempting to build a long-term relationship with the site.

Closure

Closure ends the beta test process. It is a method for ensuring that the sites understand that testing is complete and that their participation is no longer needed. As part of this process, the development team must make every effort to ensure that the software release candidate is delivered to the beta test team for distribution to the test participants.

The test sites put forth a lot of effort and normally their reward is to keep the product. When this is the case, the developers need to make certain that the beta program has everything they need. Often, the rush to release allows this task to be overlooked. The released product goes out and the sites are left with an incomplete product.

In some cases, the actual released product might be available for distribution as a reward. This usually exceeds the expectations of the test participants. Those materials should be distributed within a couple of weeks from the close of test. If there is anticipation that the timeframe will be longer, the beta team should notify the participants as such.

When the sites receive their final copy of the software, it truly signifies the end of the beta test period and they can finish knowing that their hard work went to help bring a better, higher-quality product to market.

Thank You

Taking time to recognize the contribution of the beta test participant is very important to the success of a beta test program and to the product. The beta test team will have the responsibility of ensuring that the sites are sufficiently rewarded for their work on the test. However, the marketing and engineering teams also have a responsibility.

Once a project is completed, the beta test team always takes the time to thank the test participants for their effort on the project. Of even greater value is a thanks from the developers and development team. Test participants understand that a beta program acts as a conduit for getting the feedback to the developers, and there is no expectation that anyone on the development team will say "thanks."

Therefore, a simple thank you from one or all of the developers means a lot to the test participants. Whether it is a simple group email or a personal letter sent to each of the sites, taking a moment of time to say "thank you" promotes morale and creates enthusiastic support for the product and the company.

CHAPTER 17

Making Results Pay

Beta tests do much more than discover bugs. When a beta test is effectively run, the marketing and public relations departments can mine a wealth of valuable material for a variety of purposes. From press contacts to customer testimonials, much of what is needed to properly promote a product prior to release can be collected through a beta test. With this information, a more strategic, less expensive, and carefully planned release can be orchestrated.

The Word *Beta*

Sometimes, there is a concern that the people selected for a "beta" test are inappropriate for marketing or PR use. This idea is spurned from the fact that the people selected to participate in a beta test might be too technical, too focused on testing, or not necessarily interested in helping in this aspect. Nothing could be further from the truth.

The fact is that a properly executed beta test uses candidate criteria specified by the marketing requirements document. Depending on the product being tested, the user experience can range anywhere from novice to expert. Moreover, they are only focused on the testing because that is what they have been signed up to do.

Beta sites are excellent resources for both marketing and PR, and in most cases are very willing to help by speaking with the press, providing quotes and testimonials, and completing custom marketing surveys. The average beta test participants will do almost anything asked of them as long as it is considered part of the beta test.

The word *beta* refers to the phase of testing, not the people participating. The people selected to participate in the test are actually customers, and when using the data gathered from a beta test, it does not matter if it came from this phase or not—the information they provide is valuable.

Low Cost, High Value

Beta testing selects candidates from the user community to assess the quality of a product. In exchange for feedback, the only actual payment they receive is usually in the form of a copy of the test product or an incentive. By using this program for PR and marketing purposes, a company can save a generous amount of money while gathering equal and even possibly better information.

A deviation from the rigors of testing, sites are normally very enthusiastic about participating in these nontechnical tests. They welcome opportunities to express their opinions and to share their ideas. Rather than devote valuable resources to conducting focus groups and market research, a company needs to closely examine the potential uses a beta test program has to offer.

In the following sections, some of these potential opportunities are provided. While some might stretch the role of the beta test participants, they offer a lot of flexibility. Many of the regular tasks performed by a beta test program can overlap those performed by the marketing and PR organizations. These suggestions are not meant to devalue the importance of those groups; rather, this is meant to offer methods to share the function they perform.

A low-cost and highly efficient process, beta testing is a necessary part of the product development process. By using it to its fullest potential, it effectively saves the company additional money, eliminates repetitive practices, and reduces the amount of effort necessary to get a product to market.

Public Relations

The constant source of comments about the product and the real-world experiences of a beta program are very useful for a PR department looking to promote the product through their various contacts and programs. Beta test participants are a ready, willing, and able resource for a public relations department.

Rather than invest money in market research or bother important clients to be reference accounts, a beta test participant and beta test data are far more useful and less expensive. The beta test gathers quotes, comments, ideas, opinions, and a wealth of other data. The test participants are people who are selected based on the demographics specified by the requirements document designed by marketing. This means that these people fit the customer profile for the product.

Media Contacts

The media feasts on personal interest stories. They love anything that puts real people into real situations. A company can benefit tremendously when it can get press showing real people using their products. Test participants are the perfect candidates for these opportunities. They have all the benefits and very few drawbacks.

Test participants are real people using the product in real situations. Thus, they provide actual testimonial for a product prior to its release. Furthermore, the sites are under nondisclosure, so a company can manage the information the test sites disclose during an interview.

In addition, they are familiar with the product. After weeks of testing, the sites are fairly versed in the features and capabilities of the software and can speak intelligently on the product. Because of this, they make excellent advocates for a product and can attest to its benefits.

Last, through an effective beta program, a PR department can screen the different sites and determine which participant is best suited to speak to the press. The wealth of demographic information gathered to perform a beta test combined with the sites' performance on the beta test accelerate and advance the selection process.

 ## Case Study: A Penny for Your Thoughts

Allison Sharp is the public relations manager for Thirdhand Corporation. Thirdhand designs innovative software applications that increase accessibility for handicapped people. Their latest product, *Penny*, is a human interface application for the blind and visually impaired. *Penny* takes a PC and turns it into a personal secretary. Simple voice commands open applications, write email, read Web pages, and other amazing features. In addition, *Penny* breaks new ground with its exceptionally lifelike voice.

Several magazines and newspapers are clamoring to see the new software and how it works. The product has been in a lengthy 20-week beta test with over 100 visually impaired and blind beta test participants. Allison asks Jim Turpin, beta test manager, if any of his participants might be willing to be interviewed by the press and possibly appear on television.

Jim tells Allison that he will ask them and see if there is any interest. Immediately, he finds 10 participants all interested in sharing their experiences using *Penny*. Alison tells Jim that 10 people is more than she needs, but wants to give two of them the opportunity. Jim provides her with detailed profile information about each site and tells her she can select from the list.

Allison is still unable to decide. Even with the information provided, all of them have excellent profiles for the press. She asks Jim if she could give send them a custom survey that would provide further details about their experience with the product and their uses for the application.

Jim, working with Allison, puts together a 30-question survey that gathers all the remaining information she needs. He sends the survey out and gets response from each of the interested participants. From this data, Allison selects two press contacts. The first is Mary Barberton, a lawyer in Philadelphia, and Nari Patel, a high school student from Fresno, California.

Allison also follows up with each of the eight remaining interested participants and explains that while they were not selected for the major press release, she is still interested in writing up their stories. She informs them that she will be contacting them for a more detailed interview.

Beta test participants are usually very interested in participating in press-related activities and often possess the perfect qualifications for a press contact. In our example, Allison was able to find some excellent candidates as well as gather additional material for feature articles or the Web site. Using test participants as media contacts allows a PR department to get the data they need by selecting the perfect candidates based on the criteria they specify.

Press Releases

As a product gets close to launch, the PR department is working diligently to get excitement generated about the new product. Part of this process is the distribution of press releases. The press release is supposed to provide all the details about the new product and potentially get a mention in the media.

The press release can be given extra flourish by adding quotes or comments from beta test sites about the product. Often, test participants are selected because they are technology experts or hold related positions in the industry. To this purpose, they lend credibility to their quotation and to the press release.

Press releases announcing new improvements, fixes, and enhancements can be further improved, as the PR person can see actual reports from the beta test of the product's progress and generate factual data about the performance enhancements or changes made to the software. Beta test information is exceptionally useful for understanding the state of a product.

Product Launches

Prior to release, there is very little material to promote the features and benefits of a product. Much of the information is speculative based on a design specification and marketing document that is still being implemented. A beta test actually has people with first-hand knowledge of using the product and testing those features.

While information distributed at a product launch lists the features and benefits in a specification sheet format, the information rarely shows how they impact a user. Grabbing beta test data and putting real user stories with the features and benefits will enforce the software's potential impact on the marketplace and generate more excitement about the product.

Prior to the product launch, a beta test generates a lot of new and interesting data about how the software is being used. Public relations programs can gather valuable facts about the product and can promote those that appear to have the most benefit to the user. Keying in on the features that are generating the most excitement in the beta test, the product launch will have a bigger impact.

Crisis Communications

When a company makes a mistake, the PR team has to get into action and try to control the damage. If the crisis is related to a product or a serious bug, a beta program is a quality process that can be highlighted as part of the messaging. A beta program demonstrates that a company is committed to incorporating customer input into their design and that they are concerned about what the customer thinks.

Additionally, once the fix has been made and is in test, the PR group can cite beta test comments about the product and how it is performing with the fix. Once the issue is corrected, beta feedback is an excellent assurance to the public that the problem is under control. Testimonials about the viability of the fix will help put the crisis behind.

Investor Relations

Investors want to know that their company is investing money wisely, producing quality products, and making sound decisions. Beta testing represents all three of these. Beta programs are cost-effective methods for assuring quality, and that can easily be demonstrated to an investor by showing how unpaid test candidates are being used to help perform a final qualification of the product.

Beta testing is a quality process, and simply explaining its role in this capacity should promote confidence with investors. Beta feedback is also exceptionally useful when communicating this message. Not only is the company performing extensive testing on the product, here is what the test participants are saying about it.

Finally, beta testing is certainly a sound decision for a company to make. As the aforementioned factors attest, a beta test is an investment into the product in that it is a low-cost investment to help produce a quality and competitive product. Moreover, if test participants have good things to say about a future product, what could promote confidence in a company more?

Marketing

Marketing is responsible for the planning and carrying out of the conception, promotion, pricing, and distribution of a product. Marketing achieves these objects through the collection of data, interpreting it, and then using it to make the best decisions. Beta testing is a powerful tool to help in the gathering of this data.

Market Research

Market research is the process used to gather and promote data for taking full advantage of the marketplace. Normally occurring prior to a product's development, this process is often used for strategic planning and to ensure that a design works. Beta testing achieves many of the same purposes and can compliment a good market research program.

Market research can be very expensive. Rather than spend thousands of dollars to bring people in for focus groups and surveys, a company can leverage a beta test program to get similar results. Using the beta test participants to research future products or revisions can be advantageous. The test sites cost less and have more experience with your products.

Test participants during the beta test have been using the product for a while and understand it. From this experience, they have come up with a lot of ideas about how they would change or enhance the product. Test participants also come up with many ideas for new products. Their extensive use of the product exploits needs that should be met.

Depending on the demographic you are trying to target, there might be some need to grab additional sites to gather a broader appeal. However, the beauty of a beta test is that the customer base costs little and they provide many of the same benefits of other market research tools.

Product Name and Brand Recognition

All companies aspire to have their brand become synonymous with the products they represent. Whether it is "Kleenex" or "Scotch Tape," brand recognition is an achievement in marketing. Software even has an example of this where people "Zip" up a file to archive it. During the beta test phase, a company can use this time to see what opinions sites have about their brand.

Through surveys and questionnaires, test participants can provide detailed information about the company's brand and how they view it. Everything from their view of the company in general to specific information about how the beta product fits that view can be considered. From this data, a marketing team can refine the brand messaging.

If the test participants have a perception of the product different from what marketing is trying to convey through advertising and product design, there is an opportunity to see how the company should change the product or the marketing strategy to get a closer match. Through this refinement process, the beta test participants can act as a small market research forum.

Competitive Analysis

Beta test sites are selected based on their experience with the product. In many cases, these test participants have a lot of experience with the software being tested, and more than likely, with competitors' products as well. With this in mind, a marketing program can gather valuable comparative data about their competitors.

Everything from performance data to feature comparisons, the beta test site has the ability to provide insight into how your product performs when compared to its competitors. There is even the ability to do direct comparisons in cases where test participants actually have a competitor's product.

Even without direction, test participants will provide feedback that compares a product to its competitors. It is natural part of the evaluation process. However, a marketing team can take this and work it to gather more specific and detailed information about the competitor's product and how the beta product compares.

Promotions

Marketing programs are made and broken on successful or failed promotions. Therefore, it makes sense to take a little time and test a promotion concept on beta test sites before deploying it to the world. Beta sites will provide unbiased feedback on whether they like the promotion, the concept, and whether it would encourage them to purchase the product.

Aside from expressing opinions, beta test sites can actually use promotional materials and make certain they operate properly. From completing the necessary marketing data to executing the actual promotion, the complete promotion process can be evaluated. If there is a promotional item as part of the promotion, it can be used as a further incentive in the beta program and may compliment the test.

Web Site Evaluation

When a beta test is performed, it is designed to assess an entire product. This infers everything included in the box. Conversely, limiting the product to that which is in the box is not necessarily a realistic limitation. One component that exists outside the box but is integral to the product is the corporate Web site.

A resource for the customer, the corporate Web site contains valuable information and services for the customer. Thus, it makes perfect sense to have the beta test participants evaluate the variety of functions the site offers. Clicking through its various sections, the test participants can provide feedback on the appearance, tools, usefulness, and content of the site.

Registration Process

The registration process is an important tool for gathering marketing data from the customer once the product has been purchased. Everything from contact information to detailed demographic profiles is gleaned from the registration process.

Beta test participants are in a perfect position to test the technical aspects of this function, and are also good candidates to provide feedback on the entire process of registration. Everything from the length of the form to the nature of the questions can be evaluated, and a form that is useful and effective can be designed.

Customer Support

Probably one of the most important parts of the Web site for existing customers, the support section provides all the useful tools and information for the customer's product, or at least it is supposed to. Through effective beta testing, the test participants can determine if the support being provided is sufficient.

In addition to the valuable feedback, the site can be tested for performance and the information contained relevant. Additionally, during the beta test, data is collected about the difficulties using the product. The data gathered through the beta test can also be the foundation used to build a support database about issues using the software.

File Downloads

Providing files via the Internet has become a standard. Most companies offer a download section. Inside, users find updates, demos, drivers, manuals, and other valuable material for their product. In many cases, there is a specific process needed to download files. Some files different need to walk people through an inquiry or license agreement prior to allowing the download.

For this reason, it useful to allow the test participants to try each of the files and ensure that the process for downloading the file works, and that the file itself actually works.

Material Evaluations

A product is a collection of multiple materials. Manuals, CDs, the box, and even any hardware accessories all need to be evaluated for more than their performance. Aesthetic qualities, physical design, packaging, and other factors weigh into the overall product experience and need to be assessed.

Test participants already receive a majority of these materials as part of their participation in the beta test. Gathering the additional feedback is a simple process. In fact, beta test sites often examine these factors as part of the test, and information might be available.

Custom Survey

Designed to gather specific information from the beta test site, the custom survey is a valuable tool of a beta test. A collection of questions, the survey can grab tailored information from the test participants. This information can then be used to support decisions made about the product and the marketing effort. Custom surveys allow a marketing team excellent flexibility to establish greater clarification on important marketing decisions.

The custom survey is an excellent tool to use during a beta test. Whether sent on paper or used through a Web interface, test participants are much more readily available than standard customers and closely match the demographics specified for the product.

Additionally, the use of a custom survey during the beta test process actually enhances the beta test itself. Providing the participants an additional and different task outside the normal rigors of testing, the custom survey gives the participants something interesting to do.

Project Integration

When a product is envisioned, it is a collection of different parts. Beta testing is the first instance in which all the parts of a project are assembled. This is a unique opportunity to see that they all work together. Even more interesting, this is an excellent time to experiment with other potential pieces to see if they might work as well.

Integrating the different parts of a product into one complete package is one of the biggest challenges of releasing a product. The varied components have multiple owners and need different types of information. Using the beta test to gather this information is a practical and inexpensive process.

Bringing all of the material together, simply distribute the product to the test sites through the normal beta test process. As the test progresses, introduce additional components for evaluation. Once the test is nearing completion, query the testers about the integration of these components as part of the beta test.

Price Assessment

How much a company charges for a product depends on many factors. From the bill of materials to the prices currently being offered by competitors, putting a price on a product is a complex task.

Beta test sites are experienced in using the product and they are customers. By using them as a resource, a company can determine whether the prices they are offering coincide with the perception of the public. Often, a simple survey will determine a range of prices that correlate exactly with the value the user places on the software.

Additionally, specific information on how to increase or decrease the perceived value of the product can be determined. Test participants will provide feedback on how much they feel the product is worth and can offer suggestions on how to change the value.

International Marketing Resource

Making the move from a domestic to an international product is one of the biggest challenges a marketing team might ever undertake. The complexities of the languages and the legalities of an international product make for a difficult transition.

One approach to bringing the product into these markets is called *localization*. This process makes the product feel as if it is designed for the specific local market. When this happens, a single domestic product becomes multiple applications. The manual, packaging, and accessories all have to be changed as well.

Beta testing is an excellent avenue to ensure that a product is prepared for the new overseas market. The program is able to find local people who can evaluate the translations and performance of the product in their country and language. As an added benefit, these people also become test participants and have an opportunity to further exercise the product.

The local test participants provide much more benefit than using a translation house or test service. They offer a native speaker's view of the language translations, which will provide much more accuracy. In addition, they will use the product on the international version of the operating system on locally purchased hardware. In all, the entire international verification process is much effectively tested through a beta program than through any other method.

CHAPTER 18

Product Quality = Success

C ompanies are constantly seeking ways to ensure that their name and their products represent quality. They understand that a quality product translates into success. Smart organizations implement quality systems to ensure that they not only meet the needs of their customers, but to make certain they are using the best practices possible.

Systems such as ISO 9001, Six Sigma, QS 9000, and other standards are used to help companies establish effective processes that will result in quality products. Measuring customer satisfaction is a part of every one of these processes, and beta testing is one of the most effective methods for measuring that satisfaction.

Quality is determined when customers have a high level of customer satisfaction. Through its customer interfacing and product testing, beta test programs provide companies with tangible measurements of their product's quality. Once a beta test has been completed on a product, companies can determine the potential level of success a product can achieve.

Beta Tests and the Quality Process

Companies that define quality as part of their corporate mission are looking at building a successful business based on high customer satisfaction. Their attitude about their business is that in order to win their market, they must represent the highest quality in their products. In order to determine if they are meeting these goals, they must put in programs that assess the level of customer satisfaction.

Defining quality means understanding what is and what is not a quality product. It is not purely a measurement of success or failure, but rather a system designed to ensure that the output of the development process is the best possible product. At the end of this process lies a beta test program.

Beta testing is an integral part of meeting these quality goals. It is a program designed to assess the quality of a product through customer interaction. As people use the product, they produce feedback that translates into a wealth of valuable material. From marketing quotes to engineering design issues, beta testing is a quality process designed to enhance the quality program.

When properly executed, successful products are the consistent output of an effective quality program. Beta testing is a critical component of that program. Of all the steps in a development program, beta testing is the closest to the customer. Its location at the end of the process also helps measure the output of that program.

Measuring Quality

Beta test results effectively tell a company whether a product can be considered quality. Beta testing gathers a measurement of customer satisfaction through its interactive process with test participants. The feedback produced by the beta test establishes an exit criterion for the product to be measured against.

Using customer feedback from a beta test as a measurement for quality rings true in so many ways. Since the measurement of a quality program is customer satisfaction, the only way to determine that satisfaction is by asking the customer. Efficiently run beta test programs generate generous amounts of customer feedback.

There are numerous factors in a beta test that can assess the quality of the product and provide a measurement for a quality program. Some present the subjective viewpoint of the test participant. Others present rational numbers for evaluation. However, when combined, they provide the necessary data to properly evaluate a product.

Number of Open Issues

The cumulative number of open issues discovered during a beta test is not enough data to make a decision on product quality. However, when compared with other similar products, measured against the duration of the test, and generally evaluated, the data is very conclusive.

Quality measurements should take all of these factors into consideration and establish a realistic appraisal of the product. Although the number is not necessarily something in which to base an entire decision , it certainly is a factor to consider. Products with an excessive number of open issues will ultimately be problematic after release.

Customer Comments

Beta test participants provide comments of all types. Some write concise opinions, while others write lengthy scientific evaluations. Making judgment on the quality, the best method is to review as many of the comments as possible. This factor provides excellent insight into the opinions and ideas of the test participants and can help with the review of the product.

Comments are subjective and subsequently are not an exact or scientific method of measurement. However, established criterion for quality needs to factor in this type of information because it often reveals a lot more than any statistical data can. Participant comments can vividly paint a picture of the status of a product.

Number of Feature Requests

In addition to the abundant number of issues submitted by beta test participants, there are also many feature requests. These suggestions for improvement, enhancement, or ideas for consideration are not something to use for measurement. In fact, for this process they can be relegated for later review. However, the quantity of feature requests is important.

If there are a significant number of these requests, this might be an indicator that the product needs improvement. Test participants tend to suggest these items as they use the software, and when there are continuous submissions, they are expressing a form of frustration with the product. This factor should be weighed lightly but still considered.

Overall Experience

Once a comprehensive review of the beta test data has been performed, there should be little doubt as to whether the product represents quality. In most cases, quality products have few open issues, and those that are open are minor. Comments from test participants reflect positively on the product and the company. Feature requests are negligible. With this data, a level of customer satisfaction can be derived and an evaluation of the product quality can be performed.

Quality Processes

The development process is supposed to be designed to produce a quality product. Implementing a quality program, in kind, is expected to create performance excellence. When these two fail, there needs to be some method to catch that failure. On an assembly line, there is product inspection, and in the development process, there is a beta test.

The process of developing a product is complicated and different at every company. The design of a quality program is to help standardize as much of the process as possible through the use of best practices and excellent documentation of those practices. When the practices are all properly executed to the specified process, the system works.

If only one person ran development programs, this might be an easy task to achieve. However, there are multiple people all trying to interact with one another to get the best output. Therefore, it is necessary to have some way to make certain that when there is a mistake in the process, it gets caught before a customer sees it.

Beta testing acts as the gatekeeper for a quality program. It tests every part of the product and touches each department in a company. Everything from the box the product comes in to the software itself, a beta test checks to make certain everything looks right and works the way it was designed. If this is not the case, the beta program provides feedback to that effect.

Cost Reduction

Beta testing increases customer satisfaction, reduces development time, and discovers problems before shipping. Each of these directly impacts the bottom line. Yet, these are all factors that impact the development of the product. After it has shipped, there is even more opportunity for cost savings.

Quality products have fewer support issues. Because of this, the cost to support the product is reduced. In addition, customer satisfaction with the product will be increased with fewer technical problems. Beta testing, as a quality function, helps ensure that products being released have better quality.

Beta test data anticipates the potential failures in the field and assists in addressing them before the product is shipped. This effectively reduces the rate of return on products and keeps the cost lower. In addition, beta testing can extend the life of a product by testing updates and driving product improvement.

Initiating quality through a beta test process allows companies to achieve higher quality products at a lower cost. After a product goes to market, a beta test program can continue to feed information into different organizations about improvements, enhancements, and other beta test data byproducts.

Identifying Critical Issues

The most important function a beta test serves is its ability to identify potentially critical issues before the product is shipped. This function is basically the underlying focus of a beta test. When this occurs, the test participants are directed to ensure that they can see and duplicate the issue. Once development corrects the issue, the test sites verify that the issue has been fixed.

When beta testing identifies a critical issue, there are many additional benefits besides eliminating the risk of the specific bug. How the issue was discovered is as important as the issue itself. Beta test participants are asked to retrace the process of detecting the bug, and that information is passed along with the issue itself.

The process of issue discovery often reveals where mistakes were made during the development process and generates additional issues. As part of a continuous improvement process, beta testing is not solely focused on improving the product; the development procedures are also evaluated.

Additionally, discovery of critical issues in beta testing can help a company evaluate their processes for handling situations of this type in the real world. Everyone from PR to customer support can use this test to exercise their programs and ensure that they can handle a problem of this type if it arises.

Reusable Information

Beta test-generated data is very valuable and often reusable. Not limited to issue discovery, a beta test produces many different types of productive data. From this data, companies can improve products, add new features, and innovate their design. A large part of the focus of beta testing is to produce methods to improve and enhance products.

Beta test sites often discover parts of the product that do not meet their expectations or were not included as part of the product. When they encounter these situations, the test participants submit feature requests. These requests are an excellent resource and can be reused when derivative products or new revisions are being developed.

Additionally, the information is often reviewed after the test is completed when issues are discovered through the customer support process. Beta testing acts as a support test ground, and once a product released, the data from the test becomes a resource for predicting issues and learning how to handle them.

Process Improvement

From the concept of a product to its eventual release into the marketplace, a beta test program assists with process improvement in many ways. Beta testing involves everyone on the development team, evaluates every aspect of the product, and tests multiple functions within a company.

Products entering beta test are supposed to be ready for market. When issues are discovered, they are not merely evaluated for their technical merit. An investigation into how the issue actually got into the product is also considered. In that pursuit, the process of developing and releasing a product is evaluated.

How did the issue get past quality assurance? Who is responsible for addressing this problem? Were all the systems in place when the product was delivered? These questions are asked to ensure that the product issue is not related to a process failure. How a process is done is as relevant to the development of the product as the output itself. With this analysis, the system is getting a constant check to ensure that it is servicing the company and the product well.

The beta test program revealed more than product issues in this example. Karen and her team discovered a major problem in the build process. In many cases, it is difficult to discern where or when a problem occurred. However, beta testing is designed to exercise all aspects of development and can usually determine the source of an issue.

Case Study: To Build a Fire

This is the closing beta test phase for Xenix Systems' new software. As the final candidate is ready to enter testing, serious problems, supposedly corrected, are reappearing during the beta program's evaluation phase. Because of these problems, Karen Gaugian, beta test manager, informs the development team that she is prepared to reject the candidate and subsequently slip the shipping date.

Karen's engineers are dumbfounded by the reappearance of issues that had been fixed. Even stranger is the disappearance of critical updates and improvements. In fact, they are convinced that the version submitted is closer to the original submitted at the beginning of test.

Nevertheless, the build information stored in the files and checksum information provided by David Jules, the build manager, show that the software is correct. Furthermore, the software engineers have verified that the build they delivered to the build manager does not have the problems seen in the beta test lab.

Karen is worried that the uninstall process is not working properly and instructs her team to wipe all the hard drives on their lab systems and put back clean installations of the software. She wants to verify that an earlier version of the software does not exist in any form. As a further precaution, she instructs her team to pull in some additional hardware that has never had the product installed. Nonetheless, the issues are still appearing.

The entire company has their eyes on the beta test team. Everyone is convinced that there has been some mistake during the beta test program's evaluation process and there is a lot of pressure to get this new software released. Karen stands by her team and states that the problems do exist and that she sees no choice but to hold release until these issues are addressed.

Conversely, Karen is convinced that the problem is with the build and she pushes David to make sure his team is delivering the correct software. Asking him to do the build himself, Karen wants to make sure there is no mistake in the process. David agrees and builds the CD and delivers it to Karen personally.

Once delivered to the beta test engineers, they immediately set to testing the software. To everyone's surprise, the software's issues are gone. Upon closer examination of the process, it is revealed that one of the build controllers was selecting the correct filenames but the wrong source code.

The software engineers name the components the same on each upgrade delivery, but store the source code in different locations on the network to keep them separate. When the build controller went to select the files, he was selecting from the wrong directory and using the old components.

On further examination, the source of the problem actually sits with the software engineers, as they are supposed to lock the old directories before creating new source code. When the build controller goes and creates a build, he or she is normally prompted for a password if he or she tries to select the wrong directory. The software team was not following the process properly.

All of this process improvement is for one purpose: customer satisfaction. Getting the highest level of satisfaction out of a product means that every member of a development team must be focused on executing their part of the process effectively. Quality systems are the driving force behind this effort.

As noted, a beta test program is the most effective method for measuring this level of satisfaction. When a test is being executed, the level of satisfaction with the product is apparent. Poor products reveal process problems, and good products confirm that the quality system is working. Because beta testing is designed to assess the level of customer satisfaction, it is logical to use the program to evaluate the quality process as well.

Listening and Learning

A company that makes an investment in a beta test program is effectively investing in quality. A willingness to listen to your customers is the first step in understanding how to meet their needs and produce the best quality product. With this investment comes the responsibility of listening to what is being said and learning from that information.

Beta testing often delivers both good news and bad. Everyone is always willing to step up and listen to the complimentary comments. However, when negative feedback comes in, there is often a tendency to blame someone. Nothing productive comes from blame, but if people take the time to listen, there is a way to learn where problems might exist.

During the beta testing of a product, learning is when a team examines the issue, corrects it, and evaluates how the issue occurred. When a company doesn't learn from the beta feedback, the issue is corrected but is destined to repeat itself. Learning infers that the team takes an active role in the beta process and strives to understand how bugs can be prevented.

Best Practices

A "best practice" is doing something right not just once, but every time you do it. When a company commits to a quality system, they are committing to develop and use "best practices" in every aspect of their business. These practices are usually implemented through a number of different methods.

Consultants or experts instantaneously implement other practices. Through a consultant or industry expert, a company is tapping into their experience and using it to make certain that they are doing the same. This is very valuable but often expensive. In addition, the experts aren't always there to monitor the progress of the program.

Training and investment can sometimes get best practices implemented. During the training, the company is making its own expert who will execute the best practice. However, this is a time-consuming venture and requires a long-term commitment by the company to make certain that those putting the system into operation are committed to doing the work.

Some practices are discovered over time as mistakes are learned from and systems are perfected. This is the least expensive but slowest path to achieving the goal. However, with an effective beta testing program, the effort to discover issues reveals the limitations of processes used by a company.

A beta test program is a constant evaluation of the product development process. It exercises the entire development process and often reveals the limitations in the system. From the data gathered during test, a company focused on building better systems can help build refine their processes and acquire best practices.

Corrective Action

Prevention of future issues involves listening to the customer and learning. When a customer points out a problem, a company needs to take a corrective action to see that the issue is corrected and does not reoccur. This process is a big part of quality systems. Driving toward constant improvement, quality systems strive to have the best practices.

Beta testing in its broad application can help generate corrective actions. The source of every issue is not necessarily tied to a problem with a process. However, inevitably, process problems will create issues. Thus, looking at the reason for issues is a valuable part of the bug evaluation process.

Time constraints during the development of a product make taking corrective action in the beta process unlikely. In addition, it is not the duty of the beta test program to reveal issues with the system, but rather the product. Consequently, once a product has been released, the development team should take the time to analyze the serious issues that were discovered during the beta test and see if they could have been prevented.

This time is well spent, as it will more than likely reduce the chance of the same issues appearing again. Moreover, it will help refine the product development system as a whole. Quality systems are focused on constant improvement, and using the beta program as part of the effort will effectively increase product quality and drive the best practices.

CHAPTER 19

The End Is Only the Beginning

Testing has ended. The product is released and is receiving excellent reviews because your company performed an excellent beta test. You have the marketing data from the test into the hands of the press and all of the serious issues have been addressed. Basically, you are at a point where you believe the beta test has served its purpose.

The product that just completed its beta testing is in fact complete. However, your company will continue to develop products, and there is still a wealth of information that can be gathered to assist with future products and process improvement. Completing a beta test opens the door to many more opportunities.

Seeing the Future

Having a glimpse into the future has serious implications. In one aspect, being able to see the future allows for proper preparation. We know what to expect and, therefore, we can make certain we know how to handle situations when they arise. Equally, this knowledge is a big responsibility, and ignoring it would be negligent.

When a beta test is completed, it holds a small bit of the future in it. With the abundant feedback in the form of customer comments and suggestions, the beta test participants have provided the company with what they want to see the product do. They have offered up ways they would like the product fixed, and they have given examples of how they envision the product in the future.

Taking this data and examining it is something that not only helps companies understand past issues, it helps them build products with a future. Ignoring the information makes repeating the problems more likely. In contrast, taking the time to closely consider the results of a beta test helps establish a foundation for success.

The future is not always bright and it is never certain. Beta test data allows a company to have a taste of what customers want and need. Using this data effectively is no guarantee for success, but it does provide valuable information to help achieve it.

Beta Test Cycles

Just because one beta test is completed does not mean that another isn't of value. Beta testing generates feedback from unique individuals with their own ideas and opinions about the product. It can be just as useful to run another beta test with the same product but using different users. Alternatively, run an additional test, but change the test parameters.

Depending on the level of efficiency of the beta program, getting another test together should not be too difficult. During the test participant selection phase, the beta team reviewed many different applications. Among those people might be some excellent testers. If a change in focus is decided, it is even easier to get those sites ramped back up for another round of testing.

Perhaps you might want to change the demographic or the skill level of the users. There is an opportunity to focus on a different part of the product. There might be an interest in experimenting with different fixes or variations of the same software. While multiple concepts might be considered, the end result is that another beta cycle is useful.

Forward Thinking

The product development process follows a cycle of improvement. It is a continual process designed to build upon prior successes and learn from its failures. It is supposed to be a system for refinement and enhancement. However, market changes, budgets, and other issues often stifle this effort.

Taking a conscientious look at the feedback produced in a beta test and making an effort to implement some it in future revisions is something many companies don't take the time to do. It isn't because there isn't value in this process; it is because there isn't time. The rush of project schedules and demand for fixes preempts reviewing beta test data.

The value in thinking forward is its ability to not only address potential issues, it also offers an opportunity to give customers what they want. Just because the beta test is completed does not mean the test data has lost its usefulness. In fact, as new projects begin, it is helpful to go back and see what ideas customers had for improvements.

Investing a small amount of time and seeing what the beta test participants were thinking on prior versions of products is a productive and valuable use of time. Not only will it provide insight into issues that were discovered during test, it offers ideas that can enhance new versions of the product and meet the needs of the customer.

Product Improvements

Information gathered during the test is exceptionally useful for future product improvements. Beta test sites look at the software with a completely different perspective. They are not part of the company and they don't hold the same views about the application. It is with this different perspective that they come up with different and often original ideas about how to improve a product.

Suggestions for product improvements typically come in the form of feature requests. Sometimes, they are buried inside issues. After the completion of the beta testing, it makes sense to closely examine all the feedback and review improvement suggestions. If possible, have the beta test program separate them out and deliver them.

Beta test participants enjoy providing suggestions. In fact, nothing is more gratifying to a test participant to learn that his or her ideas will actually be implemented into a product. Therefore, take time to review the suggestions they offer. Among the bug reports and the varying issues exist potential revenue-generating ideas.

Revision Management

The number of revisions generated during a beta test is a direct reflection on the preparedness of the development team for the beta test process. If there were numerous revisions, there might be a problem within the team as to what is acceptable for a beta test customer. After the conclusion of test, it might be necessary to look into how many revisions were delivered to the beta team during the test period.

At the end of the beta test, no matter how large or small the program, there should never be more than one revision per one week of testing. Sites need the time to get the product installed and time to examine it. If they are inundated with changes to the application, they spend all of their time patching and upgrading and none of it testing.

Excessive changes during the test can reduce test participation and cause confusion with the sites. Because of this, a development team should keep revisions to a minimum and work to make each change in the product a significant one. The only way to understand how this was handled is to go back to the beta test and see if it was effective.

New Product Concepts

Data gathered during beta testing is primarily focused on the product being tested. However, every so often, beta test sites will speculate on a product or feature that seems interesting to them. They might explain an enhancement they would like to see or a product that compliments the one in test. Whatever it might be, take the time to listen.

Often, simple suggestions from test participants can be expanded into viable product concepts. The information the customers convey in these reports is actually a need that they want answered. The short moment that it might take to review these suggestions is an excellent use of time. These ideas, good or bad, are opinions expressed by your customers about your products and deserve some attention.

Renewed Resources

Depending on the amount of time that has passed since the previous test, there might be an opportunity to rekindle the relationship with the test participants. Bringing a portion of the previous test participants into a new beta test or querying them about the status of the software can also help bring new and exciting ideas to a product.

Time has passed since the test closing and the beta test sites have been using the product beyond the duration of the beta program. Because of this, they might have many new ideas and insights on how to improve the product. In addition, there might be new technical data that will confirm compatibility with new versions of applications, operating systems, and software.

Going back to the beta test participant also pays them a tremendous compliment. They appreciate the company listening during the beta test, but they are astounded when a company follows up with them after the test is completed. It is an excellent representation of customer service.

Program Improvements

A beta test program should be constantly striving to improve. The focus of the beta test team is to test products, but in the same instance, it should be testing itself. With input from outside the beta program coming from both internal and external sources, it is good for anyone involved with the program to offer suggestions on improvement.

Test Participant Suggestions

Test participants often make comments about the beta program and its level of service. Since beta testing is a representation of the company to the customer, it is crucial that their feedback is heard. After the test is completed, the development team and the beta test program should make certain that all of the needs of the test participants were met.

Additionally, both should review the test data to see what comments might have been made. Suggestions on infrastructure or the design of the interface are less important than items such as customer service and responsiveness. When reviewing beta test data, any serious issues should be carefully scrutinized to discover the source of the problem.

If the issue is related to the beta test program, then it is the responsibility of that team to correct the issue immediately. Equally, if the problem is with the development team or any of its members, there should be some type of corrective action put in place.

This is not a blame game. Giving the test participants the best service possible during a beta test is the responsibility of everyone involved in the project. These people are customers, and giving them an effective, professional beta program is important to both the product and the company.

Case Study: Final Fantasy

Bravo Multimedia has just completed beta testing on their latest Web development tool. *Fantasm* is a new fantasy sports application. The program allows people participating in various fantasy programs over the Internet to have all the latest in sports news, statistics, and information in a single location.

Perry Stevenson, project manager, was extremely frustrated by the beta test process. Due to an issue discovered late in the test phase, the project slipped almost two weeks and missed the opening week of football season. While he doesn't blame the beta program for the problem, he doesn't understand why it wasn't found at the beginning of the test phase.

The problem with the software was related to its inability to talk to the stats server during the test. Test participants were unable to get their specified statistics when this happened. Had this issue been found earlier in the test period, the product could have made the shipping date. In addition, he feels that the beta program was not efficient in getting details about the issue to the proper people.

Perry arranges a beta test Post-Mortem on the beta program so he can address his concerns and allow the development team to bring up issues they might have. Everyone gathers together for this discussion, but there is obviously some hostility toward the beta team—many people blame the slip on them.

In the meeting, Brendan Keenan, beta test engineer on the project, listens quietly as each member of the development team expresses his or her concern about the server issue and the disappointment he or she feels about its late discovery. Many offer suggestions on how to correct the issue, and a few even suggest a separate beta test.

Brendan takes thorough notes and acknowledges each concern. He pays close attention and when everyone has made their comments, he tells everyone that he appreciates their concern and agrees that the issue was found too late in the process. In addition, he admits that the test did not go the way he would have liked, and on future versions of *Fantasm* he will ensure that feature is tested earlier.

Brendan finishes by asking the development team for a few things. He asks that on future tests, he would like the team to clarify their position on what should be tested first. In prior meetings, he was under the impression that the fantasy leagues conduit was the priority to test. With this clarification, he will be able to focus the testing on that effort.

Next, he asks that they take a deeper interest in issues generated by the beta program. He notes that when the issue was initially discovered, it took almost a week for anyone to look into it. While the problem did arrive late, the lack of attention made the impact of the issue even more severe. He cites that it took two meetings to finally get some attention.

Last, he thanks the team for their time and expresses appreciation for their feedback. He notes that since this is Bravo's first Internet product, it was an entirely new experience for him and that he was internally torn on what approach to take on the test. However, he believes that working together, they can ensure that their needs are met on the next test.

Perry and the rest of the development team are satisfied and agree with Brendan that some effort on both their parts will improve the process and get the most from the beta test. The team is satisfied that the issue is behind them and looks to begin work on their next revision.

Post-Mortem Analysis

At the end of any beta test, it is always good to see what went perfectly and what went horribly wrong. No process is without room for improvement, and by doing a "Post-Mortem," there might be a chance to learn valuable information about the beta test program and how to get more out of it the next time around.

Inviting key development team members along with the beta test staff, the Post-Mortem is a meeting designed to bring out areas for improvement. There should be room to make constructive criticism and suggestions on both sides. The format of the meeting should be structured and not take on the form of a complaint session. It should focus on how to improve the beta test process.

Brendan kept his composure, listened to the concerns of the development team, and made certain to address their issues. The development team welcomed an opportunity to express their frustration and take measures to resolve the issue. By making the most of a Post-Mortem, both Brendan and the team benefited.

The Post-Mortem meeting is not necessarily meant to address problems alone. In fact, it is a good opportunity to offer suggestions and compliments about the beta program as well. However, the primary objective of this meeting is to get issues out on the table and make certain that some type of corrective action is put in place.

Focusing on Success

The success of a product is not solely dependent on its quality. However, of all the factors that can contribute the success of a product, quality is certainly one that can have the greatest impact. An emphasis on quality is the foundation of a beta program, and from that focus comes the goal of a successful product.

When products are successful, everyone wins. The customers win because they have a good product that serves their needs. The company wins because they are making money from the sales of the profit. Therefore, an investment into quality is an investment into success. Thinking ahead about how today's data can be useful in the future is a way to manage that investment.

Glossary

This section defines words, phrases, and processes that are commonly used in this book and in the operation of a beta test. The definitions provided here are exclusively written for use in this book and might not apply elsewhere.

beta test   Beta testing is the managed distribution of a product to its target market; the gathering of feedback from that market; the evaluation of the feedback into manageable data forms; and the integration of the data into the organizations it affects.

bug   A bug is defined as anything that could potentially have a negative impact on the customer's experience with the product.

call   The call is an open invitation to get people to sign up for a beta test opportunity. It is usually a single-page document posted in various locations to generate interest in the beta test.

command line interface (CLI) Communicating to a product through a keyboard, the command line interface refers to using keystroke entries to provides instructions for software or hardware.

candidate   Prior to selection for a beta test, people are candidates. They must meet the test criteria and complete all the necessary documentation to become participants.

checksum   A checksum treats the all the data in a software application as numeric values. The checksum is calculated by adding all the numbers together and then comes up with a hexadecimal number representing the file. If a single file is changed in the application, the checksum value will differ.

closure   When a beta test has been completed, test participants are notified of the action that will be taken on their issues. This is closure.

compliance   A beta test participant who is in compliance is providing adequate feedback and completing the necessary tasks of the beta test.

critical path   The critical path is the schedule that a product development team uses to get a product to release. When a process is on the critical path, it means that its completion directly impacts the process.

demographics   The personal, professional, interests, and system characteristics of the beta test participants.

development team   A group of people assembled to develop a product, the development team normally comprises members from each department within a company for the purpose of getting a product to market.

end of life   Once a product costs more to produce than the revenue it generates, it is scheduled to come to an end of life. The product is no longer available, and a support path is designed.

evaluation   An evaluation is the in-depth investigation of an issue to determine whether it is a bug.

field trial   Similar to a beta test, a field trial distributes a product into the market and tests the product. However, field trials normally are very scientific and tightly managed. Utilizing control groups and placebos, a field trial is typically used in the medical, pharmaceutical, and scientific community.

functional specification   The functional specification is a detailed document that provides extensive detail of the software application and all of its components. Usually very technical in nature, it is also called a *design specification* or *design document*.

graphical user interface (GUI)   Focused on simplifying the use and interface of a product, the graphical user interface usually employs "point and click" technology.

interactive communication   Interactive communication involves communicating with beta test participants in real-time.

issue   An issue is a concern expressed by a beta test participant. Any concern about the product is an issue until it is verified to be a problem. Once it has been verified, it becomes a bug.

mailing lists   A system in which users subscribe to a list of people and receive email whenever correspondence is sent to the list, mailing lists produce an abundant amount of communication.

moderated   Moderated mailing lists and groups require that a moderator must approve an original message before it is posted to the list or groups.

newsgroups   Newsgroups are Usenet forums where varied topics are discussed in a bulletin-board type atmosphere.

noninteractive communication   Noninteractive communication is a method to communicate with beta test participants that allows time to formulate correct answers to questions, professional response to issues, and consistency in every response.

qualification   The process of qualification sorts beta test issues and determines what course of action should be taken.

quality systems   Systems designed to improve processes and achieve high customer satisfaction (e.g., ISO 9001, Six Sigma, QS 9000).

queue   The queue is an ordered schedule of projects entering projects. In a queue, projects are being worked on. If projects are coming but do not require any type of work, they should not be in the queue.

release   Once every part of the product development is complete and the product is ready for purchase by the customer, it is released. The release effectively marks completion of a product's development.

requirements document   The "requirements document" is a comprehensive document covering the rationale, feature description, target market evaluation, and specification for a product. It is also known as a Product Requirements Document (PRD) or Marketing Requirements Document (MRD).

roadmap   The roadmap is a timetable showing the logical development path for products. It presents products from conception to end of life.

seed program   Sales teams encourage companies to purchase products by using seed programs. The salesperson provides a company with a complimentary software package to get them to use it and purchase more. The initial complimentary copy of the application is the "seed."

site   A site (beta test site) is a company's customer selected to participate in a beta test. Sites are also known as *test participants*.

slip   A slip occurs when a schedule is delayed and it pushes the anticipated completion date out.

spam   Spam is a blanket distribution of commercially based mail over the Internet. Solicitations for beta test applicants can be considered spam if they are posted in inappropriate forums.

test participant   A test participant is a company's customer selected to participate in a beta test.

test plan   A test plan is a comprehensive yet concise document designed to give an overview of the beta test to the development team.

usability   Usability is the implementation of a design that follows the simplest and most intuitive method to use the product.

Usenet   Usenet is a public discussion system with global distribution and a large technical base of users. It consists of "newsgroups" with names that are sorted by subject. "Articles" are "posted" to these newsgroups by people on computers using software designed to interface with the Usenet. Once the article is posted, any reader of the newsgroup can view it.

user interface   The user interface is how a user communicates with the software. From a command line to a point-and-click design, the interface is the part the customer uses to operate the software.

viability   Viability is the point at which a product has satisfactorily stable characteristics for distribution into beta test. A viable product is ready to be beta tested.